RUBENS
by Jacob Burckhardt

PHAIDON PRESS

RUBENS AND HIS FIRST WIFE IN THE HONEYSUCKLE ARBOUR
About 1610. Munich, Alte Pinakothek

RECOLLECTIONS OF
RUBENS
BY JACOB BURCKHARDT

LONDON : PHAIDON PRESS LTD

Edited, with an Introduction, by
H. GERSON, THE HAGUE

The translation of Burckhardt's Essay is by
MARY HOTTINGER, M.A.

The translation of the Selected Letters is by
R. H. BOOTHROYD AND I. GRAFE

MADE IN GREAT BRITAIN AND PRINTED AT THE CURWEN PRESS

CONTENTS

INTRODUCTION

JACOB BURCKHARDT, *the Swiss historian (1818–97), has left us an impressive number of works on political and art history. His* Civilization of the Renaissance *is probably the best-known historical work published during the nineteenth century, but his* Rubens *was from the outset intended for a more restricted circle of readers. He appears to have felt a certain reluctance to publish the manuscript, for he laid down that the book was not to appear until after his death.*

Burckhardt could never completely free himself from doubts as to the value of works dealing with art history. He synthesized these doubts when he wrote: 'There is nothing more precarious than the life of books dealing with history and art'. It may be true that the majority of learned books 'live' only so long as their viewpoint continues to appear modern and the facts they contain do not seem to be out of date as a result of more recent discoveries. Nevertheless, there are also 'classics' which survive the changes of taste of several generations, and the value of which is not diminished by the fact that certain details have been shown to need correction. Among such works of art history we must certainly include Burckhardt's Erinnerungen aus Rubens, *which appeared for the first time in 1898. The manuscript undoubtedly dates from the last years of Burckhardt's life, but his preliminary studies must have begun at a very early period. In his book on works of art in the cities of Belgium (1842), Burckhardt had already taken up the cudgels on behalf of Rubens, whom he described as being 'in general unreasonably criticized'.*

Rubens's happy life as an artist and as a man finds an echo in the resonant words with which Burckhardt's considerations begin. Even before the author has mentioned or analysed from the historical point of view any of Rubens's works, the reader feels himself surrendering to the magic of the artist's powerful personality. This feeling that we have penetrated to the very core of Rubens's personality and work remains with us as we read on, and this is a consequence of Burckhardt's method. He does not stress the development of the artist from one stage to the next, nor does he attempt to analyse the changes in his style from his early days until the end of his life. Burckhardt likes to linger over everything which is permanent and essential in Rubens's personality and work, demonstrating these essentials by dwelling on incidents in his career, on the fundamental elements of his composition, with its tension between the transitory and the normal, on the subjects of his pictures as they pass before our eyes, on his portraits, which, together with the documentary evidence, tell us so much of his relationship to his patrons. Rubens is the only northern European painter who possessed a clear understanding of the antique and who readily absorbed Italian culture and social etiquette. For him the pictorial allegory was a welcome and simple mode of expression. That Rubens was deeply indebted to Italian art was a fact that Burckhardt, the author of the Cicerone *and the* Civilization of the Renaissance, *was naturally one of the first to recognize. But Rubens stands in relation to his predecessors in Italian painting as an artist conscious of his own powers. Burckhardt delights in following his wanderings in the South, in those countries which to him as a historian were more familiar than they were to many of his fellow art historians.*

The title of the book implies that Burckhardt did not intend to write a comprehensive monograph on Rubens. It is the only work on an individual artist which he published, but his considerations are limited to the essential elements in Rubens's artistic personality and he makes no attempt to give a clear outline of the historical Rubens. Sometimes it seems as if Burckhardt's recollections of individual pictures are a little vague, and all too often he has recourse to Fromentin's enthusiasm or to Waagen's erudition. But this throws into even greater relief what Rubens's work and personality signified for Baroque culture. The historian has contrived to make the past live again and at the same time to free the essentials from their historical surroundings.

To make a critical annotation of such a classic work is a delicate task. But the modern reader needs certain additions to the original text which will point the way to our modern conception of Rubens. During recent years research has added to Rubens's œuvre many paintings and drawings which were unknown to Burckhardt, it has arranged them chronologically and has brought to light much material which serves to clarify the relationship between authentic works and workshop replicas. I have been at pains in such cases to give the source of our new knowledge. We owe much to Ludwig Burchard, who for many years has been engaged on a comprehensive monograph of the great Flemish painter. His observations have found an echo in the articles of many colleagues who have followed up his suggestions. The notes with which I supplement this book should not be considered as corrections to the work of the great historian. His Rubens *remains the most significant book on the artist which we possess and has in no sense been surpassed by more recent works, even when these have produced other solutions to individual problems.*

The Hague, 1949   H. GERSON

SYNOPSIS

COMPILED BY BURCKHARDT HIMSELF

Rubens's career – Sojourn in Italy and first great works there – The earliest mythological pictures; portraits in Genoa – First journey to Spain; influence of Mantua and Venice – Mantegna and Leonardo; the Italian contemporaries – Influence of Caravaggio – Return to Antwerp and first great works – The first decade – First important commissions: the Jesuit church in Antwerp and the Luxembourg Gallery in Paris – Diplomatic activities – Hélène Fourment and Doralice Fioravanti – The 'Introitus Ferdinandi'; landscapes; chief pictures of the last five years – Death of the Master – Rubens as architect – Rubens's temperament and education – The extent of his power; his limitations – His talent for depicting movement; the bases of his ability to work quickly – His dominating position in art – The aim of art in his day – Rubens and the altar-piece – Altar-pieces of his school; devotional pictures for private use; his dealings with the great and his accommodating spirit – Relations with Philip IV; the Torre de la Parada – Scenes from the life of Charles V; the Stuarts – The business side of Rubens's activity – His workshop and the degree of its partici-pation in individual works; his pupils – Value and scope of Rubens's influence; his coloured sketches – General improvement of Belgian art; Rubens's engravers – Training of the engravers; privileges and sales – Importance of engravings for the appreciation of Rubens's art – Landscapes in the engravings; tapestry compositions in engravings – Form and colouring; the treatment of flesh – The male nudes – The female nudes; Susanna and Antiope; the draped female figures; the 'Pudicitia' – The pictorial value of draperies; widely differing types of beauty in Rubens's work – The women of the Bacchanals; the water-goddesses; nymphs and the daughters of Leucippus; absence of recumbent nudes – The Venus of the allegories; the 'Three Graces'; Rubens and the painting of hands – Putti – The painting of 'Romulus and Remus'; identical forms for sacred and profane putti – Murillo's putti; sparing use of putti in Rubens's work – The Holy Children in the open air; the 'Festival of Venus' – The putti in the Luxembourg; in the 'Judgement of Paris'; in the 'Andromeda'; playing with wild animals; Annibale Carracci's putti – Beauty and spiritual expression; the allegedly provincial type; Rubens's independence of Italian art – The inner conception of Flemish piety; Rubens's real ideal type – The pure blonde, and in particular the Magdalen; the older Holy Women – Talent and depth of feeling combined with moderate idealism and quick production; the full-length Holy Families – The completely personal character of the above; the type of Christ and Venetian influence – Absence of half-length figures with expressive functions; the Christ of the 'Pietà'; the Crucified Christ – The 'Raising of the Cross' and the 'Deposition'; the compassionate Christ; St. John the Evangelist – Religious expression elsewhere in Rubens's work; the 'Last Communion of St. Francis'; the 'Pentecost'; the 'St. Cecilia'; the

'Repentant Magdalen' – The demonic element in Rubens; his composition and that of his predecessors in Antwerp – Italian composition; Rubens only slightly influenced by Titian and Paolo Veronese – Influence of Tintoretto, Michelangelo and Raphael – Composition based on symmetries; equivalents and animated movement in Rubens's work – Equivalents in tranquil pictures; in animated narrative; Rubens's 'vision' – Rapid and at the same time tranquil production; more about the 'Raising of the Cross' in Antwerp – The 'Raising of Lazarus'; satisfying the eye by means of hidden symmetry; the 'Rape of the Daughters of Leucippus' – The 'Miracles of St. Francis Xavier'; the 'Battle of Amazons' – The 'Death of Decius'; similar pictures in the Munich Pinakothek – The 'St. Ambrose and Theodosius'; did Rubens overcrowd his pictures? – Examples of his economy in the use of figures; his sparing use of equivalents; of space and air; examples of simplification; seemingly overcrowded altar-pieces – The 'Coup de Lance'; the 'Adorations of the Magi'; was Rubens theatrical? – Origins of false theatricality; French painters and the French stage – Rubens's 'Tomyris'; his representation of space – His pictures in St. Augustin at Antwerp; in St. Bavo at Ghent; in St. Martin at Alost – The 'bridge steps' borrowed from Veronese; the spaciousness in pictures of the 'Last Things' – More tranquil narration; the 'Last Supper' in the Brera – Tranquillity in Jordaens's work; Rubens's flair for transforming great compositions; the 'Miracles of St. Ignatius' in Vienna and Genoa – The constantly recurring figures in the 'Adorations' – The Holy Families; the Flight into Egypt; the Child Christ with Mary and Joseph – The great 'Bearing of the Cross' in Brussels; the 'Martyrdom of St. Lievin' – The 'Martyrdom of St. Lawrence'; the 'Host of Sennacherib'; the 'Conversion of St. Paul' – Terrestrial and celestial rapes; the 'Rape of the Sabines' – 'Samson and Delilah'; the three-quarter-length narrative picture – The 'Tribute Money' and the other three-quarter-length religious pieces; the secular three-quarter-lengths: 'Diogenes', Bacchanals, devotional pictures, the altar-piece of St. Ildefonso – Parallels with Murillo; the painting in St. Augustin – The devotional painting above Rubens's tomb – Pictures of the Assumption – Italian precedents for the 'Assunta'; Guido Reni's 'Assunta' in Munich – Rubens's 'Assumptions'; inadequacy of the Madonna – The Madonna sitting on clouds; the Putti; the lower groups – The High Altar in Antwerp Cathedral – Pictures of the 'Last Things'; the large 'Last Judgement' – The small 'Last Judgement' and the 'Fall of the Damned' – Ancient mythology; mythological genre pictures – The Bacchanals; Moors, Pans and Satyrs; Nymphs; Silenus; addition of Hercules – The water-gods and their mates – Aquatic beings in historical and allegorical pictures – Hero and Leander; narrative mythologies; Rubens and Guido Reni again – Landscape in the mythologies; 'Venus and Adonis'; the 'Battle of Amazons'; Rubens's Olympus – The 'Judgement of Paris'; abundance of mythological pictures – Introduction of the comic element by means of certain metamorphoses; episodes from the earliest history of Rome – The 'Carità Romana'; 'Philemon and Baucis'; the story of Publius Decius;

oil-paintings as models for tapestries – Coloured sketches for other narrative cycles by Rubens – Allegories, their popularity and essential function – Generic allegories; the hero and Victory; the lives of men threatened by war – The Allegory of War in Palazzo Pitti – Allegorical figures in historical paintings; the Luxembourg – Restrained use of allegories – Impulse and resolve depicted allegorically; figures of evil; the 'Education of the Queen' – Predominance of allegory in the representation of general conditions; Florence symbolized as Sculpture – The 'Coronation'; the 'Reception in Marseilles'; the life of King Henri IV and the large sketches in the Uffizi – The allegorical apotheosis of King James I in Whitehall Palace; Rubens and the sketches for ceilings and vaultings – The sketches in Paris, Vienna, St. Petersburg and London, and the 'San Francesco di Paola' in Dresden – Allegorical frames for portraits; the allegories on the occasion of the entry of the Cardinal Infante – Jordaens and the large allegory in the Bosch near The Hague – The nine large religious allegories for Philip IV – Their existence in the form of sketches; of large oil-paintings and of preliminary drawings for the engravers – Content and value of the individual pictures – Rubens and the genre picture; the 'Kermesse' – The 'Country Dance'; the conversation piece; lack of such pieces in Italy – The conversation piece in Holland; and at Antwerp; social life as depicted by Van Laenen; Rubens's 'Garden of Love' – The different versions; late echo of this work in Watteau – The 'Prodigal Son' – Rubens as portrait-painter; the young couple beneath the honeysuckle; the ladies of Antwerp – Divergence of opinions as to attributions and identification of sitters; the 'Chapeau de paille'; the same female type; self-portraits; family groups – Doubtful presence of Rubens's family in other paintings; the Arundel and Gerbier family groups – The 'Four Philosophers'; individual male portraits – Portraits of princes; Mantua; the Habsburg family – The last portrait of the Infanta; some disputed identifications; the equestrian portrait of Philip IV – Carenno's copy of Rubens's portrait – Historical personages in the Luxembourg: Marie de' Medici; Henri IV; Marguerite de Valois – Rubens as painter of animals; Mantua and the first journey to Spain – Slight influence of earlier Italian animal painting – Rubens as painter of horsemen and horses; his knowledge and his insight; his equestrian portraits – Equestrian portraits and combats on horseback later in the seventeenth century – Rubens and wild animals; the help of Frans Snyders; hunting scenes and fights between animals – The hunting of the boar, the stag, the wolf, etc.; dogs and other animals in Rubens's work – Rubens and his landscapes.

RECOLLECTIONS OF
RUBENS

IT is an exhilarating task to evoke the life and personality of Rubens; good fortune and kindliness abound in him as in hardly any other great master, and he is well enough known for us to feel sure of our judgement of him. In the consciousness of his own noble nature and great powers he must have been one of the most privileged of mortals. No life is perfect, and trials came to him too, but the sum of his life so illuminates all its details that, looked at as a whole, it seems exemplary. It did not come to a premature end, like that of Masaccio, Giorgione or Raphael, while on the other hand he was spared the weakness of age, and it was in his last years that he created some of his grandest work. True, from a very early age he met with advancement on all hands, but not everyone could have taken advantage of it and made men and circumstances serve him as Rubens did, probably with the greatest composure.

He was born (at Siegen, in 1577) of an excellent mother, to whom he later remained deeply attached. His education in early childhood, in all probability at Cologne and under his mother's guidance, cannot but have been good. We know too little of his service as a page at fourteen and his entry into an artist's studio at fifteen, or perhaps only at seventeen, to estimate their influence on his development. We make the personal acquaintance of his final teacher, Otto van Veen, in the rather crowded family group in the Louvre which shows him seated at his easel surrounded by his family. In his important picture of the 'Mystic Marriage of St. Catherine' in the Brussels Gallery, Van Veen stands revealed as a disciple of the Italians and, in particular, an admirer of Correggio. The pictures in the Antwerp Gallery ('The Calling of St. Matthew', 'Zacchaeus on the Tree', etc.) show genuine religious feeling, though there is a certain weakness in form and characterization. But Otto van Veen must have impressed his pupil by what he was—a man of fine feeling, grave and dignified.

He had been court painter to the conqueror of the southern Netherlands, Alessandro Farnese, and had later entered the service of the royal couple who became Regents, the Infanta Isabella Clara Eugenia (daughter of Philip II) and the Archduke Albert (son of Maximilian II). And we can so easily imagine Van Veen presenting his pupil to the Regents, and them in their turn recommending the brilliant young artist to the Duke of Mantua, Vincenzo Gonzaga (1600).[1] In the eight years Rubens spent in Italy, he was not only able to wander about the country with commissions from his patron, paying visits, prolonged at his own free will, to Venice and Rome; as a cavalier, he even accompanied a mission to the Spanish court (1603). Although the court at that time resided at Valladolid, Rubens was almost certainly able to see all the pictures in Madrid and the Escorial, which included greater works by Titian than even Italy possessed.

In those eight years Rubens became so far an Italian that Italian remained his favourite language in correspondence. In art, however, though he must have added immensely to his knowledge, he appears from the outset as an artist of completely independent spirit, and he became a power in Italy to a far greater extent than any other Fleming. He at once took his place beside the other famous artists as if it had been ready waiting for him, and painted the same subjects as they. He might well have stayed in the South and become prince of painters there if they had left him alive. With the exception of fresco, he turned his hand to every kind of painting then practised in Italy. In addition to the copies of other masters made for Duke Vincenzo, he painted altar-pieces, among them some of his greatest and most powerful, such as that commissioned by Duke Albert for S. Croce in Gerusalemme in Rome, and 'The Gonzaga Family Adoring the Trinity' (Mantua), of which impressive remains are extant (Pls. 4–5); further, three paintings of the high altar of the Chiesa Nuova, Rome, early foreshadowings of his powerful type of saint, and an 'Apotheosis of Gregory the Great' also destined for that church, but now at Grenoble; further, a huge 'Circumcision'

for S. Ambrogio, Genoa (Pl. 6), and even in these early
days he received a commission for an altar-piece on the
'Miracles of St. Ignatius' which will be discussed below in
connexion with its much later despatch from Antwerp. At
Milan[2] where, among other things, he made a drawing of
Leonardo's 'Last Supper', he painted for an altar that 'Last
Supper' with life-size figures which does not, like Leonardo's
fresco, take as its subject the 'Unus Vestrum', but the Institution of the Sacrament. Here the full power of his composition
is already displayed. The whole of Italy had long been
competing in single figures of St. Sebastian, and to these he
made his contribution in the fine picture of the saint swooning
between angels which can be seen in the Corsini Gallery, and
above all in the great, lonely, luminous saint in the Berlin
Gallery. 'St. Jerome kneeling in the Ravine', 'an original and
splendid work', is in the Dresden Gallery (where it hangs,
strangely enough, beside Van Dyck's 'St. Jerome', also an early
work of that great master, painted at the time when he
resembled his great teacher most, and this picture actually
formed part of Rubens's estate). In the subject of the saint in
prayer, Rubens, even during his Italian years, reached supreme
power in his 'St. Francis' in the Pitti Palace. Among the
mythological pictures of this period we already find (Uffizi,
monochrome) a group of the 'Three Graces', a theme he was
to vary so brilliantly later, and that deliciously intimate picture
in the Capitoline Gallery of 'Romulus and Remus with the
Wolf' (Pl. 40), where the last tones of his palette seem to take
leave of Antwerp, and to enter into a perfectly free domain of
light and colour and of a new, delightful kind of imagination.
For the time being Rubens paid homage to the allegory beloved of his time in the pair of paintings at Dresden, 'The
Hero Crowned by Virtue' and 'The Drunken Hercules'
(Pls. 23–4); 'in one the hero conquering lust and drunkenness,
in the other the hero succumbing to both', and we shall have
more to say of their variants, particularly of the former.
Finally, Rubens could have made a position of great power
by his portraits, with which he made so brilliant a start at

Genoa[3] (Pl. 8). Since the mannerist period had produced so
many good portraitists, the famous artists of contemporary
Italy were biased by a curious idealistic snobbery against
portrait-painting as a whole, in spite of the genuine and permanent desire of the most prominent personalities to see themselves in paint, and, like Van Dyck and Sustermans later,
Rubens stepped into the breach.

But since, wherever he went, the tools of painting were
about him, it was inevitable that the great equestrian portrait
of the seventeenth century in Europe should originate on the
occasion of that first visit to Spain. He painted the Duke of
Lerma on horseback (Pl. 7) at a time when there was no other
painter in the whole country who could have produced anything tolerable in the genre. It was also at this time that he
made his copy of Titian's 'Adam and Eve' and the series of
'Heads of the Apostles', copies or replicas of which can be
seen in the Palazzo Rospigliosi in Rome, and here, at any rate,
Rubens entered into competition, in characterization and
expression, with a very living force in Spanish art.[4]

The atmosphere of Mantua, however, which always
reclaimed him, was probably still more favourable to him
than that of Rome, Venice or Florence; it did not oppress,
it stimulated him. At that time the world-famous gallery of
the House of Gonzaga, with its principal works of the various
Italian schools of the golden age, was still intact. There the
great frescoed world of Giulio Romano and his pupils still
looked down from the walls and vaultings of the Palazzo
di Corte and the Palazzo del Tè, and in the presence of the
torrential and unrestrained invention of Raphael's pupil,
Rubens may have fully realized how far removed from Giulio's
his ends and means in the great, animated story-picture were,
or rather were to be, for he had not yet tried his hand at the
genre. All the same, Giulio, whose enormous production of
narrative pictures was famous far beyond Mantua, was, taken
all in all, Rubens's most important predecessor, and in the
contours of the beautiful heads and bodies there still survived
enough of Raphael to cause some confusion in the mind of

II. SUSANNA FOURMENT
Chalk drawing. Vienna, Albertina

III. THE PAINTER'S CHILDREN
Detail from Plate 80

a younger master from another country. Yet an inward voice may have warned him that he had it in him to become a richer and more powerful painter, the master of a finer balance of composition. This invention of Giulio's, inexhaustible in subject matter and artistically indiscriminate, the lack of economy which is so particularly painful in monumental painting, his heaps of figures, often arranged in all-too-obvious parallels, the tautology in motifs and gestures, the vehement, yet often wooden and stilted movement, the stiffness in seated or reclining figures, the shapeless accumulations of clouds and torsos of divinities, and the Olympian and other teams of horses which are so conventional in spite of all their efforts to rear with spirit—Rubens was certainly able to form his own opinion of all these things from the outset, for any one of Giulio's frieze-like narratives was enough to reveal his indifference to all purer harmony.

Often enough Rubens may have quietly taken stock of all previous Italian art at this time, especially of the Venetian school, the knowledge of which had had so little influence on other northern artists. Though scarcely one immediate reminiscence of Titian can be discovered in Rubens's later work, whether of objects or of single forms, he had learned to see with Titian's eyes.[5] He found the whole mass of Tintoretto's work intact, and much of it still free of the later blackening of the shadows which makes it impossible for us to enjoy him, but he may well have been repelled by the touch of untruthfulness and lack of reticence in him, and by the crudity of a number of his compositions. It is obvious that his deepest kinship by far was with Paolo Veronese; here two minds converged, and there have been pictures which might be attributed to either, for instance a small, but rich, 'Adoration of the Magi' which the present writer saw in early, uncritical years and has never been able to forget.

When Rubens was copying for himself and not for the Duke of Mantua, whether in paint or drawing, he did so with the utmost freedom, and at times as if he wished to show the masters of the past how they ought really to have set about it.

B

Of Mantegna's nine great paintings (then in Mantua) of the 'Triumph of Caesar', Rubens selected two and blended them in one (National Gallery); he set the procession in sunshine and gave it a new background of ruins and landscape with a veritable host of lookers-on. But in many ways he remixed the composition; he turned the youthful elephant-driver on the foremost elephant into a Moor, and replaced the sheep at the head of the procession with a lion and lioness snarling at the elephant, which raises its trunk in rage.[6] In view of such liberties, it becomes doubtful how far we may take as accurate his famous red chalk drawing of the 'Battle of the Standard' (Louvre), the only surviving witness to the central group in Leonardo's Florentine battle cartoon. As for the dialogue Rubens may have carried on with Michelangelo in the Sistine Chapel, more especially on the subject of the 'Last Judgement', we shall have more to say of this in connexion with his treatment of Heaven and Hell. He had already left far behind him the spurious echo of Michelangelo in the work of his Antwerp predecessors.[7]

He found great things going on among his Italian contemporaries, who were in the thick of a great crisis—the battle between the mannerist tradition, which still persisted and was greatly appreciated, and the eclectics and naturalists. We know practically nothing of any personal meetings, and even though Rubens undoubtedly carried away some recollection of the Carraccis and their peculiar interpretation of Correggio (rather than of their treatment of form), we do not know whether he was able to see their Roman masterpiece, the Farnese Gallery, which was then approaching completion. As for Guido, whose life (1575–1642) extends exactly two years beyond the beginning and end of his own, he certainly saw his great fresco in the Cappella di S. Andrea by S. Gregorio in Rome, which shows the saint on his way to execution, but he can as yet have seen nothing of all that is so characteristic of Guido Reni for us, and the same is true of Domenichino, for Rubens may have seen no more of his work than the fresco of the 'Martyrdom of St. Andrew' (in the same chapel).

His encounter with the work and style of Caravaggio (1573–1609) was a far more overwhelming experience. Caravaggio had set the great ferment going in Rome before Rubens arrived, and during the whole of Rubens's years in Italy, he was wandering about the country and on the islands, a saturnine creature:

> Great Jove, the god of light,
> Deserted thee at birth,

while Rubens was unquestionably one of the 'bright-born, serene children of Jupiter'. Yet this very Rubens, who in all probability never saw Caravaggio, expressed his deep respect for him all his life and on important occasions; indeed this is one of the most remarkable traits in his character. His small copy of Caravaggio's famous 'Entombment' (Vatican, now in the Liechtenstein Gallery, undoubtedly painted in Rome) certainly alters a colour here and there in the draperies, but may all the same be one of Rubens's most accurate copies of other men's pictures.[8] And then, immediately on his return to Antwerp, came the great 'Deposition' for Antwerp Cathedral, which is so clear a reminiscence of Caravaggio, even in its artistic means, in the very range of blackish green, black, dull red, bright white and carnation on a background of dark, cloudy night (Pl. 18). Nor did the spirit and manner of the great Lombard remain absolutely alien to Rubens in this picture. There is a silent kinship between this 'Deposition' and Caravaggio's great picture in the Louvre, 'The Apostles with the Body of the Virgin', and Rubens may have seen it either when it was still standing on an altar in the church of the Madonna della Scala in Rome or after the Duke of Mantua had bought and removed it. Anyone who knows only the wilder side of Caravaggio will deny such a kinship, and there is, of course, no strict proof of it, but there is further evidence of a fellow-feeling between the two. One of Caravaggio's most powerful pictures is to be seen in the Vienna Gallery—the big, rich, very animated 'Madonna del Rosario'. This work, probably painted for a Dominican monastery, had come into the Netherlands in some way unknown to us, and the unprecedented happened, namely that the artists of a city united to buy a foreign masterpiece, that they acquired it for 1,800 gulden and presented it to the Dominicans of St. Paul's in Antwerp, where it remained until it was bought by Joseph II. But at the head of those artists stood Rubens, supported by the younger Brueghel, Van Balen, Coosemans and others, and it is to him that the initiative in the decision must be unhesitatingly attributed, nor does it lack greatness. It meant that the religion and the art of Antwerp possessed, in a public place, an Italian picture which that epoch recognized as a masterpiece, though less, probably, for the Madonna than for the grand SS. Dominic and Peter Martyr who are holding out to the surging crowds the rosaries they are begging for, and pointing to the Mother of God. Above, the great red curtain, which occurs elsewhere in Caravaggio, runs diagonally through the picture, and not only did Rubens borrow this curtain from him several times, but there would seem to be an echo of him in certain details of grouping. And when, in his last years, Rubens received the commission for the high altar-piece in St. Peter, Cologne, and chose as his subject the 'Crucifixion of the Apostle', there came back to him the impression made upon him thirty years before by Caravaggio's masterpiece on the same subject, in the possession of Giustiniani in Rome (now in the Hermitage, Petrograd).[9]

Rubens's return from Italy to Antwerp was followed by a time of great sorrow and a lengthy retirement. Having hurried back home on account of his mother's illness, he had arrived too late to see her alive. But good fortune at once joined forces with his own merits and he was appreciated at his true value. He did not rise by the passing whims of patronage, nor by the private tastes of the rich; powerful corporations entrusted him with their most important and solemn commissions, such as 'The Raising of the Cross' and the majestic altar-piece of 'St. Ildefonso' (Pls. 15, 93),[10] while for the Council Hall of the City of Antwerp he painted an 'Adoration of the Magi' which is regarded as the most beautiful of his pictures on this subject (Pl. 13). The Regents, who appointed him court painter and chamberlain, did not insist on his moving to Brussels, so that by far the most important centre of Flemish painting was permanently attached to Antwerp. Pupils at once crowded round him, he recognized the best of them and trained them to be the assistants his work absolutely required. Though he cast all his fellow-artists into the shade, he was on the best of terms with them, as far as they would allow. Wealth, wisely administered, began to fill his home, then came a happy marriage with Isabella Brant and a growing family of lovely children; a new and beautiful house was built, and stocked with the art treasures he had collected in Italy.

It was the situation of a king, without land or subjects, maybe, but of great social brilliance, and the attempted assassination came too. 'In the year 1622, one whom certain believed mad, sought to kill Rubens, so that the master's friends considered it necessary to appeal to the Infanta for special measures of protection.'[11] We learn of no later dangers of the kind, which he would hardly have escaped in Italy.

But Rubens had travelled far in those years, both in inward development and outward power. Religious foundations took a pride in adorning their high altars, even in Friary churches and outside of Antwerp, with some radiant work from Rubens's studio. For the Jesuits of Ghent, he had painted, entirely by his own hand, the terrible 'Martyrdom of St. Lievin' (Pl. 104),[12] and for Our Lady of Malines, 'The Miraculous Draught of Fishes' (Pl. 42), further in 1620, with the help of Van Dyck, the Crucifixion known as 'Le Coup de Lance' for the Franciscans of Antwerp (Pl. 54, Antwerp Museum). It was for the same church that he painted in 1619 his most moving legend, 'The Last Communion of St. Francis' (Pl. 48), but on the high altar of the Franciscans of Brussels his first great 'Assumption' already shone in all its splendour (Pl. 30). From studio and art-collection a fascination spread to distant lands; ready-made pictures on all kinds of subjects, even pupils' copies, attracted connoisseurs; as early

as 1616, Rubens was already painting for the distant city of
Neuburg on the Danube, among other things, the 'Great Last
Judgement', and for Duke Maximilian the finest of his 'Lion
Hunts' (Pls. 31, 34, both in the Munich Pinakothek). And the
tapestry weavers of the time made their greatest move by
employing him for whole series of huge compositions. For
Genoese patricians he designed the six 'Histories of the
Consul Decius' (Pls. 37–8), and by 1618 they were already on
the Brussels looms. Finally we can assign to the year 1619 at
latest the gem of the Munich Pinakothek, 'The Battle of the
Amazons', which many have placed in the forefront of the
master's works for its combination of his finest imaginative
power with his most superb expression (Pl. 36).

But while with this picture an old and trusted family
friend, Van Geest, received a work 'the like of which no
prince ever had from Rubens', the belief in his absolutely
creative power had grown, we may say, to fabulous dimensions, both at home and abroad. In Italy at that time it was
no uncommon thing for the frescoes of whole church interiors
—vaults, cupolas, walls—together with the entire decorative
scheme in the ruling baroque style to be contracted out to a
single artist, but the contract which Rubens concluded with
the Jesuit College of Antwerp on 20 March 1620 went far
beyond that. He had already had some say in the building of
the church in question, St. Charles, and had undertaken and
even completed great altar-pieces for it. He now agreed to
deliver designs for thirty-nine paintings on the arches, together with thirty-six paintings on the roofs of the naves and
the galleries above them (destroyed for the most part by
fire last century and only partially preserved in drawings and
engravings).[13] In 1621, however, Rubens appeared at the court
of the Queen Dowager Marie de' Medici in Paris, and designed
twenty-one huge paintings for a great gallery in the Palais du
Luxembourg, containing an allegorized history of the Queen's
life, which were finished in full size at Antwerp by 1625
(Pls. 61–7). The ambassador of the Archdukes, de Vicq, had
proposed Rubens for this enterprise, and the Florentine queen

and the great Fleming had concluded their alliance over the heads of all French and other artists. From that time on the fame of this European studio knew no bounds, while for the master there existed only the inward bounds which he found good to set himself.

Apart from the gout he suffered from in his last years, Rubens seems to have encountered no hindrance to his art but his diplomatic activities. Archduke Albert, when he felt death approaching in 1621, had specially recommended Rubens to his wife as his most devoted and most intelligent servant, and Ambrogio Spinola, who, as Field-Marshal of the Netherlands, was in a position to know, once said that painting was the least of Rubens' merits. It has been shown that a considerable part of the precious later years of his life were spent in political negotiations with agents and statesmen of Holland and England, at first in secret, then more publicly, first in the service of the Infanta, but later in the express name of the crown of Spain and its minister, Olivarez; his steadfast goal, however—peace for the southern Netherlands—was indeed one which a son of Antwerp could uphold in the face of God and man. Changes of residence, as we have seen already, never affected his work as an artist, and that work had, as far as possible, to mask his diplomatic negotiations. Hence there were long periods of absence, professional journeys to Holland (1627), during which even his young travelling companion, Sandrart, never became aware of diplomatic activities, an eight months' stay in Madrid (summer 1628 to spring 1629), which led to a mission to the court of Charles I of England (arrival in London, 5 June 1629, return to Antwerp, beginning of April 1630). But all this went hand in hand not only with repeated advancement in rank, but with the practice of his art, wherever he happened to be,[14] and on occasions with vast new commissions which soon kept the Antwerp studio fully employed. His last diplomatic efforts (1631-2), among them important conferences with Frederick Henry of Orange and later with a Danish ambassador, brought down on his head the rancour of a clique of Belgian patricians, so that, on the death of his patroness, the Infanta (29 November 1633), he was most probably relieved to be able to abandon all further diplomatic activity. The history of art, however, has to accept as a fact that one of the very greatest of creative artists was at the same time a perfectly luminous human being, who inspired confidence and understanding by his very appearance, and whose universal culture fitted him for association with any eminent personality. Even leading diplomats may have realized how timid and awkward they looked by the side of this artist. As to meetings with other artists on these journeyings, his association with Velazquez, then still young, in Madrid, will have to be mentioned, although, as people are wont to say, the great Spaniard took nothing from Rubens, for instance in the great series of portraits of the royal house (*v. infra*).

After his return to his studio, Rubens gradually carried out the vast commissions he had undertaken. For Marie de' Medici he at any rate began work on a new series, the apotheosis of her husband, Henry IV, planned on the grandest scale (Pls. 76-9), till the fall of the queen relieved him of it; on the other hand he appears to have completely fulfilled his promise for the ceiling of the Banqueting House at Whitehall (Pls. 90-1), for the series of nine great allegories, a commission from Philip IV, which then went to Loeches (Pls. 73-4), and for the entire decoration of the royal hunting seat, Torre de la Parada (Pls. 113-15). But along with all this, he created splendid altar-pieces such as (1631) the 'St. Roch' for St. Martin's church at Alost, mainly painted by himself. This picture, presented by the congregation in fulfilment of a vow at the end of a plague, was by all accounts of moving majesty, for in it the master had spent some of his deepest feeling on the little Flemish town.[15] At that time, at the beginning of the last ten years of his life, a great happiness had come to him; after the death of his first wife, Isabella Brant, in 1626, and four years of widowerhood, he had, on 6 December 1630, married Helen Fourment, then barely seventeen, whose opulent beauty and gracious expression he recorded in nineteen portraits now known, sometimes accompanied by the children of both marriages (Pls. 82, 86). These portraits alone would have brought fame to any artist, without even counting the paintings for churches and palaces in which the principal figures bear Helen's features. They are to be seen, for instance, in the several variants of the most wonderful genre picture Rubens ever painted, namely 'The Garden of Love' (Pl. 99), as well as in the superb 'St. Cecilia' in the Berlin Museum (Pl. 118). We might recall too the deliciously dewy picture of his two sons by his first wife (Liechtenstein Gallery, Vienna, replica in Dresden) and then see whether the whole of the art of the time has anything worthy to be set beside it.

The only parallel—however free and remote—might be that offered, possibly about the same time, by Francesco Albani,[16] also married for the second time to the radiantly beautiful Doralice Fioravanti, who also bore him a number of equally lovely children. He would spend the summer months with them in his little country houses, Medola and Querciola, near Bologna, which he called, in playful reminiscence of Rome, his Belvedere, his Mondragone, his *delizie Tiburtine*. He had had water laid on and had set up fountains and pools; with the luxuriant foliage of the magnificent trees and the bright distances they figure in the background of his 'Venus with Amorini', his 'Diana with Nymphs', his 'Bacchic Revel', etc., and here his wife and children served him as living objects of study. He had no desire, like Rubens, to paint portraits with names, but only echoes of a dear reality.

Rubens, however, apart from these domestic scenes, was also the main initiator and supervisor of a gigantic enterprise, a combination of sumptuous baroque architecture, sculpture and painting, namely the decorations for the main streets and squares of Antwerp on the occasion of the Introitus Ferdinandi, the state entry of Cardinal Infante Ferdinand, the brother of Philip IV (17 April 1635), and these transient splendours have been preserved, at any rate as far as subject matter and a general impression is concerned, in a number of oil sketches by Rubens himself and by his pupil Van Thulden, and in a great copper engraving (Pls. 97–8). Though already

suffering from gout, the master contributed largely to the more
important parts himself, and his last self-portrait dates from
the same year (Vienna Gallery). At that time he bought the
manor-house and estate of Steen, not far from Malines, and
it was his frequent residence from that time on at this country
seat which led to his late love of landscape. Indeed by far
the largest number of his landscapes were painted after his
purchase of Steen. If at the same time a preference for easel
pictures of moderate size begins to make itself felt, we may,
in our egoism, even be grateful to his gout, for a whole
aspect of his art, till then in reserve, only now came to full
expression, and where else shall we find the mysterious music
of the Rubens landscape? Whether the famous 'Kermesse'
(Pl. 68, Louvre), with its impressions of Brabant village life,
dates from this period or earlier must be left open to question.[1]
Beyond this, however, the last years of his life saw the creation
of deeply serious and magnificent pictures which we may
regard as genuine bequests of his art. Supreme dramatic power
again finds concentrated expression in the 'Massacre of the
Innocents' (Pl. 102, Munich Pinakothek), and still more in the
moving 'Bearing of the Cross' (Brussels Gallery, finished in
1637; Pl. 92). In the 'Stigmatization of St. Francis' (Pl. 29)
the master found an ultimate expression for Franciscan piety.[1]
For the high altar of St. Peter's, Cologne, as has already been
mentioned, he chose the 'Crucifixion of the Apostle', and
painted the whole picture with his own hand. The wonderful
picture of the 'Horrors of War' (1638, Pitti Palace) shows
that he had not lost his command of the great symbolic
allegory, and that none of the richness and splendour of his
palette had faded (Pl. 111).

Finally, though not without objections, the altar-piece in
the chevet chapel of S. Jacques, Antwerp, has been assigned to
these years. A supreme solemnity has been imparted to this last
religious painting, not only by the glow of the colouring but
also by a quite personal fire (Pl. 105).

Rubens died at the age of 63 on 30 May 1640. We may
omit here all the details that are to be found in every work of

him—the wise provisions of his will, his artistic property and its subsequent fate.

There was in his life infinitely much that brought him happiness, above all the independence of his position and the spacious freedom accorded to him in his work, but we, the later-born, have reason for gratitude too. We may tremble to think what might have happened if Rubens had had to develop under the domination of Louis XIV, and to become his Lebrun. He might have been born a few decades later, and in France, he, the greatest since the great Italians, the only supreme master whom Nature had in store.

For his general characteristics as a man, we may refer the reader to all that has been discovered and told by others, especially to Waagen's beautiful description[19] of his joyous serenity and his nobility of character, his warm-hearted sympathy on all occasions, great and small, and that unselfishness, helpfulness and kindness to other artists which has been most unjustly disputed.

In spite of his great wealth, he was exceedingly temperate; that and the unceasing care for the further development of his very fine culture, and the choice of social intercourse worthy of it, is what Fromentin[20] summed up in the phrase: '*l'hygiène fortifiante et saine de son génie*'. And further, in describing how nothing could dazzle or blind him: '*la fortune ne l'a pas plus gâté que les honneurs. Les femmes ne l'ont pas plus entamé que les princes . . . C'était une âme sans orage, sans langueur, ni tourment, ni chimères.*' Finally, as to his manner of working: it was calm, but inspired, '*en combinant bien, en se décidant vite*'.

On the summer house in his garden there were inscribed those famous lines from Juvenal (X, 347 ff.) which are among the most consoling that Latin poetry has given us; they speak of the *mens sana in corpore sano*, of the desirable strength of a soul free of the fear of death, of anger and desire, and of the gods, who judge what is good for us better than we can, and who love man more than he loves himself.

As regards his relationship with architecture we can, for all essentials, refer to the work of C. Gurlitt, which investigates and characterizes it.[21] What follows are a few remarks and a postscript containing facts which only became known from a more recently discovered source, and which would hardly find an appropriate place later.

Rubens's long years in a royal environment, where architecture was a perpetual topic of conversation, the inevitable acquaintance with Italian ecclesiastical building, then in a period of vast efflorescence, his close association with great gentlemen of Genoa who possessed famous and perfect mansions, were particularly beneficial to a mind which noted and assimilated formal art in all its aspects. When he returned to Antwerp in 1609, there was probably nobody in the whole of the Netherlands who could, like him, have become the great herald of Italian architecture, and perhaps he might have done so but for more immediate obligations. Nevertheless his advice was sought in many quarters, and the Jesuit church in Antwerp, for instance, can hardly have been built without his assistance. A description and illustrations of his house and garden will be found in Gurlitt.[22]

Suddenly he revealed a desire to exercise a direct influence on a broad basis. The man who secured Caravaggio's great altar-piece for Antwerp (p. 8) published in 1622 his *Palazzi di Genova*, containing the ground-plans, sections and elevations of a dozen of the finest Genoese mansions, most of them in the Strada Nuova, including masterpieces by Galeazzo Alessi, from whose personal estate the drawings may have come. The work was published without letterpress, but with a foreword of one folio page which makes Rubens's intention quite clear. He does not wish to put forward suggestions for exceptional buildings, for courts and princely residences, but to present typical buildings as models for wealthy modern Europe of the north in general, *una opera meritoria verso il ben publico di tutte le Provincie ultramontane*. Whether the work attracted attention and imitation we do not know, but with this publication he took his place as the *grand seigneur* commanding the means of publishing his own ideas of the beautiful and appropriate, and his censor, a canon of Antwerp, not only

calls him *Belgicae nostrae Apelles*, but emphasizes the exemplary
character of the work, since it stands as a *paradigma* for all
practitioners and lovers of the art of building *ad nova et illustria
operum miracula patranda*.

In the setting of his pictures, Rubens gives only as much
architecture as the subject requires or can bear, unlike Paolo
Veronese, who has a taste for enframing his stories with
elaborate edifices, generally in symmetrical arrangement. But
what Rubens gives has its own appropriate richness and force,
and contributes wonderfully to the general light and colour.

It would really seem like predestination that Rubens should
have been entrusted with a commission of the greatest importance in the field of temporary decoration, a type admirably
suited to and eagerly practised by the barocco. Architecture,
sculpture and painting were combined at that time to satisfy a
reckless taste for the most ornate catafalques (so-called *castra
doloris*), triumphal arches, fantastic porticoes, splendid taber-
nacles for the exhibition of the sacrament during the forty
hours' contemplation, theatrical scenery, and so on. Examples
of all these things were important enough to be engraved, so
that we possess fairly full documentation about this very
perishable genre. Rubens was engaged for the decoration of
the city of Antwerp at the state entry of the Cardinal Infante,
the Introitus Ferdinandi, in 1635, which we have already
mentioned and will often have to refer to again. The whole
matter was arranged by him, he was its artistic supervisor, and
he even helped in the execution with his own hand, and of the
extant oil sketches for a number of separate 'spectacula',
especially for triumphal arches, some are recognized as his (Pls.
97–8), while the chief assistant, Theodor van Thulden, was
one of his favourite pupils. As to the architectural language
of form, which range from the most brilliant and ornate
late Renaissance to the boldest rustica, we may question
whether they are really always architecture, but we should do
better to rejoice again in the master's good fortune, since he
was enabled to give free rein to his most magnificent imagin-
ings in a style to which, after all, he had been born. And so

whether the stucco figures, mostly in vehement movement, were placed in front of or beside the architectural erections, or whether they gesticulated freely into the air above, they still formed part of the whole; in the painted stories and allegories occupying the great main fields, however (which were often treated in a very slapdash fashion on such occasions), Rubens here and there displays his most brilliant powers, and we shall have to consider some of these paintings in greater detail later on. The whole, as we see it in the copper engravings and the sketches, is certainly the most amazing setting for pageantry which the seventeenth century produced.

By a lucky chance, further information about Rubens the architect and decorator has come down to us in the shape of architectural and ornamental sketches, all Rubens's own ideas, with the exception of a few drawings or recollections of Italy. Nor is any doubt of their authenticity possible. A still earlier, though not quite contemporary, owner carefully collected them in a folio, which has now been acquired by Russia, fortunately for a public institution. In the execution, they range from the most fugitive of pencil sketches to fairly exact pen-and-ink drawings. It is as if there had been somebody near Rubens who took good care that not the most fleeting improvisation by that inspired hand should be lost. There are no ground-plans at all. What we have are all details of elevations, doors, windows, dormer windows, panelling of the most varied kinds, altars, pulpits; among the more elaborate pieces there are more especially monstrances, and of large-scale architecture half-elevations, or even partial elevations of church façades, steeples, and quite particularly, domes. In the style and feeling a few details are still Gothic, for instance, the open-work spires; with that exception, however, everything, every filling, framework, moulding, festoon, belongs to a very individual conception of the baroque. The master has made the freest use of broken and curved gables and volutes of all kinds, and has had no hesitation whatever in embellishing the architecture with plastic ornaments. It is, however, the designs for domes which are of supreme interest, not only on accoun of the rich variety of their outer shells, but also, and mainly, on account of their extreme slenderness and the concave curve of the attics, above which the calotte sometimes rises, and finally of the soaring and ornate lanterns which recall, for instance, the lantern over the dome of Sta Maria di Loreto in Rome by Giacomo del Duca. North of the Alps domes were still rare in the first part of the seventeenth century, and the building of them was left to Italians (Salzburg Cathedral) who gave them no great height. Rubens, on the other hand, reveals an ambition for supreme slenderness, and his finials recall the most elaborate forms of ships' masts.[23]

The designs for altars, in very varying degrees of elaborateness, are remarkable in themselves in so far as they show how Rubens wished to see his own altar-pieces framed and placed.

*   *   *

It would be a wonderful task to analyse the various aspects of Rubens's artistic temperament and education. As a rule, however, he takes care that the spectator shall be caught up in a single great wave and borne beyond analysis. Even in his early youth, we ask in vain the question that constantly arises with other great masters of the past—where did they get their education, and even their learning? Only one thing is certain, his education was innocent of our modern system of schools and examinations. But if we ask for the artist who formed him, tradition, for instance, has nothing to tell us as to the teaching methods in Otto van Veen's studio, and during Rubens's eight years in Italy, we only become aware of the freest assimilation of Italian art, past and present, without being able to prove any association with Italian contemporaries. We ask in vain, too, where he learned his perspective, both spatial and in the extremely bold movement of his figures. And where, later, did he find the model for so many didactic treatises? What we can prove from extant studies of the most varied kind is that he never lost sight of nature, in spite of a prodigious memory for form which enabled his imagination to find true and genuine expression even in more hasty sketches. Even in daily life, scenes that passed others by without a trace must have unconsciously impressed themselves upon him—in the street, by the Schelde, at home in distinguished society, among clergy of every rank or among the great.

In him, then, the great Renaissance of Flemish art dawned on the horizon. This 'Italy of the North' rises from the manneristic eclipse to resume its former sway, and it was he who was its standard-bearer. Immediately after his return from Italy, in the great state commissions already mentioned, his vast powers developed as if of themselves, and no man could guess what could thenceforth be expected and demanded of him. There is no further sign of fluctuation, nothing tentative. What he could do—whether it suits our taste or not—he could do at once perfectly. In him an unparalleled inventor is combined with a brilliant colourist, and the sunny daylight he prefers quite obviously and radiantly expresses his own sunny nature. But what he could do in other directions is shown in the 'Old Woman with the Brazier in the Grotto' (Dresden), while the terrible power which invests the sombre glow of Hell can be seen in the 'Fall of the Damned' (Munich Pinakothek) and the 'Lesser Day of Judgement' (Pl. 69, same gallery), and nowhere else.

The attempt has often been made to sum up the essential qualities of the master's greatness, yet no one has ever got far beyond mere asseverations. We all feel ourselves in the presence of a tremendous power; most of us feel it to be a lovable one, and catch a hint here and there of a personality whose dignity and nobility went hand in hand with that power. Nor is it necessary to make allowances for its gross and savage elements; we shall expect them from the outset, in order that the phenomenon may be complete. But the scope of the phenomenon is vast and touches the farthest bounds of painting. This great painter of history could, as we know, have treated genre on his own account instead of buying seventeen of Brouwer's pictures for his pleasure, and in the 'Garden of Love' and the 'Kermesse' (Pls. 99, 68) he did justice both to Low Life and to High Life. Animal painting as a genre

IV. THE PAINTER'S FIRST WIFE
Detail from the Frontispiece

V. RUBENS AND HIS SECOND WIFE
Detail from Plate 99

first achieved true and splendid freedom with him. His wonderful intercourse with elemental nature speaks its own language in some fifty landscapes, and not even Titian can strike it dumb. In problems which had existed long before him, it is as if he were founding a genre, because for him there always exists an entirely fresh way of depicting everything, and where he has something of his own most personal feeling to give, he is really moved, and has passed far beyond mere calculation.

In the description of the static, of pure being, he has, so to speak, no more than his own place beside other great masters, and will enchant or repel us according to our temperament and mood; what he cannot do is to leave us indifferent. Sensitive minds find the full-bloodedness of these brilliantly healthy figures distasteful; but his ideal need not be anyone else's ideal, and there are more noble, delicate and blissful things in the heaven, on the Olympus and on the earth of other masters. But as soon as it comes to 'glorifying man in all his powers and instincts', as soon as he embarks on his own great theme, movement, he goes his own way. Here, in countless pictures, 'the fire and truth of his physical and spiritual motion' provoke a perpetual amazement which no other artist has even approached. His enthusiasm and his enormous capacity for 'happenings', whether in the subject as a whole or in single figures, make him launch out without misgivings where others would have reflected and considered. Was he too servile and yielding? Whatever tasks were set before him, whatever wishes he had to fulfil, particularly if they could find expression in movement, he saw at a glance what was paintable, and then it was worthy to be painted. Once given a subject, he had no need to wait long for the right 'mood', for he lived in a permanent 'mood' for any problem, religious or secular, and no matter how great, which his time and civilization presented him with. 'Everyone according to his gift! My talent is of such a kind that no commission, however great in size or varied in subject matter, ever daunted me', he wrote in 1621, when just about to begin work on the paintings for the great

C

gallery of the Palais du Luxembourg. Even in the apparently
most intractable material, he senses its paintable aspect and
answers: Give it me. He will and must do everything because
he can. Yet the feeling in his painting, however stormy it may
be, is nearly always pure and deep. Today, however, nobody
can be expected to share the master's terrible visions of the
Apocalypse or fare forth with him in the fight with the
wildest beasts of the wilderness.

Hence his methods and his mass of studies, the figures
which seem to move before the spectator's eyes, the unerring
fusion of colour, tone and light, and finally his enormous
output. Rapid painting, *la furia del pennello*, which, as Bellori
(p. 247) [24] says, is one of the certain roads to ruin for lesser men,
did not in him mean superficiality; it was born of the steady
power and ripeness of the vision from which it sprang. We
might see a radical distinction between him and other artists
in the fact that his inspiration responded most readily to any
theme, i.e., that he could paint more subjects with pleasure
than others could. If we grudge him that privilege, let us say
so; his own time and ours have not done badly out of it.

The only seventeenth-century artist comparable to him in
personal authority and artistic influence was Bernini. In Rome,
a man like Arpino could, by despicable methods, bar the
way to all others, eclectics or naturalists, and even set about
exercising pressure abroad. [25] It must never be forgotten that
Cardinal Richelieu, whose reputation as a connoisseur stands
so high, tried to supplant 'Rebens' by that very Arpino [26] in the
last commission of Queen Marie de' Medicis, the series of
the Deeds of Henri IV; in the meantime, of course, it suited
him to overthrow the queen and drive her out of the country,
so that the commission was never carried out. The later
French artists, however, under Louis XIV, for all their talent,
only won their great name in the world because the king and
his Colbert used them as one of their many means to dazzle
or subdue the world, and in the end the greatest of court
architects was within an ace of being superseded by Bernini
in the extension of the Louvre. But a power such as Rubens

exercised is genuinely founded on evidence and can wait for the greatest courts to seek it out. Its advertisement is in its works alone. It needs no literature, not even an Aretino.

The most stirring heralds of Rubens's art, which spread his fame abroad all over Europe, were unquestionably the great and powerful engravings of his pictures, which no engraver's workshop in Europe could rival for many a year to come.

*   *   *

The material situation of European art as Rubens found it is a matter of common knowledge. Yet we shall always feel the need of recalling in detail his world of patrons and artists as a contrast to our own. Above all, the ground from which art sprang was not that of our great cities of today, with their mobile and hence very fluctuating wealth. There was no public opinion feeding on perpetual novelty; no press to serve as the voice of that public opinion, and to cast its net even over the art of the place and make the artists subservient to it. And no novel with its programme of ceaseless invention in the terms of the day and dedicated to the representation of its people and events, whatever they may be. No sudden vogues to carry away the so-called 'cultured' classes of the great cities, only to make way for another soon after. In a word, no public on which everything and everybody, including the artists, depended, and no exhibitions in our sense of the word.[27]

What still existed to yield Rubens the matter of his art was an established stock of ideas, forming a single whole blended of the ideal world and a recognized sphere of the real world, and predominantly southern in character. The Bible, vision, legend, mythology, allegory, pastoral, history, and even a piece of the everyday world, figures as well as scenes, still formed a whole, and a mighty naturalist, inspired by his own fullness of life, undertook to maintain all these things at the right temperature. Rubens never really broke through this horizon, which he had absorbed in his early years in Antwerp, and still more in Italy. He was no wilful dreamer of strange fantasies, but only the mightiest herald and witness of that great tradition. His vast power of invention was essentially occupied in an ever-fresh response to it and an ever-new expression of it. It was as if religion, princely power, saga, the myth and poetry of all times, his own family and circle of close friends, even elemental nature, both in the animal kingdom and in landscape, had turned confidingly to him that he might take them on his eagle's pinions.

Finally, it was extraordinarily fortunate for the Catholicism of the entire north to find so great, so willing and so happy an interpreter, who was himself fired with enthusiasm for the life of all the great religious figures. On the other hand, it was to Rubens's advantage that there was no throne near him, that government was solely in the hands of the extremely devout Regents, Albert and Isabel, that Antwerp was not the seat of the Papacy, nor even the centre of the greatest Flemish school of theology, for that was at Louvain. Any religious information he needed he could get from the Jesuits of Antwerp, and still more from the Dominicans of that city, for whose church he painted the famous 'Scourging of Christ' and helped to buy Caravaggio's 'Madonna del Rosario'.[28] And doubtless these monks' way of thinking was shared by the rich corporations and spiritual communities who commissioned the great religious pictures, and by individual patrons, such as Burgomaster Nicholas Rockox, one of Rubens's most devoted friends, who bought a large number of his pictures. But in Rubens's work the restitution of all that the terrible Flemish iconoclasts had destroyed in 1566 reaches its climax. The Flemish mannerists, possibly the aged Floris, then Martin de Vos, the studio of the Franck family, and so on, had been the first to provide the churches with new altars. Rubens, however, even as early as his return from Italy, painted the greatest of altar-pieces, and his fame for the genre soon spread, as we have seen, far into the Catholic south of Germany.[29] Till the end of his life he revered the splendour of the altar, and thus bestowed his best powers on the Flemish popular saints (St. Bavo, St. Amandus, St. Lievin, etc.). It was not the custom of the Netherlands to adorn whole cloisters with cycles of legends in fresco, as the Bolognese had done for instance in the pillared octagonal court of S. Michele in Bosco; instead of that the more important churches throughout Brabant and Flanders were provided by the pupils, assistants and disciples of the great master with altar-pieces proportional in number and value to those of the contemporary churches of Italy and Spain. Rubens painted few pictures for domestic devotion, though one or two of them are of the first rank. It appears that the older domestic altars, of which such large numbers still exist in Antwerp in our day, were hardly or not at all affected by the image-breaking, and continued to be the centres of family worship.

When it came to dealing with those in high places, Rubens had probably realized a good many things even in Italy; above all their impatience, which could only be satisfied with work at high speed, further the range of their ideas and culture, their family pride and ostentation, and their love of allegory in every sense and its introduction into narrative scenes in the way which had been customary ever since Vasari's *Sala de' cento giorni,* or even earlier. And there were artists who went unpaid, or who had to wait because ready money had been spent on some passing pomp or political necessity, while the house of Farnese had paid off Annibale Carracci in a way that can only be called niggardly. But Rubens always managed to recover part, if not all, of what was due to him, and the rest was probably part of the game. What he sought and found was by no means mass commissions, like Federigo Zucchero and the later 'subject' painters of the Doges' Palace at Venice, but occasions, since even fugitive and vague hints may have fired him with the vision of great, animated scenes. Incidents which others would have regarded as hardly paintable he, so to speak, dared himself to attack, and while the kings or their confidants were still speaking to him, that swift pencil may already have been at work on a first sketch. And the noble patrons were most likely delightfully surprised at the beautiful ideas they had, while the artist will certainly not have disillusioned them in the course of further conversations. We cannot imagine the gallery of the Luxembourg—whoever else may have been consulted on questions of learning—coming into being without the liveliest discussions in Italian between the queen and the artist, who had long been familiar with the family pomp of the Medici. And if the taciturn Philip IV hardly spoke more than a few words the whole year round, it was notorious that he made an exception in the case of artists; he would climb the scaffolding and hold most confidential conversations even with the Bolognese ceiling painters,[30] and thus he may not have remained dumb even at Rubens's portrait easel, but will have given some kind of idea of the great series, both sacred and secular, which he wished the artist to paint. Here we must think less of the eight big histories (in part, at any rate, Roman) for the great hall of the palace at Madrid,[31] than of the nine huge allegories of the Triumph of Faith (Pls. 73-4) which will have to be discussed in detail later, for in them a way of thinking quite personal to the King must have been taken into account.[32]

Further, this is the best place at which to mention a royal commission which presupposes the artist's unbounded confidence in his own powers. The commission was for the newly built hunting-seat of Torre de la Parada (Pls. 113-15), and here, in view of the lack of native painters in the genre desired, the obvious thing would have been to send to Italy for first-class frescoists. Titian, however, had established at court the tradition of painting on canvas, and now, according to one account, Rubens himself took the measurements for a series of scenes from Ovid's *Metamorphoses*, while, according to another source, these measurements, and even the canvases themselves, were sent to him later (1636?) at Antwerp. The paintings were to be contiguous;[33] not only the wall surfaces above doors and windows (*sopraporte e soprafenestre*), but all the rest, even in the corridors or on landings, were to be covered with them, while in a few anterooms there were to be animal paintings (*scherzi d'animale*) for which Rubens's great assistant in such things, Frans Snyders, was to be called in. The work actually executed as a whole (probably for the most part by the hands

of pupils) and sent to Spain in 1638, was not confined to
Ovid; it was 'a series of scenes of the chase and the woodland,
mythological, realistic and courtly-allegorical'. As to the
subsequent whereabouts of this great work—since patronage
for hunting-seats is particularly unreliable—a number of pictures, and probably the best, were removed to other royal
residences, and when Palomino (Chap. 106) speaks of
pictures from the *Metamorphoses* by Rubens which had been
brought to Madrid for the King's apartments, we may be
pretty sure that they came from the Parada. But how much
that is now in the Madrid Gallery came from the same place
we cannot say ('Mercury and Argus', 'The Rape of Hippodameia', represented in the Brussels Gallery, along with a 'Fall
of the Giants' from the Escorial, by three sketches?—'The
Rape of Proserpine'?—'The Suckling of Hercules'—perhaps
even the Madrid 'Judgement of Paris'?).[34] If the delightfully
conceived picture of 'Latona with the Lycian Peasants' in the
Munich Pinakothek comes from the Parada or was painted for
it, it is possibly not the only Metamorphosis taken from the
humorous side. In Dresden, a 'Diana with Nymphs Hunting'
may be traced to the same source with some certainty, and as
some of the nymphs are portraits, we may imagine that the
whole shows 'a distinguished society in mythological guise'.[35]

A further great enterprise, however, may have been touched
on in the conversations between Charles V's great-grandson
and the Antwerp artist. The Berlin Museum possesses a
wonderfully spirited battle-sketch, with a magical radiation
of movement and light from the centre, not unlike that in the
great unfinished picture of the Battle of Ivry (Uffizi). The
moment selected, however, is the decisive victory of Charles V
at Tunis (20 July 1535) over the army of Hayraddin Barbarossa.
Is this perhaps only one of a number of scenes from a life of
Philip IV's great ancestor which the King's dreamy mind was
pondering?[36]

Finally, the house of Stuart, surveying Europe for an artist
to create a monument to its own glory, found that it could
not do without Flemish art and Rubens. Charles I, even as

Prince of Wales, had dreamed of great paintings for the Palace
of Whitehall while it was in building, and now, as king, he
came to terms with Rubens, who was in England on a
diplomatic mission, for an allegorical apotheosis of his father,
James I, to fill nine fields of the ceiling of the Banqueting
House (Pls. 90-1). Beside the sketches for these, Rubens
painted several other pictures in London, and also designed for
the King the cartoons for eight tapestries on the subject of
Achilles (Pls. 87-9). According to the scenes known to me in
engraving, this latter work must have been rather perfunctory,
while the ceiling in Whitehall is said to display the master's full
creative powers (completed and delivered to London, 1635).
That he was later still in great demand at the English court
can be seen by the fact that shortly before his death, negotiations were under way for three pictures on the story of Psyche
for the ceiling of Queen Henrietta Maria's bedchamber in
Greenwich Palace.

The business side of this kind of work might be prosaically
summarized as follows: a great master of the art of allegorized
historical painting, living in a European country which was
to all intents and purposes neutral, at a time when the artistic
renown of Venice was in eclipse and neither German nor
French art counted, who was already in the habit of receiving
and executing commissions from other countries, was, by the
intermediary of an agent of the Archdukes at the French court,
brought into touch with the Medicean ambitions of the Queen
Dowager of France, and so, in a place which was long the
meeting-ground of all Europeans of rank, attained supreme
fame with a series of pictures; further, the impression made
by his personality was such that it resulted in an unprecedented
combination of art and diplomacy and personal contact with
the great, who, it would appear, chose him to be the interpreter of their personal emotions—while side by side with all
this there went, as a matter of course, the designing of great
series of tapestries. It may have dawned on these people that
they had in him the greatest story-teller of all time. These
commissions, however, were executed exclusively in the

Antwerp studio, where the master was surrounded by a selection of assistants unique at the time, and from that studio, the paintings, rolled up, were sent all over Europe, followed at times by anxious thoughts lest they should suffer damage on the way. This is quite a different world from that of the fresco painter, who moved about from church to church, from palace to palace.

This studio, however, was far from being the only one of standing in Antwerp, and others plied a thriving trade beside it; indeed, the head of one of them, Jan Brueghel (the younger Brueghel, d. 1626) was a close friend of Rubens, and even collaborated with him in important pictures (Pl. 60). Further, the work of the studio was by no means confined to the huge commissions from abroad; it was actively engaged in all kinds of current work. Early in his life, Rubens's position was high and secure enough for him to create, or direct the creation of, works which might be sold or remain in his possession. The regular occupation of the pupils working under him at any given time would of itself create a stock of replicas of work already finished, to which he would give finishing touches with more or less interest. Thus there arose the range of work— the pictures painted entirely by his own hand, those with the main parts finished by him, those merely retouched, the studio picture of varying degrees of excellence, the pupil's painting after the master's drawing, the copy which may never have seen the studio, and finally mere imitations, some made abroad. In his correspondence of 1618 with Carleton, the English minister at The Hague, which contains a list of the stock in hand, at least as far as it seemed expedient to Rubens to give it, we can clearly distinguish several of these stages, along with the proportion of pupils' work.[37]

In the course of thirty years, the personnel of this famous studio naturally underwent great changes. The 'Crown Prince', as Fromentin called him, standing out above all others by the side of the master, was Anthony van Dyck. According to recent research, he at times gained a very great influence over Rubens himself, and his fame, like his master's, was destined to spread far beyond the Netherlands. The next strongest personality to these two, Jacob Jordaens, though he was a friend of Rubens and absolutely dependent on him in his art, is now no longer counted among his pupils or even collaborators. The assistants specialized in definite parts of the pictures; for animal painting and animals in other scenes, as well as for accessories, by far the most outstanding was Frans Snyders, who was only two years Rubens's junior, and was, by his noble and attractive personality, as we see it in Van Dyck's portrait in Vienna, worthy to be Rubens's friend too. In landscape, the names of Lucas van Uden and Jan Wildens are most frequent. How Rubens employed the others according to their special gift may possibly be seen in many individual details of his pictures. For the work on the gallery of the Luxembourg, in addition to the assistants already mentioned, we find the names of Justus van Egmond (born in 1601) and Pieter van Mol (born as early as 1580), Cornelis Schut (born in 1597), Jan van den Hoecke (born in 1611, and hence probably too young?), Simon de Vos, Deodat Delmont, etc., and in parts their work can be traced with some certainty.[38] Among Rubens's later assistants, the chief name is that of Theodor van Thulden (born in 1606). Abraham van Diepenbeeck was at any rate an outstanding pupil, and it is disputed whether the beautiful composition of the great Cloelia picture (Dresden) is by him or his master.[39]

In so far as we are in a position to judge now, it was perhaps one of the happiest studios we know of. Quite apart from the master's other human and artistic qualities, we cannot imagine him otherwise than as the perfect teacher, and it is as if all these other talents had been waiting for him. Under his eyes they developed—not into slavish imitators, but into very estimable artists on their own account. They did not become mannerists, because they did not imitate the master's way of feeling, but followed his principles and artistic methods. And the spirit of Rubens has entered quite freely into the finest works of men who never at any time enjoyed his direct teaching, such as de Crayer and Van Oost, and even into his opponent Janssens and his pupil Rombouts, not to speak of others, while a power radiating from Rubens finds most felicitous expression in the whole of Belgian genre painting, and not in Teniers alone.

If, however, we return to the actual studio, it is not so very easy to imagine the day-by-day manner of collaboration between master and assistants. According to Waagen's suggestion, Rubens made the drawings for the pictures, then had them very carefully coloured by his pupils after colour sketches, and then put more or less finishing touches to them.[40] We cannot, however, deny that by far the largest number of the colour-sketches by Rubens now in galleries give the impression of 'first ideas'; they are often mere brush sketches rendered in a reddish or greenish tone and very hastily roughed out. And even in those that are much more highly finished, which go far beyond this shorthand in two colours and show the distribution of space and light in the finished picture, we must allow for a great deal of work to be done by the master at a later stage. We only have to look at even the most highly finished of the sketches for the Luxembourg gallery in the Munich Pinakothek,[41] for instance, to be convinced that pupils would have found them far from adequate to work by (Pls. 61–7). We shall never be able to guess how, in each case, Rubens gave his later and more detailed instructions, if only for the final colour scheme and the general tone, and how he then relied on the individual assistant's intelligence and feeling, or, to put it in a more general way, his grasp of what was meant and how it was meant.

As we have already seen, we can draw no clear line of demarcation between the heritage which Rubens left to his school and the total heritage of all the studios of the southern Netherlands (as far as Liége), yet a note on Rubens's influence may not be out of place here. In industry, all competitors, down to the smallest, can be paralysed by a great accumulation of strength (capital), and even a big shop can force a large number of smaller ones to go out of business. In art, fortunately, things were different at that time. The studio of a great artist might deliver fourteen hundred pictures, but that only meant that the whole country benefited by the increase of artistic activity and opportunities of disposal. A general prejudice in favour of that country grew up, there was a gradual rise in its relative standing, because, with the great master, a general supremacy in art was created which outlasted the century, very much in the same way as in Holland. Both countries, in their likeness as in their contrasts, together created the great pre-eminence of those times which is still recognized today, for the great artists of Louis XIV had long since ceased to be regarded as masters in their own home, and Italy, which appeared to be resuming the leadership of Europe with Pietro da Cortona, Luca Giordano and the ecclesiastical artists who derived from their manner, had lost it again entirely. But Spain, with all its artistic power, was never made to be a leader.

*   *   *

A second retinue of the royal master was formed by his copper engravers, and with them too his relations, both in art and in business, must have been excellent and absolutely free, for they also worked after other famous masters. Lucas Vorsterman, Paulus Pontius, his particular friend Schelte à Bolswert, P. Soutman and Suyderhoef, not to speak of all the others, made an imperishable name with their craft. In the Netherlands, where the art of engraving may have originated, it had been practised most actively for a century, and had numbered, after Lucas van Leyden, such masters as Hendrik Goltzius and the Sadelers as its own. But Antwerp had long been the most important centre and greatest publishing place for all work of this kind, from the large artistic engraving to mass-produced book illustrations. It was precisely the painters of the local mannerist school who had been most widely propagated in engravings, some of which represented the highest that contemporary craftsmanship had to show, not excluding the Italians, and thus for Rubens and his company, a great road lay open, a great business tradition existed.

Under his leadership, however, fresh impulses and new achievements set in. Whatever the origin and training of the engravers who came to him, they had first of all to set about learning to draw as he understood drawing; their burin, their etching needle, leaving Goltzius far behind, had to learn to render that modelling of forms, that texture of materials, that gradation of light and shade, of foreground and background and finally that disposition of the whole which were the master's in a host of sometimes very crowded scenes. We cannot even imagine their work without constant supervision and collaboration on his part, but then they could rest assured that they would travel much farther under his guidance than would have been possible anywhere else. Further, they must also have been assured of their due share in the financial profit from these huge engravings. Rubens himself, as the actual *entrepreneur*,[42] protected the individual sheets against copyists by royal Spanish, royal French and even Flemish state patents, and it was worth while to do so. For while the contemporary engravings of Italian artists give the impression of having been made merely for other artists, Rubens appealed to a large purchasing public all over Europe which bought eagerly for religious purposes and pure pleasure in art and found more altar-pieces in this one source than in the whole of Italy. The French copyists anticipated in a very delightful fashion the French notion of the protection of industry by representing to the authorities that, given the great demand for engravings after Rubens, the prohibition of copying was sending a great deal of money out of the country. The question even arises— who was in the greater hurry, the vast circle of purchasers or Rubens himself? For great and important engravings, in spite of the inscription *Rubens pinxit*, were not engraved after the completed picture, but after early or preliminary sketches, which were to undergo important and highly desirable alterations, especially in the way of simplification. The 'Raising of Lazarus' in the Berlin Museum, as compared with Bolswert's engraving, may be taken as an example. These designs may have been coloured sketches, or they may have

been cartoons, and in many cases it can be proved that they
were in grisaille, painted by Rubens in grey or brown monochrome; a number of them have been preserved. Besides,
when there was an engraving to be made, Rubens often
handled finished pictures with the greatest freedom. 'The
Virgin with the Parrot' resulted in an engraving containing
only the Mother and Child without Joseph, without the
parrot, without the landscape and with only a hint of the
architecture, and thus there was created a Virgin for Everyman
which lacked the peculiar intimacy that breathes in the famous
picture in the Antwerp Museum (painted in 1614).[43]

In the engravings, the great colourist appears before the
public without colours, and won brilliant and personal fame
merely by his composition, form and light. And he might
well feel a lively appreciation of that fame, and allow the
great, very animated scenes in particular to be widely propagated even in their early, and perhaps somewhat overloaded
version. Those who knew his work well could in any case
often deduce from the engraving the colours and whole colour
schemes which he intended or had already applied. That he
had an eye on the fairs too, now and then, can be seen by the
woodcuts of Christopher Jegher, a German who had settled in
Antwerp, and it was for him that Rubens composed, among
other things, the lovely 'Rest on the Flight', and drew, in his
last years, a specially arranged version of the 'Garden of Love',
when the fame of that scene, which was originally intended
only for the few, had broken all bounds. Otherwise the
engravings held on their majestic course, and they are indispensable to a knowledge of Rubens's total *œuvre* in more than
one direction. It is possible that certain mighty animal fights,
for instance, are only extant in the engravings. The most
terrible 'Boar Hunt' exists, to my knowledge, only in the
engravings by Soutman. But how far the school had pro-
gressed in the grasp of these subjects too comes out particularly
in the superb example of the Munich 'Lion Hunt', since we
can compare Bolswert's magnificent engraving with the long
famous original.[44] Landscape had long been one of the most

amous expressions of the artistic spirit of Antwerp, in painting nd engraving, and now Rubens entered the lists too, and at quite special moments in his career, from his Italian years on, he reated those works, now scattered over Europe, ranging from he simplest view of nature to the highly fantastic scene and the huge natural convulsion, which we shall have to consider later, nd again it was Bolswert who made a great deal of this imperishable art accessible to everybody in a series of masterpieces. Without personal and thorough studies, more especially of woods, under the master's guidance, he could not have done so.

Finally, it was possible, in special circumstances, for engravings to be made which surpass in effect the original pictures. The nine allegories of the 'Triumph of Faith' for Philip IV (Pls. 73-4), so far as I have seen them in the Grosvenor Gallery in London and in the Louvre—very big, in oil on canvas, executed by lesser pupils and partly in a very poor state of preservation—cannot stand comparison with Bolswert's engravings (of which we possess four), for the latter give the impression of a higher art of representation. Rubens had put more of his best powers into these compositions than the taste of today is ready to admit; he may not have been particularly interested in their execution in tapestry, for which they were intended, and may even have had some doubts about it, and since, instead of the tapestries, it was the great painted canvases that were despatched to distant Spain, he obviously rescued them from oblivion by careful drawings which his great engraver used as models, and those drawings were pretty certainly by his own hand.

Those Frenchmen, however, of whom we have spoken, had followed a sound instinct in providing themselves plentifully and in good time with engravings of spirited works by Rubens. The time, after all, was not so far distant when all that would be set before them was to be the cold dishes of Lebrun and his like, not excluding Poussin, in engravings by Edelinck, Nanteuil, Audran and others, which were of much greater perfection and elegance than those of Antwerp.

*   *   *

The judgement of Rubens's form and colouring is essentially
a matter for artists, and all that the layman can allow himself
is a few remarks on the position of individual works within
the total *œuvre* of the master. But here Rubens himself renders
any clear statement of fact difficult, because everything in his
work is so much a part of, so much a factor in the general
effect of an intensely living whole that we can see it only in its
relative aspect.

As for his personal taste, he admits (1618) to a 'passion for
antiquity'. But he fully realized that colour is not stone, and
that vast range of beings 'from heaven through earth to hell'
which he had to depict in living form had to become his own
creations if he was to have any joy of them. It was his personality in mysterious union with a magnificent education
and training and with those traditions common to the civilized
world of his day, by which any other artist might have
profited. That is what the admiration or disapproval of later
times has to reckon with when the fascination becomes too
strong to be ignored. Now whether Rubens is to be regarded
primarily as a naturalist, whether, by and large, he must be
taken as a descendant of the Venetians, whether his power and
originality were in some way determined by them, are
questions we cannot go into here. Admittedly his figures,
from the skeleton outward, lack ideality, and his selection of
types was not always aimed at perfection, as we can see at
times in the ugly and ungraceful stride of his male figures.
Before going further, however, we must realize that this is
counteracted by the enchanting splendour of his treatment of
flesh in itself, especially in paintings by his own hand, by the
famous beauty of his nudes and their setting in light and
chiaroscuro, by his general use of the nude in his work, har-
monized by an unparalleled range of tones, of deeply luminous
or softly shimmering colours in the drapery and setting. This
flesh, too, passed through its own development from the
light yellowish tone of the Italian period, to vermilion and
ultramarine, and to the carmine which replaces the shadows
in youthful nudes. Indeed, even early paintings, for instance

VI. SELF-PORTRAIT
Detail from Plate 120

VII. Detail from 'The Garden of Love'. (Plate 99)

'Jupiter Disguised as Diana with Callisto' (in Cassel), are
famous for the perfection of their modelling with practically
no shadows. Further, he could render with perfect verisimilitude the skin of his figures, which varies so widely with sex,
age and social rank.

As regards the male nude, there is no dissentient voice in
the admiration for the body of Christ in the great 'Deposition'
of Antwerp Cathedral (Pl. 18), both for the quality of the
modelling and the beauty of the foreshortening, which has
not only never been surpassed, but never even equalled in any
other 'Deposition'. Opinions, however, differ greatly when
we come to the '*Christ à la Paille*' in Antwerp Museum, to the
various 'Pietàs', to the recumbent, violently foreshortened
body of Christ in the Trinity pictures, and finally to the
treatment of the Crucified Christ, whether alone on a dark
background of clouds, or as the central figure of a 'Crucifixion',
or in the 'Raising of the Cross,' for instance in the famous
version in Antwerp Cathedral (Pl. 15). The authenticity of
some of these, however, is disputed or denied. There is a
peculiar dignity and beauty in the body of Christ in the great
'Pietà before the Grotto', an early work in the Brussels
Gallery. Among the figures of Christ in motion, it is agreed
that there is supreme mastery in the 'Scourging' in St. Paul's,
Antwerp (though only partly authentic) but the effect is
dubious. Christ, though bound to the column, seems to be
attempting to escape his torturers. In the superb 'Christ with
the Great Penitents' in the Munich Pinakothek (Pl. 44), the
body is only moderately idealized, while that in the 'Intercession of St. Theresa' (Antwerp), is, on the whole, an inferior
type of body, though there is a high Venetian nobility in the
head. As to the 'Christ with St. Thomas' (also in Antwerp), it
has been sharply criticized. On the other hand, the great (and in
other respects universally acknowledged) critic Fromentin,
who shares that opinion, singles out for supreme praise the
rich vitality of the nudes in two fishermen in the 'Miraculous
Draught of Fishes' (Pl. 42, Notre-Dame de Malines). Other
heroic nudes attain even in the Italian period a perfection of

D

vitality such as no contemporary Italian at any rate could surpass. Yet they are all spontaneous creations, freely drawn from personal study. We have, for instance, only to see how his huge river-gods, while owing something of their corporeality to Roman statuary, from the Nile God of the Vatican onwards, are perfectly original in the motifs, for the master always created his motifs afresh. The youthful nudes begin in the Italian period with the grandly plebeian 'St. Sebastian' in the Berlin Museum, which, though executed in the yellowish tone customary at the time, is wonderfully luminous. It is still undecided whether Rubens or Van Dyck is responsible for the beautiful body of the same martyr in the Corsini Gallery, Rome, leaning against a tree-trunk with an equally beautiful young angel loosening the bonds from one of his feet.[45]

Other more important and in part draped angels can be seen, for instance, in the 'Flight of Lot' (Louvre), in the Munich 'Adoration of the Shepherds', and as the avenging angel hovering over the 'Martyrdom of St. Lievin' (Pl. 104, Brussels) etc. The classical nude of the ideal type, which is not frequent with Rubens even in the mythologies, is well represented in the gallery of the Luxembourg, for instance by the Genius in the 'Birth of Louis XIII', while in the Apollo of the Olympus (so-called 'Government of the Queen') Rubens has obviously transposed the 'Apollo Belvedere' into swift movement.

There was a great desire for female nudes, and there is evidence that Rubens fulfilled it gladly and spontaneously. Where do the old poets write, or where do we find in classical reliefs, or on vases, that the three daughters of Cecrops, Herse, Aglauros and Pandrosos, were nude when they discovered the snake-footed child Erichthonios in the open basket? But in the superb painting in the Liechtenstein Gallery, Rubens depicted them so, in bright light in front of the moist gloom of a river-head, the stances wonderfully varied, and added to them a draped muse, a busy *putto* and a small dog, further a sculptured nymph on a fountain and a horned Pan as Hermes

outside in the sunny glade. Even 'Susanna Bathing', conceived
by all the artists and patrons of the time as a demonstration of
the nude, displays, in the picture in the Munich Pinakothek,
a definite intention in the presentation of the figure from the
back, and, quite spontaneously, Rubens used this theme again
in an 'Antiope' in the Antwerp Museum (also foolishly mis-
called '*Vénus refroidie*'). All the same, we cannot fail to see a
hint of the comic in both pictures, especially in the two
Elders in the first, one of whom is peering ecstatically through
the branches while the other is on the point of vaulting over
a balustrade, and there is farce too in the Jupiter in the guise
of a Satyr in the 'Antiope'.[46]

In the construction of the female figure, Rubens makes,
first of all, a quite obvious distinction between the draped
figures and the nudes, giving the former the privilege of
tallness and slenderness, as we can see in the Holy Women in
the St. Ildefonso altar-piece (Pl. 93), in those on the outer
panel of the 'Raising of the Cross' and even in the St.
Domitilla on the high altar of the Chiesa Nuova in Rome.
Among these figures there is also to be found what is probably
the only example of Rubens's borrowing directly from a
classical theme, namely the so-called '*Pudicitia*'. It is the
standing draped figure, extant in a number of excellent marble
examples, with the right hip projecting; the right hand holds
up the veil falling from the head while the left either sinks on
to the left thigh or turns over towards the right hip. It appears
in a number of the paintings already mentioned, and is quite
particularly beautiful and relevant to the subject in the 'Holy
Women at the Sepulchre' (Czernin Gallery, Vienna). But
in addition, Rubens even introduced it in the form of a statue
into the so-called 'Ceres' (Hermitage) surrounded by vivacious
putti busily engaged in adorning the niche of the statue with a
magnificent garland of fruit. And otherwise Rubens has an
inexhaustible variety of movement in his draped female
figures, as can be seen, for instance, by the most cursory
glance at the gallery of the Luxembourg, and as for clothing
as such, both idealized, so-called classical drapery and the

elegant and opulent dress of his time, he is and remains our
most important source of information. True, the great total
pictorial effect to which all this is subordinated is, as a rule, of
such a nature that the spectator only becomes aware gradually
of these precious details. We must further note the perfect
ease with which all his figures, male and female, wear their
clothes, whatever they may be, for they look as if they had
never worn anything else, even to the heroic battle habit
somewhat casually adopted from Roman monuments, and
to all the glittering splendour of velvet, silk and jewellery
which the eye takes in by the way as if they could not be
otherwise.

But as we have already seen, the female nude can, by the
mere beauty of the skin blended with light and chiaroscuro
captivate the judgement before we can even realize the poetry
of the subject and the beauty of the form. Anyone who wishe
to feel this magic once and for all should, for instance, take the
Berlin picture of 'Andromeda liberated by Perseus' (Pl. 51)
and study this creature, in herself so fat and insignificant, in
all her luminous plenitude, from head to foot. Rubens, moreover, has given us a very curious personal confession of the
bounds of the beautiful, which were, for him, set so wide, in
the famous picture known as '*Het pelsken*' in the Vienna
Gallery which shows his wife, Helen Fourment, on her way
to the bath. (Obviously a very late picture and entirely by
the master's hand.) Against the velvet, furred cloak, held
lightly by one hand, and some fine linen, the neutral background and the red carpet, a quite wonderful body and the
most delicious of heads stand out to incomparable effect, and
the spectator will, for the time being, entirely overlook the
fact that the movement and form of the legs and the bladder
pouches of skin on the knees are anything but perfect.[47]

The female figures, indeed, vary very much in beauty
according to the general intention and the setting, and further
differences enter with the degree of authenticity and state of
preservation. Even in pupils' work there are transparent
laughing, glowing flesh-tints and luminous, golden hair

In the many scenes devoted to the rout of Bacchus and Diana, nymphs and maenads are occasionally superb in presentation, though far removed from nobility, and the general atmosphere is often completed by the addition of Moorish women and female Pans. We could hardly expect the mates of the river-gods to exhibit much delicacy of nurture, yet the beloved of Poseidon in the famous Schönborn picture (Berlin) is more nobly formed, and the chiaroscuro itself confers greater distinction upon her. In the 'Farewell of Adonis', a small, magnificently executed picture in the Uffizi, the Three Graces approaching from the left are beautiful both in form and movement, and in the 'Three sleeping Nymphs surprised by Satyrs' (Pinakothek, Munich, landscape by Jan Brueghel) we may find much to blame in the less noble poses, however truthfully the weariness of the chase comes out in their abandonment, but the modelling is most pure and delicate.[48]

Rubens's greatest achievement in nude goddesses in tempered movement is 'The Judgement of Paris', as we see it in the last, most perfect version (Pl. 103, National Gallery).[49] For impetuosity and fully developed splendour of the body, where the magnificent contours of two nudes form, by their contrast, a perfect balance, the 'Rape of the Daughters of Leucippus' (Pl. 39, Munich Pinakothek) has probably never been equalled. From this picture, the vast power of Rubens's art radiates in many directions, and we shall have to discuss it further; beside it, every other Rape falls into humble obscurity, and vehemence alone cannot work such miracles.

Rubens had certainly seen the best examples of the recumbent, sleeping nude (generally called Venus) of the great Venetians from Giorgione on, and had certainly heard of similar figures by subsequent Italians, but his taste, or that of his patrons, did not lie in that direction and he probably never painted a picture to be kept behind curtains. The only exception to my knowledge is sharply concentrated on a moment, and the sleep is not a natural one; it is the little picture by Rubens's own hand in the Vienna Gallery which shows Ariosto's 'Angelica in the Power of the Hermit', who has put her to sleep by a spell (Orlando Furioso, VIII, 28). With all its lack of ideality and its ugly foreshortening, it is one of the most beautiful, effulgent bodies the master ever painted (variant in The Hague).

In those allegories which, in several variants, depict earthly happiness threatened by war (one in the Munich Pinakothek, cf. also Pl. 80), there are unquestionable portrait elements in the nude figure in the centre, which has been interpreted as Venus or as Family Love. The same is true of the painting in the Uffizi which is erroneously entitled 'Hercules at the Crossroads', where a hero is shown torn between love and the duty of battle, for, in spite of his lion skin, he need not be Hercules at all.[50] On the other hand, the nude in the latest and most splendid of these pictures, 'The Allegory of War' in the Pitti Palace (1638; Pl. 111), is one of the most beautiful idealized creatures in the whole of Rubens's work, and he himself refers to it in a letter as Venus.

To complete this list, we might mention his pictures of the 'Three Graces', or the 'Three Horae', which present the figures in ever new forms and ever new combinations (Madrid Museum, Uffizi, Vienna Academy, etc., cf. Pl. 119). To obtain any idea of the master's fecundity of invention as displayed in a group which would seem condemned to repetition, we should have to lay side by side these groups which were painted many times during that great career. We should find every conceivable aspect of the nude standing in repose, from the almost complete profile to the full front and full back view, every beautiful turn of the head, every graceful and easy entwining of the arms and movement of the hands. Rubens remains entirely independent of the antique models, of the Siena group and the reliefs, while the Pompeian paintings were not yet excavated.

A brief digression on the hands in Rubens may not be out of place here. In this respect he was not only a great master, not only a man of breeding, but a man of delicate perceptions too, and his long acquaintance with the Italian people and its language of gestures had not been without effect. We never

find in him the fingers stretched in exclamatory gesture as in
the Roman school, in Caravaggio, and later in the French
school. His fingers are always softly curved towards each other
and are suited to express every noble and powerful feeling.
Every touch is graceful and, even in boisterous or low-born
figures, never rough, although he is perfectly well able to
shape the huge fist of the soldier. For special purposes he can
use a special language; he shows a hand, held out in wonder,
beautifully foreshortened, from the front, while the hands of a
blind man are seen waving or groping forward (Pl. 47).
Female hands, whatever their gestures, are of a noble sweetness, and we cannot look at the six hands and six feet of a
picture of the Graces, such as that in the Vienna Academy
(where the Graces are carrying the basket of fruit) without
a steadily growing amazement. Above all, solemnity and
holiness find supreme expression in the hands. In the pictures
of the Assumption, beauty succeeds beauty, from the Virgin's
hands bestowing blessing to those of the disciples raised in
ecstasy. A deep feeling speaks here which far transcends the
mere fecundity of an incomparable art. Praying hands, whether
merely curved towards each other or clasped, have their own
peculiar beauty, which can stand comparison with anything
that Guido Reni or Sassoferrato have to show, while the
wrung hands of the 'Penitent Magdalen' (Pl. 28, Vienna)
will probably never be surpassed. And when, in the same
gallery, St. Ambrose refuses the Emperor Theodosius admis-
sion to the church (Pl. 45), the spectator, moved by the
wonderfully dramatic whole, may yet note how the hands and
arms of the stalwart Emperor and his suite are balanced by the
great Archbishop's mild gesture of rejection. And what can
we say of the hand of the miraculous healer in the gesture of
blessing, that unforgettable right hand of 'St. Ignatius with
the Possessed' (Pl. 46; same gallery) which precisely marks the
upper centre of this great picture! And while this hand stands
out on a dark background, the right hand of 'St. Francis
Xavier bestowing Life and Health' (Pl. 47; same gallery) is
set against bright cloudy atmosphere, while his left hand

points to heaven. Rubens's 'Emmaus', only known to me in engravings,[51] which tells the great moment of recognition, is almost completely contained in the eight visible hands. Fine hands of sleeping figures, one propped up, one hanging and two lying, can be seen in a very secular picture in the Vienna Gallery, the story of Cimone from Boccaccio, and finally we might mention Rubens's last self-portrait (same gallery), where the left hand rests nobly on the hilt of the dagger, while the right (the painting hand) is gloved, perhaps as an allusion to gout. His engravers, whose hands are almost always excellent, were probably specially trained by him for them.

*   *   *

The *putto*, or naked child, which entered on the period of its most lavish use in painting with the seventeenth century, had already a long history behind it. The Flemish tradition of the latest, mannerist period probably meant little or nothing to Rubens on this point, and he had to tackle the problem afresh in Italy. There he already found a profusion of cherubs in religious, mythological and decorative art, though it must not be forgotten that the type and the study of it had been maintained at a fairly high level by the two Holy Children, Jesus and St. John. Among the masters of the past who may have made the deepest impression on Rubens in this direction, we may guess at Andrea del Sarto, and above all, Titian, with the cherubs of the 'Assunta', of the 'Madonna del Pesaro' and 'St. Peter Martyr', while it remains uncertain whether Rubens saw at that time the so-called 'Festival of Venus', or 'Children's Festival', once the property of the d'Este family, for in those years it had vanished and it was only much later, when the picture had passed into the ownership of the King of Spain, that he copied it along with the others. He was certainly enchanted by many an antique marble figure of a child, both in relief and sculpture, though he knew from the outset that that world and his were divided.

Then quite independently, and, so to speak, with a quite naturalistic delight, he painted his first secular picture of

children known to us, 'Romulus and Remus with the Wolf'
(Pl. 40; Capitoline Gallery), based on absolutely personal
studies and, more particularly, free of any infection from all
the agitated *bambini* and cupids of Giulio which beset the
art-lover in Mantua. A certain arbitrariness in the modelling,
which recurs even in Rubens's later cherubs, cannot quite
be denied, but the artist has at least given to the first nude
child he painted the expression of joy; while Remus sucks,
Romulus jubilates, obviously at having found a nurse, while
the wolf turns her head, as if in amazement, towards the two
children; calm and unheeded, the Tiber god and his lovely
mate recline in the tall reeds, and earthly life sends a messenger
to the miraculous event in the person of Faustulus, the good
shepherd. All honour to learned research in mythology, but
would we not do better simply to yield ourselves up to the
complete credibility of this splendid scene?

Soon after his return home, Rubens painted the unsurpassed
cherubs in the upper part of the central picture of the St.
Ildefonso altar-piece (Pl. 93), and perhaps these may have
been the earliest of his hovering child angels.[52] But the latter
are, and remain in Rubens, practically of the same race as the
secular *putti*. There are boys and girls, fair and dark, tender
and bold, while in the peculiar world of the Bacchic revel,
little child Pans are added. And if we had nothing of Rubens
but this host of children, they would seem enough in themselves to fill up a good part of the life of a great artist; but this
is not the only part of his work to create that illusion. Quite
often he paints hosts or garlands of these delicious creatures,
and in the 'Virgin with Angels' (Louvre) this has a special
meaning; the forty or more children who crowd hovering
round the Virgin with the lovely *bambino* represent the Holy
Innocents, for they have no wings, and some carry martyrs'
palms in their hands. But who could ever forget those two
pictures in the Munich Pinakothek, 'The Garland of Flowers'
and 'The Garland of Fruit'? In the first, one of the sweetest of
Madonnas presents the Infant Christ in majesty, while eleven[53]
superbly differentiated cherubs in liveliest intercourse hover

around and support the sumptuous oval wreath (by Jan Brueghel) which enframes her. In the second, Rubens has transformed an old familiar theme of Italian art, *putti* carrying a continuous festoon, into a wonderful group of seven lively children who, some intent on their labours, drag along a huge and lavish garland of fruit. In this gallery, which contains such a wealth of Rubens's work, the eye may fall on many another cherub which is worthy of special remembrance. In the great picture of the 'Trinity', a studio production, the feet of the Divine Persons rest on a floating globe with three cherubs; one helps to carry it, the second is attempting to embrace it, and the third, clambering up it, simply has to be seen. In the 'Massacre of the Innocents' (though actually there is nobody to compete with him but Raphael and Guido), he has put forth all his powers to depict the child at the moment of its last scream (Pl. 102). And finally, we find in the same gallery a small improvisation by his own hand of 'St. Christopher with the Hermit', which reappears on a colossal scale in the outer panels of the 'Deposition' in Antwerp Cathedral, where it may be only too easily overlooked. Facing the searching light of the hermit's lantern, the Christ Child is throwing open the scarlet cloak of the kindly giant which had been wrapped round him: Lo, it is I!

Forty years after Rubens, Murillo (1618) was born, and his are the only cherubs that can bear a general comparison with those of Rubens. Murillo too was a man of happy temperament, a point which may not be without significance in this connexion. The myth with its attendant cherubs finds no place in his work: even the cherubs on earthly business bent, which find their own particular consummation in the wonderful Beggar Children of Seville, are little assistants of holy persons, verging here and there on the humorous, and here Murillo is at times closely akin to Rubens; afterwards there came his Infant Christs and St. Johns, which surpass all the rest of the seventeenth century in their spirited conception and supernatural beauty, and finally we have the world of hovering *putti*, the retinue of the divine persons, in particular those in the altar-piece of the 'Conception'. In joy and sadness, these lovely creatures, which seem to be drifting lightly into the picture, reveal in the tenderness of their shape and movement what no later master was ever able to express, and even Rubens's most beautiful hovering cherubs look somewhat muscular beside them. Yet Rubens himself foreshadowed many things in his cherubs. The bright bloom of the flesh in the silvery clouds, the light hovering of these *oiseaux célestes* (Fromentin), the avoidance, as far as possible, of the head-down position, the general grace of the foreshortenings, and finally the Titianesque shimmer caught from the Venetian altar-pieces (p. 44) produce an impression which may have had its effect on Murillo when, as a young man, he studied the pictures in the royal collection in Madrid and the Escorial. Among them there were many important pictures by Rubens, and it may be that there were some which contained cherubs of this kind.

In his altar-pieces, apart from the Ascensions, Rubens tends to be rather sparing with his cherubs, in contrast to famous Italian contemporaries, who only too often placed the Madonna of the ordinary devotional picture up in the clouds and gave her a whole retinue of angels as well as *putti* and cherubs' heads, instead of leaving her in the midst of the saints. Rubens only allows these children to appear in a definite function relevant to the whole. For instance, in the 'Trinity' in the Antwerp Gallery, two very vigorous ones, bitterly weeping, present the instruments of torture. Indeed he can create special situations for them. In the 'Rest on the Flight', the woodcut mentioned above (p. 34) which is his own design, the Child asleep on His mother's lap might be wakened by the noise of the two cherubs pulling at a lamb, but a third warns them to be quiet by pointing to the Infant. Further details of the life of the Holy Children in the open air can be seen in a delicious picture in the Vienna Gallery and its excellent studio replica in Berlin; the Infant Christ and St. John reclining on the ground, attended by two winged cherubs, one of whom is leading the lamb to St. John, whose cheek is being thoughtfully stroked by the Heavenly Child. He is clearly distinguished by the greater nobility of his bodily form and by that miraculous fairness which Rubens gives his elect. In a number of variants, the two Holy Children appear alone, busy with the lamb, in a forest glade—again a kind of forecast of Murillo.

As regards the secular *putti*, there is an example of extreme lavishness in the splendid 'Festival of Venus' in the Vienna Gallery (Pl. 100). On the garland of fruit and the drapery which hangs in the tree-tops, a whole cloud of them comes floating along, the main body dances in front of the goddess, while a second group dances to the left, and there are single ones scattered throughout the picture in every possible function. We get the impression of a very free improvisation on Titian's 'Children's Festival', which was one of the pictures Rubens had copied during his second visit to Madrid.[54] But what Titian was aiming at was a careless hurly-burly of quite small children, and this work, painted when he was about forty, belongs to his prime of life. Beside it, these *putti* of Rubens certainly look somewhat conventional in execution, even where the design is most spontaneous and spirited. But that Rubens tended as a whole to economy, even in secular painting, can be seen in the historical allegories. Of the five *putti* in the 'Allegory of War' (Pl. 111; Pitti Palace) four are indispensable to the action. In the whole of the gallery of the Luxembourg, only the 'Exchange of Princesses' has an ethereal dance of welcome, while in other pictures *putti* are the exception, but then they are exceptionally beautiful and appear at telling places, as, for instance, the two riding with torches on the team of lions drawing the chariot of the city of Lyons. In the more perfect and mature version of 'The Judgement of Paris' in the National Gallery (Pl. 103), several of those which figure in the ten years' earlier version in Dresden have been omitted.[55] Apart from the 'Festival of Venus', the master brings them in only where he has work for them to do, and occasionally with the most charming humour, for instance the five in the 'Andromeda' in the Berlin Museum (Pl. 51), who unloose the bonds of the nude figure of the heroine, and help each other to climb up and groom the winged horse of Perseus, that friendly dapple-grey. They play and shout round the most frightful wild beasts, and even Romulus and Remus seem quite at home with the wolf (Pl. 40). Now every artist in Rome for a century past had known Love with the Lion in classical sculptures, and also the colossal Nile God of the Vatican, where the *putti* sport not only with the ichneumon, but with a crocodile too. But it was the great Fleming who, in the famous 'Four Rivers' (Vienna), armed with the full glow of his palette, combined the most real and living of his wild beasts with his loveliest and merriest *putti*.

In a building in Rome, now demolished, Annibale Carracci had painted in a free fresco style those scenes from the story of Psyche which were recently transferred to the Capitoline Gallery, and it is possible that Rubens saw them. Large subordinate fields show *putti* playfully taming wild beasts, a lion, a lioness, a wolf and an ass, probably in allusion to the metamorphosed Lucius in Apuleius. There is a touch of grandeur in the whole, and since I cannot share the general disparagement of Annibale, it would seem very fortunate that two great masters of the same period should have given their versions, in different styles, of wild beasts with *putti*. But just as Rubens recalls Titian here and there, Annibale, in the modelling of these *putti*, looks back to those of Raphael in the Camera della Segnatura, where, in the frieze in the Hall of the Legislature, the three seated women, Wisdom, Temperance and Fortitude, are grouped with five magnificently modelled and animated children.

* * *

In the art of later times, and quite particularly in superior female heads, beauty cannot be imagined apart from soul. Here Rubens can be very instructive, whether in fugitive sketches or in carefully finished pictures, in work by his own hand and in studio paintings, in scenes of calm and scenes of dramatic movement, wherever the hand of the master is to be felt in any way. Given the vast range of beings who owe their existence to him, it should be possible to draw some more general observations from his female figures. People have spoken all too heedlessly of the provincialism of their opulence, and we hear, for instance, of 'Flemish grossness' though Antwerp at all times belonged to Brabant. But even when this point has been cleared up, it might be well to see at first hand whether the type can still be regarded as dominant in our own day, either among the people or in such old families as still survive. For Rubens's own time we can turn to the female portraits, which are exceedingly varied in type; apart from royalty, the sitters were, in all probability, patrician ladies of Antwerp.

It may be that general but one-sided conclusions have been drawn too freely from the voluptuous beauty of Helen Fourment, together, perhaps, with that superb figure which occupies the central place in a number of Jordaens's pictures and also exists in a portrait. This is Jordaens's wife Catherine, the daughter of Adam van Noort, who had been Rubens's teacher at one time, and Rubens must have seen her often from childhood on. But it was certainly not she who determined his type.

Above all, those features which were his ideal in great and important passages were certainly bodied forth out of his own most inward imagination, and they are by no means those which Europe had long regarded as the highest attainable namely those of the holy women of Leonardo, Raphael, Fra Bartolommeo and so on, which so many Flemish artists had admired, and had been struggling to imitate for a hundred years. Nor are they those of the Venetians, and Rubens resisted in Titian not only the 'Assunta', but also the enchantment of those faces among which the 'Flora' of the Uffizi takes the lead. Nor were matters otherwise with the living women he encountered in Italy. The Italian beauty who emerges, for instance, very clearly from several of Van Dyck's Madonnas can be recognized nowhere in Rubens, and he left it to his contemporary Guido Reni to find inspiration in the Niobides of classical antiquity. The new and living creation which impresses us even today does not, in its actual features, represent a native Flemish type, yet, by virtue of a mysterious divination, it corresponds to the inward feeling of his race. It is in this sense that we are to understand what Fromentin[56] says in connexion with the 'Crucifixion' and the 'Deposition' in Antwerp Cathedral (Pls. 15-20): 'In these pictures Rubens revealed the Gospel in Flemish terms and established the Flemish type of the Virgin, the Redeemer, the Magdalen and the Disciples'. Two centuries earlier, the Netherlands had achieved a great transformation of the kind and succeeded in imposing it as a model of form and expression even on German, French and Spanish art. But in Rubens's time an independent and powerful method of expressing holy beauty was living and growing in Italy and Spain, with elements of ecstasy and sweetness which we never or rarely find in Rubens. It was the transfiguration of types different from his, and we should not take this as a misfortune, but as a sign of the creative power of the epoch.

First, what we might call his more normal type must not be sought in figures highly charged with feeling, in the Mater Dolorosa of the 'Deposition', of the *Christ à la Paille*, of the 'Pietà' of the Vienna Gallery, nor in great apotheoses, such as the 'Assumption', but in works for domestic devotion.[57] What we see here is a brunette, the face full and already rather matronly, with a prevailing expression of lovingkindness, the dark hair very heavy, the eyes and mouth of a peculiar and extremely attractive shape, the texture of the flesh rich, yet not voluptuous, and the whole without any kind of resemblance to Isabella Brant, although she was a brunette. Such is the Madonna of the St. Ildefonso altar (Pl. 93), of the 'Virgin with Angels' in the Louvre, and of the 'Adoration of the Magi' in Antwerp (Pl. 70). In the 'Holy Family with the Basketwork Cradle' (Pitti Palace) it approximates to a more popular type, while the 'Virgin with the Parrot' (Antwerp) has a more patrician air, and the type reaches pure beauty in the 'Garland of Flowers' (Munich Pinakothek—the Madonna with Eleven Cherubs). The same features will be found again

in the secular and mythological pictures, for instance in th
female figures in the 'Four Rivers' (Vienna Gallery) and eve
in larger histories, where Rubens gives a place to this, his ow
peculiar creation, side by side with portraits and direct obser
vation of life. But it was the rich blond that had the master'
preference, both in religious pictures and mythologies, i
draped and in nude figures, the very light and shining ha
being wonderfully attuned to it. In the pictures of the 'Hol
Children' (Vienna and Berlin) it is this fairness which
together with the expression in the eyes, clearly distinguishe
the Infant Christ as the Lord from the other three childre
The features are softer than in the brunette type, the expressio
milder, with even a touch of lovely sadness. Yet the figur
that comes to mind in this connexion is an expression c
deepest sorrow, the Magdalen at the foot of the cross in th
famous picture known as the '*Coup de Lance*' (Pl. 54; Antwer
Museum) where she is unquestionably the centre of attentio
With her, not only were all the master's Magdalens dedicate
to fairness, but all the female figures in other pictures t
which he wished to show special favour too, for instance, th
Veronica in the 'Bearing of the Cross' in Brussels (Pl. 92
Rubens also set fair and dark in the most vivid contrast, bot
of form and expression, for instance in the picture of th
'Daughters of Cecrops' (Liechtenstein Gallery) already di
cussed, while there are many instances of this contrast whic
came about of themselves.

The aged holy women, Anna and Elizabeth, sometim
accompanied by an old woman of the people, the mother
the adoring shepherds, have in Rubens a superb expression
benevolence and happiness. I do not myself share the all-to
prevalent tendency to recognize members of his family in h
religious pictures, but we cannot help feeling that he has he
recorded the features and character of his own mother. Lon
ago, an altar in the Carmelite Monastery in Antwerp w
resplendent with the picture (now in the museum) of th
'Education of the Virgin' containing the most beautiful S
Anna Rubens ever painted.[53]

VIII. Detail from the 'Portrait of Marchesa Doria'. (Plate 8)

IX. Detail from the 'Ildefonso Altar-piece'. (Plate 93)

These types, of course, appear in every kind of modification and verge at times on the purely individual. Here Rubens clearly betrays an entourage of beautiful women of rank; the 'Garden of Love' (Pl. 99) is their glorious common memorial.

We may abandon further attempts to demonstrate prevailing 'types' in Rubens, though we might, for instance, recall that recurring heroic head of a man in middle years which some have believed to be his own.[59] It would, however, be more important to consider the scope and depth of his feeling, which is too little realized even now. Some observations of his Holy Families and Christ, both in action and suffering, may at least make some points clear. While Rubens never achieved, in form and expression, that idealism of the great Italians of the mid-Renaissance which has never been paralleled since, even in Italy, we nevertheless find everywhere in his work both truth and life, and often grandeur and beauty. In big, quickly painted pictures, in scenes of crowded action, he certainly extemporized many a face from his vast and vivid memory, and the whole must make up for the detail, although the range and depth of his psychological experience never abandon him entirely. The great organized pictures, in which his hand is visible throughout, are a different matter, particularly when there is less action in the scene.

First of all, it is characteristic that we find nowhere in Rubens the single half-length figure whose only function is to express feeling, especially longing. This includes not only the Madonna, but also the Magdalen, the Sibyl, etc., for Rubens has no feeling whose origin lies outside the picture, and the St. Cecilia in the Berlin Museum (Pl. 118), which we may regard as the sole exception, may have her special *raison d'être*. The half-length figure itself hardly occurs in all his work outside of the portraits, not even in the Madonna and Child. In its place he nearly always gives us a picture with several figures in momentary action, whether in the form of the Holy Family in the narrower sense of the word or in intercourse with angels and cherubs. Except for a few, though excellent, three-quarter-length pictures, for instance of the

E

'Holy Family with the Basketwork Cradle' (Pitti Palace) and
another in the Turin Gallery,[60] all his figures are full-length.
We see a happy young mother with her family in the quiet
enjoyment of a delightful moment, and the artist was here
quite true to his personal experience, for he was the painter of
the momentary and a happy father and he certainly fulfilled
the needs of Belgian piety, although his feelings only attained
full freedom in Italy. In the 'Annunciation' (Pl. 11; Vienna),
painted earlier at Antwerp and almost an example of the local
manner, Maria is still without a soul.[61] It was only later that
mothers with children appealed to him as a subject, as we see it
in the Holy Families, the legends ('The Miraculous Healing
of St. Ignatius', Pl. 46), the Sabine Women and the portraits of
his two wives. Whether the Madonna appears as a woman
of the people or as a lady of rank, she is always gracious, and
her expression of joy finds its reflection in the garlands or
flowers and even whole festoons of cherubs, as we have
already seen. Otherwise the scene is frequently set in the open
air, with trees and verdure. The Infant Christ, where he is not
solemnly presented for adoration, caresses his Mother or the
child St. John, or (in a studio picture in the Pitti Palace) St.
John's lamb, on which St. John is actually riding astride,
while the *Bambino* looks up to his mother with an expression
of loving tenderness. There is also a St. Anna, smiling kindly,
while Joseph, a rugged, homely figure, retreats, humble but
happy. We can see by the pictures of the 'Visitation' and
the 'Education of the Virgin' (Antwerp Museum) that the
artist gave greater distinction of expression to the Virgin's
father, Joachim, than to Joseph, as he also did to the aged
priest Zacharias. We may well ask whether all the art of the
period has a Holy Family to show comparable to the 'Holy
Family under the Apple-Tree' in the Vienna Gallery (Pl. 96).
It is, as is well known, a composite picture, made up of the
former outer panels of the St. Ildefonso altar-piece, which
were later sawn off and reassembled with supplementary
painting. Thus the deep desire for a union of the families of
the Infant St. John and the Infant Christ is, so to speak, satisfied.

—two parent couples, two children, and above in the treetops
two cherubs plucking apples have been fused by wonderful
contrasts into one grand pictorial effect with a supreme balance
of forms and expressions.

As regards the spiritual representation of Christ, the art of
Antwerp possessed, in addition to all the great creations of the
Flemish Primitives, a high authority in Quentin Matsys, who
was still held in high honour (quarter-length figure of Christ
in Antwerp Museum, National Gallery and Louvre, of more
or less certain authenticity), and Otto van Veen's Christ reveals
at any rate the intention of great nobility. But in Italy, Rubens
had become most familiar with the Venetian conception of
Christ; he had also, in all probability, seen Titian's famous
'Tribute Money' (then at Modena?),[62] and he betrays here and
there the impression it had made on him ('Intercession of St.
Theresa', Antwerp Museum). Yet even here, the influence of
Italy on his art was liberating rather than determining.

Firstly, as with the Madonna, there is no single, half-length
figure of Christ with a purely expressive function, no single
head, such as we find in the Carraccis, in Guido, Guercino and
a host of others, ranging from the calm and majestic head with
steady gaze to the head crowned with thorns, the Ecce Homo.[63]
It is as if, in Italy, this theme had been the test of the artist's
capacity for religious art. On the other hand we find in
Rubens outstanding 'Pietàs', though these, with the possible
exception of the 'Christ à la Paille' have been oddly neglected
in comparison with Van Dyck's, which have attracted all
attention to themselves by the nobility of the holy suffering
and the more subtle selection and finer development of the
forms. Rubens is not at all afraid of crass foreshortenings, as,
for instance, in the head of the 'Christ à la Paille' and the early
'Pietà' (1614) in the Vienna Gallery, and in the outstretched
foot in the same 'Pietà' and the 'Trinities'. And just as, in his
'Holy Families', many feel him to be inferior to Van Dyck's
appealing sentimentality, his attendant figures in the 'Pietàs'
lack some of Van Dyck's tenderness of feeling. It is only after
deeper consideration of the Vienna picture that we can do

justice to Rubens's greater seriousness and admit the pro-
foundly moving power of the great 'Pietà before the Grotto'
Rubens may have seen one or another of Carracci's pictures
overloaded with figures and gestures, with the inevitable
swooning Madonna and the resulting dispersal of interest,
but they could not lead him astray. Even the sorrow of St.
Francis in these pictures, which may be called declamatory in
Annibale (Parma), is in Rubens veritable grief.

The figures of the Crucified are absolutely Rubens's own,
and in any case he came too late to see any of Guido's much
admired altar-pieces with the solitary crucifix on a background
of clouds (S. Lorenzo in Lucina, Rome; Modena). In view of
the relatively large number of studio pictures, engravings and
imitations, and the competition of Van Dyck, whose work is
particularly difficult to distinguish here, we can mention only
the life-size 'Crucifixion' in the Antwerp Museum, an early,
authentic picture with its wonderfully noble head at the
moment of the cry: 'Why hast Thou forsaken me?'[64]

In the 'Raising of the Cross' in Antwerp Cathedral (Pl. 15)
the high light is concentrated almost exclusively on the Christ
against a dark, rocky background in the upper half of the
picture, a powerfully expressive figure with a truly tremendous upward look, surrounded by the sullen crowd of hire-
lings, soldiers and mounted men, to the left the women and
children of Jerusalem in loud lamentation. The great 'Deposition' (Pl. 18; also Antwerp Cathedral), with its grandiose
unity of design which gathers up every figure into the action
and feeling, is perhaps the absolutely ultimate and supreme
solution of the problem, both emotional and artistic, and is
far superior to Daniele da Volterra's work in Trinità dei
Monti in Rome, not only in effect, but in power of feeling. If
Daniele worked after a composition of Michelangelo's—and
opinion on the subject is divided—Rubens's picture is a victory
over Michelangelo, too.

Outside of the Passion, the Christ of consolation and
succour takes on different features and a different expression,
and it cannot quite be denied that something of the artist's

own personality had entered into it, for instance in the superb
picture in the Munich Pinakothek which shows 'Christ with
the Four Great Penitents' (Pl. 44), and equally clearly in the
profile figure of Christ in the 'Raising of Lazarus' (Berlin
Museum) and possibly also in the 'St. Thomas', while elsewhere (see above) there would seem to be a revival of
Venetian impressions.

St. John the Evangelist, who appears in all the Passions and
Assumptions as a powerful, succouring figure of a still youthful fair-haired type, is again entirely Rubens's own, and he has
put a great deal of his finest feeling into this disciple. In the
great 'Deposition' it is St. John who receives the body in his
strong arms.

Religious feeling will be found movingly expressed throughout Rubens's work, but it achieves wider scope in the 'Last
Communion of St. Francis' (Pl. 48). Rubens left Italy too early
to see Domenichino's solution of the same problem in his
famous 'Last Communion of St. Jerome' (Vatican Pinacoteca),
and the feeling in his picture is totally different. His saint, the
embodiment of spirituality, still youthful, not sinking back
but leaning forward towards the priest with the sacrament,
the onlookers—probably monks of the Carmelite community
at Antwerp, for whose church the picture was painted—not
carefully selected and placed, but crowding round in longing
and all deeply moved, and finally the extraordinary pictorial
qualities of the work—all these things together give it a place
apart in Rubens's total œuvre in virtue of the peculiar sublimity
of its inspiration.[65] But even in comparison with famous works
by earlier Italian artists which Rubens must have seen, we can
feel in him, now and then, a far greater depth of religious
feeling when he takes up the same problems. Titian's 'Pentecost' in the Salute at Venice is composed and painted with
every concession to beauty and variety—in the centre, beautiful heads of women, private conversations among the bystanders and a number of seated figures. For Rubens's handling
of the same subject we are dependent on a studio picture
(Munich Pinakothek) and an engraving by Pontius which

does not quite correspond to it, yet how much deeper is the gravity with which he renders the one rapture inspiring the fifteen figures standing and kneeling round the Virgin! Rubens's Apostles, dramatically distinct in his Assumptions, are here united in one mighty moment.

It may be that the enhanced expression of feeling is not always intended in a strictly religious sense. Had Rubens really, seeing but unseen, watched his Helen Fourment in a moment of ecstatic devotion when he painted her in the guise of St. Cecilia (Pl. 118; famous picture in the Berlin Museum), or was his essential purpose—long before Carlo Dolci—to show beautiful hands in movement on the organ keys? Four enraptured cherubs, elaborate architecture and a rural vista complete the sumptuous scene. Even the 'Repentance of the Magdalen' (Vienna, Pl. 28; old copy at Cassel) is somewhat questionable and the noble grief of his opulent blonde figure is less successfully rendered than the wringing of the hands. And incidentally, the prevailing interpretation of the picture gives rise to some misgiving; beside the principal figure, which stands out with such wonderful brilliance against the background of a red curtain, there sits waiting in the half-shadow, against cloudy atmosphere and a column, a creature in a black veil who is generally taken to represent Martha, the Magdalen's sister, but she looks more like a pretty maid, wondering whether the repentance will soon be over or whether it is going to last, so that she may fall heir to the fallen jewel-box (and perhaps the lovers too). In that case, what we have here might be an ironic comment on the way of the world, like the 'Samson and Delilah', which will be discussed elsewhere.

We shall, however, come in time to recognize the tenderness of Rubens's feeling in many places where we least expect it. In the Cassel picture of 'Callisto with Jupiter in the Guise of Diana', how appealing is the creature in her state 'between yielding and misgivings'.

But finally, as an extreme contrast to all this, Rubens proves to be one of the very greatest masters of the demonic in human nature, and in the men possessed by devils in the two altar-pieces of the 'Miracles of St. Ignatius' (Pl. 46; Vienna and S. Ambrogio, Genoa) he may have touched those confines accorded to great art in his time and demanded by a general conviction. In his pictures of Heaven and Hell the boldness and power of his mind has created beings far beyond the range of humanity in ways utterly different from the grimacing masks of the ordinary run of Flemish phantasts.

$$\star \qquad \star \qquad \star$$

The sublime power served by all Rubens's separate capacities and individual conceptions may for the time being be subsumed under the name of his composition. At first sight it seems a miracle, to be revered as such, yet it might be desirable even here to follow up certain details and to consider some of the conditions which made it possible for this most sane of natures to lay hold on what suited it best. That nature certainly appears to be under the unerring guidance of a genius born with it.

Rubens's predecessors in Antwerp, the mannerists, had older traditions, all kinds of respectable individual talents, and a great store of diligence, but the whole was spoilt by a false conception of modelling and an artificiality of feeling due to the Roman school, whose traditional gestures and poses showed to peculiar disadvantage in Flanders. Further, they overcrowded their compositions at the cost of all artistic economy, as if they could mend matters by mere multiplication. Here Rubens's chief task was to forget what he had been familiar with since boyhood, yet the first multitudinous impressions he received in Italy could not improve things very much. He certainly saw the paintings of great masters of other times, preserved in far greater number and much better condition, but the art he found not only alive, but tyrannous there, and the talk and opinions that went with it, were again largely those of the mannerists. Yet it was just with Venice, to which he felt most akin, that his most decisive encounter took place. True, he found there, in contrast to the mass frescoes of the rest of Italy, oil painting on canvas on walls and ceilings showing the freest and most brilliant command of all artistic means and a feeling in the characters and the life depicted which was very close to his own.

But in the narration of events and in the selection of what was to be communicated, his feeling was entirely different. We must not overlook the fact that Venice at that time possessed little of what was most important to Rubens, namely, Titian's spirited subject pictures. His historical paintings in the Great Hall of the Doge's Palace had long since been destroyed by fire, and though one of them, the 'Battle of the Bridge' (or 'Battle of Cadore'), is generally believed to have furnished Rubens with the dominating motif of his 'Battle of the Amazons' (Pl. 36), he can only have seen the picture in copies[66] or in Fontana's engravings. He must have been enraptured with Titian's 'St. Peter Martyr', and he certainly admired the ceiling paintings of scenes from the Old Testament (now) in the sacristy of the Salute. On the other hand, he took nothing from the 'Presentation of the Virgin in the Temple', from the 'Pentecost' mentioned above, nor from the 'Fides with Doge Grimani', at least as far as subject matter is concerned. He far surpassed Titian's 'Martyrdom of St. Laurence' in the design of his own picture, while the great 'Ecce Homo' in the Vienna Gallery, which he may have seen, is designed in a spirit directly opposed to his own, for all its rich pictorial effect. But even his revered Paolo Veronese had, as a rule, not troubled to do more than extract what was absolutely necessary from the scene as he saw it, and then simply add the rest, the subsidiary figures, according to his desire for pleasing colour and effective variation, so that his pictures, in spite of a superb general effect, are lacking in the sense of a higher unity. Above his legends of saints, St. Justina, St. George, St. Sebastian, he adds, as a kind of second part, a whole glory, a cloud-group of the Madonna with saints or angels, or at any rate (in the 'Marriage of St. Catherine', Pl. 75) a swarm of angels and cherubs, while below, a number of side figures, excellent in themselves, are none the less mere supers, and here we find Rubens borrowing, namely the flanking groups of horsemen on the right-hand panel of the 'Raising of the Cross' at Antwerp (Pl. 17), but they are vital to the picture, and not supers. Tintoretto, for all his gifts, must have repelled Rubens by his sham instantaneity, with bending and reeling figures (even Paolo is not quite free of them) and by his complete lack of artistic economy, for to Rubens the given space and content of a picture were from the outset something sacred.

But as Rubens became familiar with the real Michelangelo in Rome, he must have come to ignore the spurious Michelangelo who still lived on in Tintoretto, as well as in the mannerists of Antwerp. What he now had to do was to create his own world of beings to set beside Titian's creatures of Heaven, earth and hell, while from Titian as a frescoist he felt himself worlds apart both in means and aims, a feeling which may have been very consoling. The mute dialogue between Rubens and Raphael is much more difficult to interpret. The only directly recognizable influence from Raphael came from the 'Battle of Constantine',[67] and Rubens had long been familiar with this picture in engravings, but what his state of mind was before the 'Transfiguration' in S. Pietro in Montorio, we cannot divine. It is not until quite late in his life that we find, in his 'St. Roch' at Alost, that superb fusion of earthly wretchedness, dawning hope and supernatural consolation, and here, at a century's distance, kin may have called to kin.

Of living Italian artists, as we tried to show above (p. 7) by examples, probably Caravaggio alone left any strong impression on Rubens's mind. While the rest might serve him as examples or warning in various directions for the so-called technique of painting, he was already inwardly superior to them all in composition by the mighty double gift of his nature, of which he must now have been fully aware—the delight in living invention and representation and the premonition of laws which, while setting bounds to them, supremely enhanced the appeal of the picture. His means and qualities, taken singly, are those of all higher painting, they are all, in themselves, recognized and natural, appear in great perfection in other artists, and even form part of recognized doctrine, whatever scorn may be cast upon it. Since the end of the old schools, which deemed their duty done, particularly in religious art, by serious, unemotional representation of detail, the more so when they had added all they could by way of splendour and delicacy of execution, a free consciousness of visual effect had gradually developed, and the eye had become ready to respond to it; how, for instance, the colours, with their wide range of tones, cool, warm or glowing, should act upon each other and succeed each other effectively in the picture, was a thing that could be learned entirely from the Venetian school in its heyday. A tradition also survived from earlier art as to the arrangement in space (which the mannerists of the time had so often sacrificed to a riot of details which they found interesting), namely, the desire for an even, fairly symmetrical arrangement of the figures and incidents, since the picture had to be not merely a description of something or other, but, by an approximate balance of its parts, a beautiful thing. This symmetry, however, though it dominated the whole, had to be concealed as far as possible, and suppressed here and there. Now although this was recognized as a primary law of painting in the heroic age, Rubens must be regarded as the first great initiate and master in this domain. For only in Rubens do we find the richest symmetrical manipulation of a variety of elements of equal value, of equivalents, in the picture, combined with a most animated, or even agitated incident to produce an effect which triumphantly captivates both eye and mind. The horses of his sun chariot are fiery creatures, but he would not let them run away with him.

These equivalents, of course, do not appear separate, they interpenetrate: when, for instance, a light and a dark mass correspond in symmetry, or when one plane of colour is set against another, quite different contrasts of form and expression come into being, and, above all, visual values can be counterbalanced by ideal values. Even movement, when it

balances repose, can have its place here, and, in particular,
moral and spiritual importance can balance moral and spiritual
subordination. This list could be made much longer; we
may sum up by saying that stresses varying widely in nature
and significance can be found together in the same picture.
A true and satisfying distribution of such stresses may be
demonstrated by a beautiful example of the simplest kind,
the three-quarter-length picture of the 'Resurrected Christ
with the Four Great Penitents' (Pl. 44; Munich Pinakothek),
where, merely as a visual impression, the Christ, a bright
nude in three-quarter view, balances the group in the shade
opposite him consisting of the Repentant Thief, St. Peter,
King David, and the Magdalen bowing low before him,
though she really belongs to the mass of light. But it is the
Christ who takes up almost half the picture and bears the
supreme spiritual emphasis, in spite of the deeply expressive
quality of the other figures. In a splendid picture with the
same intention (Cassel Gallery, repetition or old copy in the
Nuremberg Museum) with full-length figures, it is the calm,
enthroned Madonna with the two Children who fully balances
not only the Four Great Penitents, but also the four saints
attending them, although the latter are deeply moved by the
sinners' repentance and St. Dominic, in his emotion, has
grasped the arm of St. Francis, who kneels in prayer.

It is, however, only when a power and intention of such a
kind are combined with vivid, even vehement narration that
those amazing works come into being which can only be
explained by some inward process peculiar to Rubens. A vast
imagination, even in full inspiration, would of itself have
produced nothing more than a worthless profusion of detail.
On the other hand, a patient, conscious building-up of the
picture by equivalents would have led him no further than
other artists. In Rubens, some other power must have been
at work.

We like to think that great masters had their moments of
vision when future works appeared before them complete.
This vision would appear to have been of a peculiar kind in

Rubens. He saw at one and the same time a restful symmetrical arrangement of the masses in space and vehement spiritual and physical motion; he saw light and life radiating mainly from the centre, and his triumphant colour harmonies, his near and far distances and scheme of light and shade rose before him, as they could not but rise, till all was matured to the harmony and power we have spoken of. Then he set to work. But he worked calmly; as Fromentin[68] remarks: '*la brosse est aussi calme que l'âme est chaude et l'esprit prompt à s'élancer*'. When work began, he was perfectly clear in his mind and absolutely at home with most formidable problems. The same author speaks with profoundest insight when he says of the Antwerp 'Raising of the Cross' (Pl. 15); '*tout paraît être sorti à la fois d'une inspiration irrésistible, lucide et prompte*'. The existence of preliminary sketches merely means that the master, at various stages of work, set down, for his own use or by order of his patrons, a general idea of the final effect of the picture. It is just the sketch (Louvre) for the last-named picture that might furnish further evidence in this direction. According to old custom, the Council of St. Walpurga's church required a triptych for their high altar, and it would have been difficult for Rubens not to give them a preliminary idea of the distribution of the action over the central and outer panels, which form one in the drawing.[69] Here we may turn for comparison to the deplorable expedients Tintoretto resorted to in his 'Raising of the Cross'—not of Christ but of the Repentant Thief (Scuola di San Rocco). In Rubens, the powerful exertions of a definite number of herculean figures to set up a heavy tree trunk so that it will stand firm are realized with incomparably greater force. What they have to do, they do with a will and obviously. But on the tree, as it rises across the upper centre of the picture, the face of the Crucified hangs in the high light with an indescribable expression on the features. With the balance and contrast of these two extreme accents of movement, Rubens becomes absolutely supreme in the rendering of the instantaneous. Further, a profound sense of the symbolic told him that light and shade were here the vehicle of expression, and he added colour only in a subordinate role. The background is a gloomy precipice with bushes.

The 'Deposition', on the other hand, is one huge central unit of design with many rays, and all participate, spiritually and physically, in a wonderful gradation (Pl. 18). There is no swooning Madonna as the centre of a second subsidiary group, such as we find in Daniele da Volterra, nor has anyone time to stride along, helplessly ranting, like Daniele's St. John.[70]

The 'Raising of Lazarus' (Berlin Museum) is one of his great achievements in the mastery of spiritual and pictorial values. A preliminary composition, which is reproduced in an excellent engraving, was well filled with members of the family, Pharisees and gesticulating onlookers, and would roughly correspond to the very best that the minds of such artists as Francesco or Leandro Bassano could produce. But in this authentic painting, he has compressed the whole action into six indispensable figures. To Christ he has given the most majestic bearing, a powerful striding approach in profile and the red cloak, to Lazarus his swift rise from the abyss and his look of gratitude. Peter turns, deeply moved, to Christ, and another apostle looks upon Lazarus; there is a similar arrangement of the two sisters kneeling in the centre, Martha, who is loosening the last cerements of her brother and Mary Magdalen, whose head occupies the centre of the picture, looking up to Christ.[71] Compared with this wonderful and fiery unity, the much more famous picture by Sebastiano del Piombo (National Gallery) gives the effect of a construction coolly calculated and calmly executed, and the Lazarus (said to have been painted in by Michelangelo), though certainly a very learned nude, exudes all the icy chill of intention.

In Rubens's very great pictures of momentary action, what the spectator enjoys, at first unconsciously, is the combination of dramatic movement with a mysterious visual restfulness, and it is only later that he becomes aware that the separate elements cohere by a furtive symmetry, or even by a mathematical figure. Rubens certainly never set to work with such

a figure in mind, but it certainly entered of itself into his vision
and grew in his imagination along with the rest.

In the 'Rape of the Daughters of Leucippus' (Pl. 39;
Munich Pinakothek), the two female figures form an almost
uniform mass of light exactly in the lower centre of the picture,
round which the rest is disposed like a cloud—that is, the
Dioscuri, Castor and Pollux, the two horses and the two *putti*.
These eight beings fill out the exact square of the picture on the
background of a bright, lush landscape. But it can further
be seen that the two magnificently developed female figures
are precisely complementary, that the one presents exactly
the view not presented by the other, and that the artist has
isolated them from each other by an intervening space so that
they nowhere overlap. And all this is fused in the incredible
fire of the moment. No other artist, at any time or of any
school, could have created just this.

A perfect contrast to this huge, single event is offered by a
picture with a number of quieter incidents which is, in its
turn, based on a restful symmetry—'The Miracles of St.
Francis Xavier' (Pl. 47). Five accents of widely varying importance form a quincunx; in the upper right, on a stone pedestal,
the saint and his companion; to the upper left, the sick, noble
Hindu with his black servant and torch-bearing retinue; in
the middle, somewhat farther into the distance and beautifully
distributed to left and right, native onlookers and a Portuguese
in armour, the former gazing at the saint and the latter at the
Hindu; in the foreground, bottom left, a man raised from the
dead and the grave-diggers who were to have buried him;
bottom right, the halt and blind seeking healing. A further
means by which repose emanates from so crowded a composition is that the heads of all the figures in the different groups
are roughly at the same height, so that the planes in which
they appear become perfectly clear; there is also a great deal of
atmosphere and a wonderful sunbeam, and, in the upper part
on the heathen side, a temple with a falling idol and people in
flight, while over the saint, in the clouds, there is a Fides with
angels. Some may pity Rubens because he had to paint such

hings, yet we must marvel at his own joy in the mastery with
vhich it was done. But pity is altogether out of place with
Rubens and may spend itself elsewhere in the history
of art.

In the 'Battle of the Amazons' (Pl. 36), it is the stone arch of
he bridge which, as a restful mathematical figure, dominates
he tumult in quite a different way from the bridge in Titian's
battle-piece mentioned above. While in Titian (according to
Fontana's engraving) it bears only one galloping rider, in
Rubens it bears aloft the whole main group which, being
nearer, is relatively much bigger. That group is unsurpassed in
he dreadful beauty of its action. Exactly in the middle under
he feet of the combatants, a headless corpse confronts the
spectator, below the bridge there is a bright vista on to the
iver with pursuers and pursued, and in the foreground, on
both slopes, a savage destiny overtakes horses and Amazons in
contrasts which create an incomparable balance of effect,
vhile in the centre of the picture there is a restful conclusion
for the eye in the light on the bodies of two Amazons who
have attempted to escape by swimming.

Of the six great paintings in the Liechtenstein Gallery (de-
igned for execution in tapestry for Genoa, cf. p. 10) which
depict the heroic history of Consul Publius Decius, the 'Death
of the Consul in the Cavalry Battle' (Pl. 38), has always
roused the greatest admiration. This central theme occupies
group in the foreground, while farther back, in a second
ight, the thick of the battle moves from left to right. There are
hree horsemen, Decius on a rearing white horse, his adversary
on a bay kicking backwards, while a third, whose horse is
hardly visible, has just thrust his lance into Decius's throat; in
he lower foreground a dead horse, human corpses and two
bodies in their death-throes. We may long have admired the
indescribable fire of the action and the splendour of the
colour scheme before we realize that this group forms,
visually, an almost regular, flattened hexagon. The heads of
he man with the lance, of Decius and of one dying man are
almost vertically above each other in the middle of the

picture, but the light falls exactly from above on to thi
central group.

In the Munich 'Lion Hunt' (Pl. 34), that incredibly instan
taneous moment composed of seven men, four horses and two
lions, the heads of the helmeted man in the act of striking, of
one lion and the falling Arab again lie in one and the same ver
tical, while the helmeted man again forms an equilateral triangl
with the two lying on the ground—one dead, the other stil
warding off the lioness with his dagger. It is true that this can
only be seen if it is looked for. As a rule nobody realizes any
thing of the pyramid which secretly dominates and lend
repose to the 'Garland of Fruit' (same gallery) by grouping
together the three central *putti*.

The same Munich Pinakothek contains, in the 'Massacre o
the Innocents' (Pl. 102), one of the most powerful examples o
concealed symmetry and the secret operation of equivalents
Some spectators may feel the subject to be distasteful, and be
repelled by the uncompromising realism of its presentment
yet no one can fail to feel the mastery. There are three group
clearly distinguished by visible intervening space; in th
middle, patrician women lament, but to right and left women
of the people savagely assault the slaughterers; to the left
dark prevailing on a light architectural background, to th
right, mainly in the high light, a Doric temple giving the effec
of darkness.

In the same gallery, however, as if to reconcile the eye, w
find that scene before a threatening battle where the women
in the high light, enter the space between Sabines and
Romans, kissing and holding up their children[72] to the hostil
husbands and fathers to left and right; the prominent figures
mounted or on foot, are balanced merely by contrasted detail
of movement and form.

Of the 'Banquet at the House of Simon the Pharisee', an
early work by Rubens's own hand (Hermitage, excellen
sketch in Gallery of the Academy, Vienna), we may say tha
pictorial and spiritual equivalences are wrought into an abso
lutely wonderful harmony.[73] In three great and famous picture

x. Detail from the 'Raising of the Cross'. (Plate 15)

XI. Detail from the 'Landscape with Castle Steen'. (Plate 107)

on the same subject (Brera, Turin Gallery and Louvre) Paolo Veronese had so represented Christ that he seemed to be speaking to the others, and thus was hardly aware of the Magdalen wiping his feet. But Rubens's picture, first, was not designed to cover the whole wall of a refectory and to include splendid architecture; it is a moderately sized oblong picture with the figures about life-size, while a single column and a curtain against the outer atmosphere suffice for the setting. The principal incident, however, Christ's look and speech, and the grief and beauty of the Magdalen, is in Rubens really the power which informs the whole. In the repentant sinner kneeling in the foreground, the formidably difficult problem of the hands touching the foot of Christ is perhaps more nobly solved than anywhere else in pictorial art, while the looks and attitudes of those present are related partly to her and partly to the Redeemer. 'Deep compassion with the penitent is expressed in the noble countenance of the Christ, and his lips can be seen moving in speech' (Waagen). Sitting alone at the end of the table, against the background of the dark curtain, he, along with the three boldly foreshortened disciples, balances the close-packed and very agitated group of Pharisees and youthful servants on the left. It may be that the spectator will hardly be ready to acknowledge the restful symmetries which, in their turn, dominate the whole, the linen-covered table exactly in the centre of vision and the almost perfect semi-circle of high lights in the foreground which takes in Christ, the Magdalen and the robe of the Pharisee sitting nearest to them.

Finally, among the many examples which should find a place here, there is one of equivalences of telling simplicity, the picture by Rubens's own hand already mentioned (p. 43) —'St. Ambrose refusing Emperor Theodosius admittance to the Church' (Pl. 45). Here the two groups are balanced, spiritually and visually, with exquisite precision; to the left, the manly Emperor with his three adjutants, any one of whom could settle the question by force, but the group is seen against the light, and lower by the two steps which Theodosius is just

F

about to mount; at the top of the same steps to the right, the saint with his serene, for the most part aged, attendants, physically helpless, but in the high light, in shining robes, with majestic bearing and venerable features.

*   *   *

There are still some remarks to be made on Rubens's composition in general and on his movement in particular, in so far as it is pre-eminently characteristic of him.

Can Rubens's composite figure subjects be called 'over-crowded'? The commission and subject might of themselves require, or at any rate, occasion a large number of figures—should he have refused them? After all, he had nothing to fear and he must often have invented and proposed the subject himself. What leads to overcrowding in a picture, moreover, are things with which Rubens has nothing to do. First, there have been gifted artists who have no gift for arrangement and produce an effect of overcrowding with no more than four or five figures, where another will look effortless and right with three times that number. Further, however, especially among the mannerists of Italy and Flanders, the pictures were really overcrowded by the addition of figures, particularly heads, which have no true relevance, or even no relevance at all, to the moment represented, but which the artist valued for some reason or other. Here Rubens was perfectly clear that whatever is not directly relevant to the moment weakens it, and all his figures take their share in the life of the moment, as it in them. They all have room to move, and do move, then light and colour come to unite them, and a true colour-scheme of itself prevents any effect of overcrowding. Rubens is an enemy of overcrowding because it could only prejudice the delicate balance of his pictorial and spiritual equivalents; further, he possessed, and imparted to the spectator, a distinct feeling of the space represented and an abundance of atmosphere, and in this respect he agrees with Veronese rather than with Tintoretto and the mannerists, whose backgrounds are at times simply walled up with figures and heads. Further, in cases

here we can still consult a composition in its earlier and later
ages, there is direct evidence that Rubens simplified, and has
crificed details, or whole passages, to the interests of a finer
fect. Where engraving and finished picture exist side by
de, as in the striking example of the 'Raising of Lazarus',
uoted above, this is almost the rule, while the 'Judgement of
aris', also already referred to, is a particularly convincing
xample of the same difference between an earlier and a later
ersion in oil, as we see it in the examples of Dresden (c.1625)
nd London (1636, National Gallery; Pl. 103).[74] In this latter,
vonderfully executed by Rubens's own hand, two *putti* have
een omitted, with a great gain in effect. Further, we must
redit the master with a rule of his own in certain large
tar-pieces which had to be placed high and produce their
fect at long range. The picture-space is well filled, but the
gures are few in number, large in scale, grand in character,
nd flooded with light. It was not for the Antwerp Museum,
here it now hangs, but for the high altar of the Carmelite
Monastery that Rubens, commissioned by Burgomaster
ockox, created that unparalleled Crucifixion which is famous
nder the name of the '*Coup de Lance*' (Pl. 54). The three
rosses in the diagonal occur before him, e.g. in Tintoretto;
e adds nine living figures, to the right, the Virgin with St.
hn and a female companion, and a soldier on a ladder
aning against the cross of the Unrepentant Thief; to the left,
deep shadow, two horsemen, one of whom is thrusting his
nce into Christ's side; farther back, the 'people', reduced to
vo partial figures, but in the centre, falling on her knees, the
Magdalen, a noble, blonde beauty, her arms raised in an
stinctive, yet wonderfully helpless, gesture to the soldier with
e lance; apart from Christ, the full light rests practically on
er alone. Is there in the whole of great art a Magdalen at the
ot of the Cross comparable to this? It is true that the Vene-
ans had long since mastered the art of interrupting some
reat story in the middle by a beautiful female figure, and
itian's use of this motif in his 'Ecce Homo' (Vienna Gallery)
nly makes his picture the more frivolous. Among these

pictures for altar-pieces in tall oblong form with large scale figures, there are also Rubens's 'Adorations of the Magi', which begin with a space in the lower foreground from which a rising path leads backward for the retinue and the onlookers crowding after them; no further simplification of the scene was possible in view of its huge precedents; all Rubens could do was to enhance the power of the principal figures. The picture in the Brussels Museum, painted for the high altar of the Capucins at Tournay, has the more gracious features and a more beautiful expression, while that in the Antwerp Gallery (Pl. 70), painted in 1624 for the high altar of the Abbey of S. Michel, is more dramatic in development and in the distribution of the lights, is powerful in its construction and incomparably bold in its long-range effect. The slightly raised centre of vision is occupied by the eyes of the Moorish king gazing at the Infant Christ; Mary, standing on the right with the Child and magnificently isolated, spiritually balances the entire semi-circle of eight standing and two kneeling figures and two horsemen; behind, against the air, camels and soldiers. (Other 'Adorations' for high altars, Louvre, Hermitage and S. Jean, Malines.) Anyone who finds such works overcrowded might consider which figures could be eliminated as superfluous.

*   *   *

Further, there are people who have considered Rubens 'theatrical', and certain individual figures which are posed and self-conscious may be thrown as a sop to this Cerberus, for instance, the 'St. Sebastian', in itself so magnificent a figure in the great 'Marriage of St. Catherine' in St. Augustine's Antwerp (Pl. 75), and even the Christ in the 'Great Last Judgement' at Munich (Pl. 31). But beyond examples such as these, the criticism requires scrutiny. Above all, both stage and picture are subject to one and the same absolutely legitimate demand—the beauty, truth and life of the scene presented, and even an individual moment of an individual actor may inspire the artist by making him feel that his own

ntuition of the theme and the moment have possibly been sur-
assed. Since, however, we have no knowledge whatever of
ny connexion of Rubens with the stage actually existing in
ne countries he knew and lived in (and since, incidentally, he
vas not called upon for theatrical scenery, as was many an
talian artist), we must abandon that possibility, the more so
s the source of life within him made such a stimulus quite
uperfluous. But false theatricality enters into painting even at
mes and in places which have practically no stage, namely
vhen, in default of imaginative power, the excitement of an
ncident must be created by reflection, the artist himself,
nough lacking actual experience, really imagining himself an
ctor. In Rubens the absolute opposite of such a state of affairs
 clearly visible. Consider how seldom his figures are shown
n loud, emotional speech, how they never rant, how his
ands, with all their abundance of beautiful gesture, never
esticulate, then turn for comparison to the French artists of
,ouis XIV. In France there was a famous drama which could
ot but become the accomplice of painting, although the two
rts did not necessarily appeal to the same audience. The
ctor can force a situation, just because it is momentary;
e can also expand the character to its utmost limits. But
vhat happens to the artist who imitates him? Antoine Coypel,
Racine's friend, also associated a great deal with the famous
ctor Baron. Now Baron, for all his mastery of character and
ituation, transgressed the bounds of truth and nature in his
fforts 'to avoid the commonplace', and 'distorted the already
ontorted', and Coypel's figures obviously suffered from the
ontagion. Compare, for instance, in the Louvre, as a specimen
f colossal theatricality crowded with gesticulating hands, the
icture of 'Athalie being led away after her Fall' with the
Raising of Joas'. This sharing of power with the stage brought
bout a general preference for excess of expressiveness, but
hat expressiveness, continually repeated, became monotonous
nd stereotyped in painting, and that is the worst fate that can
efall. Le Brun was able to give the formulas of expression in
is book of recipes: *Conférences sur l'expression des passions*.

From that time on every artist of this school had scenes from
the stage in mind, even in biblical pictures. Let us imagine a
scene such as that of 'Queen Tomyris receiving the Head of the
slain Cyrus' in the style of Lebrun and his like, and compare it
with Rubens's great work (Pl. 52). (We have only an engraving
which probably corresponds to the picture in Darnley House,
but not to the version in the Louvre.)[75] In the middle, the only
figure in motion is the almost naked, half-kneeling slave
holding the bleeding head over an ornamented basin, to the
right the group of bystanders, oriental nobles and soldiers in
armour with hardly a whisper going on, to the left, standing
on two steps, the Queen with her attendant and three other
ladies in waiting, all silent and scarcely smiling; the only two
figures in actual conversation are the two young pages holding
Tomyris's train. The only clear sound comes from a little dog
barking at Cyrus's head. The scene is a superb hall with
drapery above and a vista through to the open air. Even
Paolo Veronese, whom Rubens approaches more closely in
this picture than in any other, would have spent more action
and dramatic expression on it. The picture is, so to speak, a
magnificent stage scene, but it is instructive in having not the
remotest hint of theatricality.

*   *   *

In connexion with the sumptuous hall so appropriately
introduced into this picture, a note on Rubens's representation
of space in general may not be out of place. Although he was
familiar with all the rich effects of the late Renaissance (cf
supra p. 19) he only used as much of them as his subject
required and as was compatible with his composition. Even
the gallery of the Luxembourg, compared, for instance, with
the halls of Paolo Veronese, reveals a totally different mentality. He composes the interior of magnificent buildings with
the utmost freedom, and when looking at the 'Miracles of
St. Ignatius' (Vienna version, Pl. 46), for instance, we have
some difficulty in recalling an actual church with such an altar
His mastery of architecture and perspective, however, come

ut most vividly where we are not looking for it and are
ardly even grateful for it—in the ease with which he estab-
ishes the various planes in which his figures stand, walk,
nount, sit, kneel and so on; steps, flights of stairs, bridges,
rches, etc. create the necessary differences of level and distance
nd the reposeful horizontals which give welcome rest to the
ye. This has already been referred to in connexion with the
Miracles of St. Francis Xavier' (Pl. 47; Vienna Gallery). We
only realize after long familiarity with this picture what its
ffective unity owes to steps, balustrades and pedestals which
nay easily pass unnoticed. True, when Rubens had to unite
ourteen saints in a 'Mystic Marriage of St. Catherine' in
St. Augustine's at Antwerp (Pl. 75), he could only do so with
he help of a very visible base in the middle, a few steps in the
oreground and flights of stairs at the sides. Above, to the left,
he first columns of a colonnade run diagonally into the air, in
he way Titian had introduced into certain of his backgrounds,
n order to give the impression of a huge building standing
outside of the picture (St. Mark with the Four Saints, the
Madonna of Casa Pesaro). But this effortless mastery only
omes fully home to us in one of those pictures in which two
ctions of one and the same person had to be presented in the
ame picture-space (childishly, as the world of today imagines),
nd since the altar-piece was of necessity an upright rectangle,
hey had to be shown one above the other. This is no less a
icture than the great 'St. Bavon' of Ghent, which even today
an hold its own, side by side, with the world-famous altar-
iece of the Van Eyck brothers.[76] Bavon, a Flemish nobleman
f the seventh century, after a wild life distributed his goods to
he poor with the consent of his wife, and presented himself
efore Bishop Amandus and Abbot Florbert to do penance.
he subject, therefore, was one of those alms-givings which
vere common at the time, and in Italy probably found their
upreme expression in the 'Charity of St. Cecilia', Domeni-
hino's fresco in S. Luigi de' Francesi in Rome. But in Rubens
oo, St. Bavon with his two servants and the poor with their
hildren form one of the most beautiful of groups in motion,

with the wife and two attendant ladies in the clear light beside
it, and all this was made possible by the concealed expedient of
a flight of steps. Above, however, the same flight of steps runs
diagonally through the picture, with the saint swiftly mounting it, followed by a superbly depicted retinue, while the two
prelates with their attendants await him in a church portico.
The two events are in no way linked, but we must leave it to
artists to tell us how and why the wonderful pictorial unity of
the whole impresses every spectator. In the magnificent
plague picture in St. Martin's, Alost, the bridge-like arch in
front with the sick below it and St. Roch with a hovering
Christ and an angel above, seems to have been suggested by
the prison-like nature of the masonry, and the saint actually
died in prison. Once Rubens's imagination seems to have been
caught and held by an arrangement of the kind. There was a
picture, also an upright rectangle, by Paolo Veronese, a
'Visitation' on some organ panel, rather loosely composed—
possibly only known to us in the old engraving by Le Febre.
Here the arrival of Mary and her two companions is made
clear by their mounting a few steps resting on an arch, and
above the arch, in front of the house, Elizabeth is standing
waiting with Zachariah and a serving-maid, but under the
arch at the lower edge of the picture, Paolo has set three almost
purely decorative half-length figures, perhaps servants. When
Rubens in his turn came to paint a 'Visitation' for one of the
inner panels of the Antwerp 'Deposition' (Pl. 19) in a still
narrower and taller picture-space (1:3, while Paolo had more
room to move with 1:2) he simply used the arch for the
ascent where the two couples[77] and their maidservant meet
and below he added a vista into the open. In spite of the
wonderful effortlessness with which this beautiful group of
figures is arranged in the narrow space with a creeper-
covered Dorian portico, he seems, as it were, to have regretted
the necessity; in a freer arrangement for the engraving
he loosened up the action, gave quite a fresh arrangement
to the portico with the creepers and, as if further to accentuate
the impression of an arrival from a far distance, added a

stalwart manservant with a pack-animal turning back towards the main group. Yet even in this complete rearrangement of the scene, there follows, at the bottom of the steps, the arch with the view open on to the distance. And we find Paolo's arch in other variants of the same theme, even when there is nothing underneath it but hens pecking about for food, and we must leave it to our own century, which is very precise in such matters, to decide whether this is plagiarism, and laudable as such.[78]

But the picture in which Rubens's mastery of space finds its ultimate expression is the 'Fall of the Damned into Hell' (Munich Pinakothek) in the series of Heaven and Hell. Created as a continuation, a prolongation, of the so-called 'Lesser Last Judgement' (Pl. 69), in an indescribable state of mind and with utter self-dedication, presumably without any commission or suggestion from outside, the picture takes us into a dreadful night of cloud and torrents, filled to the farthest distance, depth and height with the tossed and scattered bodies of the damned. But the incredible spatiality is brought out by a powerful light falling from the sky on to every ghastly group. If we survey the art and poetry of all times for a comparable imaginative power, we shall most probably recognize it in its exact opposite, namely in a horrible description of non-space. But the speaker is Mephistopheles in the second part of Faust, and he is giving Faust instructions for his journey to the 'Mothers'. Thus by totally different roads, men like Rubens and Goethe arrive at the same goal—the stirring within us of profoundest mythological feeling.

*   *   *

While Rubens was primarily the great painter of living movement in a general way, and in particular of historical scenes in action, he was also confronted with the absolute necessity of painting subjects in which there was emotion, but no motion. Yet even here we shall not find him wanting. He was probably still in Italy when he painted the 'Last Supper' for a great altar-piece (now in the Brera), though not the moment which expresses the certainty of the betrayal, as Leonardo did.[79] He has chosen the blessing of the bread in the Institution of the Sacrament, the chalice standing on the otherwise empty table, which is pushed forward cornerwise; round it, crowded together with great mastery, are the disciples with Judas in the foreground in chiaroscuro, forming together a moderate-sized pyramid with a disciple sitting opposite to him in the light and with Christ; the light, coming from the last glimmer of day and two strong candles,[80] is truly unified and mysterious. It may have been about the same time or not much later that Daniele Crespi painted the same moment of the Institution (now in the Brera) but in bright daylight, with a table running, not diagonally, but straight upward through the picture, and still covered with dishes and plates. In good old Milanese fashion he surpassed Rubens in the homeliness of his Apostles' heads, but they are all so busy gossiping among themselves that none pays any attention to Christ.

There was, however, in Rubens's neighbourhood a master who was his disciple in great artistic means, but who was averse from the action they are so pre-eminently suited to express, and the comparison between the two is instructive. What Jacob Jordaens had acquired from Rubens was the plenitude of his modelling of the human body, his light, his glow of colour and rich rendering of materials, but as far as possible he left his figures standing, or even sitting or lying, in repose. The consequence is that his biblical pictures look over-crowded, his Bacchanals look comical, with the mythological rout comfortably seated, while his great bean-feasts and domestic concerts show how much noise these seated persons could bear.[81]

In comparison with him and others, Rubens, as far as his subject permitted, is all fire and action. Very little of it can be expressed in words, yet this specific power must be illustrated by particularly striking examples.

From the outset, we may wonder at the fecundity which permitted him to discard completely great designs which already existed in great finished pictures and create them

entirely afresh. Of the huge altar-pieces of the 'Miracles of
St. Ignatius', that in the Vienna Gallery (Pl. 46) is probably the
earlier and completed before 1620, that in S. Ambrogio in
Genoa was promised as early as 1606, but only delivered at
Genoa in 1620 and we must regard it not only as the later,
but as the more perfect version, and, at the same time, as one of
the greatest examples of a design being transformed while the
chief subject is completely retained, so that it is difficult to
distinguish the two pictures from memory alone. In both
cases we have the healing of the possessed on the left, on the
right there are mothers with healthy children, appealing to
the saint for his blessing or intercession. In the Vienna version,
the first group greatly predominates, with the madman,
foreshortened with terrifying effect, falling backward on his
head and the woman in the grip of a satanic convulsion,
both surrounded and supported by their horror-stricken companions, while the Genoa version shows only the madwoman
with her family, and, in perfect balance on the other side, a
much richer group of mothers enlarged by worshippers from
among the people. The greatest change, however, has come
over St. Ignatius himself; in the first case he is pronouncing the
exorcism in the half-light with that wondrous gesture of the
hand; in the second he is in the high light, and turning in
another direction, with outstretched hands, his eyes raised to
heaven, obviously rapt in intercession with God for the sick
and the mothers. Further, in the first picture, a number of
monks are placed in a row receding into the picture; in the
second, they form a close-packed, rather distant group, while
on both sides of St. Ignatius youthful acolytes look down on
the lower groups with the most beautiful expression of pity. In
the Vienna picture, which is by far the more powerful from the
pathological standpoint, Rubens obeyed the inward impulse of
a divination of the demonic, and explored that experience
which his people believed they possessed; in the Genoa version, having outlived the Vienna phase, he sought a gentler
kind of expressiveness and the beauty of balanced harmony.[82]
We see another kind of freedom when Rubens designs

subjects common at the time with figures which are identical
or similar in character and attributes, but always new in
arrangement and action. Especially in his Adorations of the
Shepherds or Magi, whether upright or horizontal in shape,
old familiar figures recur again and again, and it is hardly
necessary to name them. The Moorish king and his retinue
were based partly on studies from life (the Brussels Museum
has recently acquired a picture by his hand of four heads of a
more or less complete negro type[83]) which could also be of
service to him as secondary figures, for instance in his Bacchanals, while for oriental costume, he had that huge, ponderous
Levantine whose portrait, in sumptuous costume, is now in
the Cassel Gallery. The essential thing, however, is the
veracity and honesty with which these figures always appear
and the ease with which they are freshly and naturally drawn
into the life of the picture. There is never a hint of mere
academic padding, such as we find, for instance, in Guido
Reni's great historical pictures. In the 'Adoration of the
Shepherds', the devotion and delight of the same simple folk
have every time their special *raison d'être*. In the twelve compositions of the 'Adoration of the Magi' too, of which ten are
extant as finished altar-pieces, Rubens always created fresh
aspects of the subject by means of light and colour, variation
of motion and repose, and equivalents in a general way; he
obviously came to love these familiar beings, and never tired
of them, for they could always be depicted in a fresh anti-
thesis.[84] Yet the feeling in this subject is very quiet and one
can imagine the solemn moment as one without a sound. As
regards the setting, Rubens, like many an Italian and even
Venetian of the sixteenth century before him, made no use of
the splendid ruins in classical or Renaissance style, preferring
an insignificant wall or a raftered building or the space in
front of it. What is peculiar to him is the deep love with
which he allows the light to play over it, and takes into his
picture rustic paraphernalia of all kinds—baskets, utensils and
so on. In the discreet arrangement of the two characteristic
animals, the ox and the ass, the greatest animal painter of all

ime has surpassed himself, and there are often superb dogs, oo.

Even in the Holy Families, however, untrammelled movement sets in again exulting. An attempt has already been made p. 54) to give some idea of what is expressed by the 'Holy amily under the Apple-tree' in the Vienna Gallery (Pl. 96); he imposing presence and radiance of the restful Madonna group is balanced by the eagerness of Zachariah as he holds out the apple and by the Infant St. John's struggles to escape from Elizabeth's hands to the Christ Child. In the 'Flight into Egypt', Rubens has combined haste and danger with supernatural help in most moving fashion. This is the magical little picture of 1614 in the Cassel Gallery (Pl. 26); a woodland brook at night, to the right, in the distance, a sheet of water reflecting the moon, while with enigmatic beauty the Presence passes before the spectator's eyes—the Child in its mother's arms as the sole effulgence; the ass on which she rides is being drawn through the stream by a stalwart young angel, while a second, hovering on a cloud, points the way with a staff. Joseph, striding swiftly forward, looks anxiously back, for in the distance a horseman, probably one of the pursuers, is galloping. This work is remarkable at the same time as one of those partial plagiarisms (mentioned on p. 5) in which Rubens, stimulated by some other artist's work, begins by copying it only to show in the end how the first should have set about it. His model was Adam Elsheimer, whom Rubens had met, and apparently come to admire very much, in Rome. Elsheimer's Flight into Egypt', of which there are several replicas (one, for instance, in the Munich Pinakothek), has in common with that of Rubens a certain general arrangement of the whole and the proportions of height and breadth, as well as the journey by night, which also occurs in Elsheimer (perhaps for the first time) and is intended as an allusion to the growing danger. But Elsheimer has no angels, and in his picture the light is shed by a torch held by Joseph, while a second light comes from a big shepherds' fire in the distance, not to speak of other differences.[85]

The Infant Christ between his mother and foster-father was painted by all schools of the seventeenth century as a solemn and restful altar group, usually elevated into a Trinity by the addition of a glory. (Famous pictures particularly by Albani and Murillo.) Rubens, on the other hand, according to an engraving by Bolswert, expressed his peculiar feeling for the scene by setting it in the open air. The Child is walking across the fields between Mary and Joseph; both hold his hands, but he drags them forward, and the title of the engraving: *et erat subditus illis* (St. Luke ii. 51) is only partially fulfilled; God the Father and the Dove above remain unheeded.[86]

Violent action, however, is powerfully and tragically blended with one of the great moments of the Passion, and here Rubens has carried emotion to its climax in an absolutely original way; this is the great 'Bearing of the Cross' in the Brussels Museum, painted for the Abbey of Afflighem and finished in 1637 (Pl. 92). This work is known in four stages: a preliminary engraving by Paulus Pontius, two small oil-paintings and finally the finished altar-piece, and at every stage the story becomes simpler, more powerful and more terrible. The spectator is made part of the long and patient suffering, the procession moving up a steep and narrow mountain path, seen from behind, yet in such a way that the main figures turn round, facing forward. It is only in the last, maturest version that St. Veronica, the women of Jerusalem with their children, and one of the soldiers holding up the cross, all grouped round the swooning Christ, form that almost symmetrical mass of light in the centre of the picture, but in this version, the two thieves are seen as half-length figures, dragged from the lower edge of the picture by soldiers; according to the engraving, they had before moved with the crowd, almost unnoticed, but here they movingly reinforce the sombre effect of that 'upward'.[87]

Rubens was no more able to evade horrors than his famous Flemish predecessors in the fifteenth century when commissioned to paint the martyrdom of saints. He painted with his own hand the 'Martyrdom of St. Lievin', the patron saint of

hent, for the Jesuit church of that city, and in light and
nality it is recognized as a masterpiece (Pl. 104; Brussels
useum). The centre of the picture has a strong accent in the
arlet cap of the torturer who is holding out in tongs to a dog
e saint's tongue, which he has just torn out. To the left St.
ievin himself is being dragged to the ground by an executioner
ho has him by the beard, and there are other distasteful
etails. But above, in the air, over the terrified soldiers and a
aring white horse, we see at any rate no heavenly concert
was customary in contemporary Italian martyrdoms, but
enging angels. The whole scene of torture to the left finds
astonishing equivalent to the right; the whole right lower
rner is occupied by a halberdier whose head is still turned
wards the heavenly apparition, yet who is already rushing
vay as if maddened—a truly Rubenesque fusion of the past
d the coming moment.[88]

In the 'Martyrdom of St. Laurence' (Munich Pinakothek,
ry much restored) Rubens may have been perfectly well
vare of his rivalry with the famous Titian in the Jesuit
urch at Venice. The great Venetian had been able to rely on
e beauty of detail, especially on the body lying stretched out
1 the gridiron, the three distinct lights, a great architectural
ckground and other attractions. Rubens, on the other hand,
ade the saint, sitting on the gridiron and being forced back-
ards by torturers, the exact centre of a composition which is
furious action, yet is made restful to the eye by a great
rizontal. It is superior to Titian's looser arrangement in that
is firmly self-contained. All the causes of action are greater
d the effect unified.

In this picture, Rubens still remained within the limits of
e altar-piece, which he always treated with great reverence
d devotion, while otherwise both biblical and mystical
enes could offer him the opportunity of giving full rein to
e force of a moment of action. About the time, roughly
om 1617–19, in which the Munich 'Lion Hunt', the 'Battle
the Amazons' and the pictures of the 'History of Decius'
ere created, he painted, for instance, the 'Destruction of the

Host of Sennacherib' (Pl. 35). In the Bible, it was the angel of the Lord who, in one night, smote 'an hundred, four score and five thousand men'. What is obviously meant is a camp plague, 'and when they arose in the morning, behold, they were all dead corpses'. What Rubens makes of this scene is a wild and raging tumult of flight caused by heavenly apparitions, with men, mostly mounted, fighting against an unearthly enemy; even the horses are beside themselves, and over the whole there pour streams of light and night. In the same Munich Pinakothek which contains this picture, we find its obvious and contemporary counterpart, also of exactly the same measurements—thirty-eight inches high by forty-eight inches wide—'The Conversion of St. Paul'; here too the heavenly apparition, consisting of Christ with child angels, appears as a rent in the night sky, and on the earth a tumult with no earthly enemy, but in quite a different arrangement. The group extending right through the picture in the middle distance, men and horses in superb confusion, is separated by an illuminated tract of country from the foreground with St. Paul, who has fallen from his horse on to his head, and three companions. Who can say how many such visionary tumults of men and horses still slumbered in the depths of Rubens's imagination? Nobody would expect such a subject from any artist of later times, but then, and to him, it could not but occur.

It was, further, inevitable that Rubens should inherit from the painting and sculpture of the whole Renaissance the great theme of the Rapes which are dominated by superb female nudes in vehement action. Such abductions may take place on earth, and the 'Rape of the Daughters of Leucippus by the mounted Dioscuri' has already been discussed as one of the most powerful and beautiful of the master's scenes of action. Then Pluto appears with horse and chariot to carry off Proserpine, in several versions, some of a rather frieze-like character, from Soutmans's engraving to the picture in the Madrid Gallery. But Rubens could not avoid a special predilection for aerial abductions, since the contour of the female nude can

XII. LANDSCAPE: SUNSET
1635–8. London, National Gallery

XIII. Detail from 'War and Peace'. (Plate 80)

hen stand out in perfect freedom and beauty, and where it is
held aloft by the nude figure of an old man, it was generally
believed in the schools of the time to represent Truth carried
away by Time.

Now it is admitted that, in the last picture of the gallery of
the Luxembourg (Louvre), the figure of Truth, one of Rubens's
most beautiful nudes, held aloft by an old man, is not represented as carried away, but as preserved and rescued by Time
(*la Vérité soutenue par le Temps*). A quite incontestable, and
even violent aerial abduction, however, is that (Vienna,
Academy) of Oreithyia by the aged Boreas, who puffs out his
cheeks, and what the attendant *putti* hovering with them
carry in their hands are great hailstones (by Rubens's own
hand, with a wonderful colour scheme taking in all the
colours of the floating draperies).

The theme finds its climax, even as early as the fifteenth
century, in mass abductions, occasionally by horsemen. We
find the 'Romans under Romulus and Remus carrying off
the Sabine Women' (Pl. 101), and we may ask whether the
subject was suitable for pictorial treatment. What was beyond
question was that Rubens would one day paint it in this
fashion. The beautiful picture by his own hand in the
National Gallery is not intended as a kind of pendant to the
Munich picture referred to above, which shows the reconcilia-
tion between Romans and Sabines; it is much smaller in scale
and quite different in feeling. Force, resistance and lamentation
are shown in astonishing variations, but in the three foreground
groups, especially in the fine, stout woman clasping her hands
—*unam longe ante alias specie ac pulchritudine insignem*, as Livy
says (I, 9)—and in the masterly group to the right, where a
horseman is being helped to lift a Sabine woman on to his
horse, there is gaiety in Rubens, and the transmutation into
the comic was most likely conscious.

But what are we to think of 'Samson and Delilah' (Munich
Pinakothek)? Earlier artists had shown the hero asleep on the
knees of the courtesan, who is quite calmly cutting off his
curls. Now if memory does not deceive me, Rubens was the

G

first to reduce the scene to one keenly dramatic moment by
painting Samson starting up from sleep when he has already
been overcome and is being fettered by the Philistines. Later
we have Van Dyck's 'Samson' in the Vienna Gallery, a mere
variant as regards the design, but with important psycho
logical alterations, then comes Rembrandt's version (Cassel)
and Jan Steen's (Antwerp), a picture disintegrated into mere
details of infamy and scorn, and from that time on it was only
possible to paint Samson as vanquished. But as more refined
scenes of the 'way of the world', conceived both tragically
and ironically, only Rubens's and Van Dyck's composition
can be taken seriously, and the pupil was able to surpass his
master in the aristocratic indifference of Delilah's dismissal and
the grief in the eyes of the hero fixed on her, for in Rubens, the
hero's eyes are turned away from her. What both picture
have in common as moralities is the treachery of the courtesan
and the defeat even of the noblest of men by the crowd when
his hour has come. In Rubens, the old woman behind Delilah
has, quite rightly, the same expression as she, though on
different level and in profile.[89]

*   *   *

The story with three-quarter figures, biblical or secular
could not appeal to Rubens, if only because movement, his
peculiar gift, depends mainly on the complete presentation of
the body. He would have had no lack of examples of the genre
especially among the Venetians, and he must have seen Cara
vaggio's three-quarter-length pictures; indeed his own
'Tribute Money' closely resembles a work attributed to
Caravaggio. In itself, it is one of the subjects best suited to
three-quarter-length treatment; the showing of a coin,
conversation and its reflection in the faces of those present—
indeed, we might go so far as to say that this perfectly quiet
subject, based almost entirely on facial expression, could not
be expressed in full-length figures. We have to judge by one
of the many copies, without being able to say where the
authentic original is to be found, but even here, the whole at

and wisdom of Rubens stands out clear in the simple beauty
with which the action is represented with the light falling on
Christ, and we may conclude that the original is also a miracle
in the modelling and gestures of the hands, on which so much
depends in this subject.[90] A similar inspiration, though drawn
from a higher world, has given us the 'Delivery of the Keys to
St. Peter', with a transfigured, half-draped Christ (engraving).[91]
'Christ and the Woman taken in Adultery', a scene painted
by every great Venetian, is said to exist in England in three
variants by Rubens, presumably with three-quarter-length
figures too.[92] The 'Christ with the Four Great Penitents' (Pl.
44; Munich Pinakothek) must be mentioned again here, even
though it is not actually a narration, because of an obvious
kinship in the nature of its pictorial effect. Rubens, however,
was quite right in feeling that a great moment such as that in
the inn at Emmaus, which was often painted three-quarter-
length at the time, required full-length figures if the disciples'
deep emotion was to find full expression, and all the beauty
and power of his feeling lives in the work already mentioned
on p. 44. Pictures such as the '*Christ à la Paille*' and 'Christ
with St. Thomas' (both in the Antwerp Museum) being
destined for tombs, could not exceed very moderate measurements, and while the life-size was desirable for fullness of
expression, the moment could be rendered with great power
in three-quarter length. In the picture of 'St. Thomas', the
saint is accompanied only by two other disciples, nor does he
touch the wound in Christ's side, as in the picture by
Guercino, who takes the thrusting of the finger into the
wound so literally; the wound in the left hand is enough (St.
John xx. 24 ff.).

The chief example of the secular three-quarter-length figure
is 'Diogenes in Search of a Man', though we can only
form an opinion of it by the doubtful copy in the Louvre
(Rubens's own sketch, Staedel Gallery, Frankfurt[93]). The
philosopher's retinue consists of three women; a mother with
a child, another with a basket of fruit, and between them the
famous laughing Moorish woman; in front of Diogenes and

his lantern, everybody is taking to his heels, and two men are
climbing up a column; in the centre there is a charming woman
who seems to be waiting to see whether Diogenes will find
humanity in her. The figures which are not in action are
crowded together with great mastery, yet with a freedom
quite beyond the power of Jordaens, to whom the picture has
sometimes been attributed. On the other hand, Rubens left
to Jordaens and such painters as Theodor Rombouts, etc., the
great genre painting in three-quarter, as well as half-length and
full-length figures, but the best of them, all the same, derive
from Rubens's influence.

In the Bacchanals, which will be discussed later, the main
thing to decide was whether a complete impression could be
given at all in three-quarter length, and representations in full
length certainly had the advantage that *putti*, child Pans, etc.
could join in. Yet certain three-quarter-length pictures are
among the most beautiful we have and some of these are also
rich in movement, for instance where a Moorish Pan is
attempting to caress a superb nude tambourine player, while
a male Bacchant strides swiftly forward blowing his flute, or
the drunken Silenus is being led by more or less sober companions. What really matters here is whether we can enter
into Rubens's joviality, and whether the picture is anything
like authentic.

*　　　*　　　*

We possess only a few devotional pictures for churches and
great altar-pieces of the Madonna with Saints by Rubens, yet
they all count among his most important extant works.[94] The
contemporary Italians had a number of excellent devotional
pictures to show, but even these are cast far into the shade by
the great triptych in the Vienna Gallery, the 'Altar-piece of St
Ildefonso' (Pl. 93). The central panel shows the saint, Archbishop of Toledo, kneeling to receive a chasuble from the
Madonna. She, a royal, benevolent being, seated on a splendid
throne, is accompanied by four holy women of the most
vigorous type, arranged with complete unconstraint, their

yes resting on St. Ildefonso, and even the three cherubs
hovering above are among the finest Rubens ever painted.[95]
Further, there is in the picture, whose source of light is
internal, a visionary golden haze, the exact like of which
cannot be found even in any of the great earlier Venetians; it
is, however, most remarkable that the Archduke Albert and
the Infanta Isabella on the outer panels, presented by their
name-saints and kneeling at *prie-dieux*, are shown, not in that
haze, but as it were outside in evening light under colonnades
with red draperies. The whole is one of the most amazing
sights in modern art, and at the same time an incomparable
votive picture of royal piety. At an earlier time, Rubens had
painted the Gonzaga family kneeling in reverence to the
Trinity still more devoutly (Mantua, Pls. 4–5, two fragments)
but since then his power of animation and his command of
light and air had grown immensely.[96] Finally, in the course of
the century, Murillo's 'St. Ildefonso' (Madrid Museum) came
to take its place beside that of Rubens; there is far more narration in it, since, instead of the holy women, four angels are
present and are actively drawn into the presentation of the
chasuble; the light (judging from a photograph) is daylight,
silvery atmosphere and a mass of clouds with a host of *putti*
and cherubs. It is immensely satisfying to see how the heroes
of Antwerp and Madrid can be mutually exclusive without
harming each other in the spectator's memory.

Further, in 1628 Rubens painted for St. Augustine's church
at Antwerp, and most likely for an altar containing relics of a
number of saints, that famous picture discussed above in connexion with the distribution of space (p. 75; Pl. 75). One of
Correggio's great efforts had been to reduce the devotional
picture to a single dramatic moment, and also in Raphael we
find it rendered in this way, for instance in the 'Madonna di
Foligno'. But in the altar-piece of St. Augustine's church, no
fewer than fourteen saints had to be brought into relation with
the Holy Family above, justice had to be done and life imparted to every figure, and none might stand in the way of
another. A more solemn whole might be imagined in an older

and more austere style, but the many smaller repetitions an
engravings show how perfectly Rubens suited the taste of h
time and his country. It would be useless to attempt to de
scribe in words the abounding life within the firm structure o
this picture, in which the figures, taken as a whole, form a
almost regular circle and the loveliest symmetries are con
cealed in the details. It is now extant in a very damage
condition, but it was once specially famous for its color
scheme. Since a number of saints are generally misnamed
it might be well to give an authoritative list,[97] beginnin
at the top; on both sides of the Holy Family with St. Catherin
at the moment of her espousal to the Infant Christ, St. Joh
the Baptist and SS. Peter and Paul; farther down on one sid
the crowded group of St. Mary Magdalen, St. Clara (with th
scales), St. Agnes and St. Apollonia; then in the lower fore
ground and larger in size, St. Nicholas of Tolentino (with th
bread), St. Laurence and St. Augustine with the flaming hea
in his hand, and, as a counterpoise, that superb St. Sebastia
described above as theatrical, in eager converse with S
George standing on his dragon; in the midst of these five, S
William of Acquitaine in armour mounts the steps wit
his back turned to the spectator. The cherubs are used sparing
ly here too and only in entirely relevant functions; the litt
one scattering flowers on the betrothal of the Infant, the tw
with St. John the Baptist's lamb, and one hovering over th
Virgin's head with the wreath. It is characteristic of suc
pictures as a whole that the Madonna's eyes are bent, not o
St. Catherine, who is kneeling close to her, but on the midd
of the picture, and, we may add, on the worshippers. Bu
when the picture was in a perfect state of preservation, ho
beautiful must have been the transition from the high light o
the lower group to the ethereal light in the upper group, wit
a great beam of light from heaven!

The world-famous 'Madonna with Saints' over Rubens
tomb in the chevet chapel of S. Jacques in Antwerp (Pl. 10
is obviously intended to convey some special message to u
and was also painted with special devotion, probably durin

...e master's last years, but whether for his own tomb is
...oubtful. Some happy interpreter may one day penetrate its
...cret meaning, but the first condition would be that he should
...ease to interpret the heads as 'Rubens and his Family'.
...abella Brant and Helen Fourment are represented in none
...f these holy women, not even in the Magdalen and the
...Madonna, and Rubens resembled the St. George with the
...anner who appears here at no time in his life. If such an
...aterpretation were possible, it would have to start with the
...bviously principal figure, the prelate or cardinal kneeling in
...ae middle of the picture who is holding the Child's hand to
...is lips, and who is quite arbitrarily denoted as Rubens's
...ather. In the foreground, the very agitated pose of St.
...erome is probably only intended as a counterpoise to the
...wift stride of St. George. What the real significance of the
...igure is would first have to be discovered.

*　　*　　*

...ubens painted the Assumption of the Virgin in ten compo-
...tions, most of them very big altar-pieces, and he was the first
...followed by German masters trained in Italy, especially
...rescoists) to bring the latest version of this great theme to the
...iorth: the Virgin wafted upward among angels and clouds
...bove the Apostles assembled below, generally round the
...arcophagus. Till that time, the last great consummation of
...ae Virgin's life had been interpreted in the north as the
...Coronation of the Virgin by Christ or the Holy Trinity.[98]
...n Italy, both this subject, the *Incoronata*, and the Assumption,
...he *Assunta*, had long been frequent in altar-pieces and
...rescoes in churches, and gradually the Assunta had taken
...recedence. As early as 1518, Titian had rendered it in
...upreme majesty on the high altar of the Frari in Venice. But
...ater, this climax of religious art, which should have remained
...are, was repeated by lesser hands, and from the Assunta
...here passed to mere devotional pictures the habit of placing
...he Madonna up in the clouds with a large retinue of angels

and cherubs, and with an expression of ecstasy, while in earlie
times she had been enthroned among the saints. The new and
vigorous artistic spirit which arose in Italy at the end of the
sixteenth century adopted this state of things, and that is wha
Rubens found there. He did not yield to the Italians in th
devotional picture, but left the Madonna surrounded by saints
and thus preserved what he cared for most—the great unit
both of design and colour. The 'Coronation of Mary by the
Trinity' can be seen in a very attractive studio picture
(Brussels Museum) which he at any rate touched up, but the
Assunta became one of the very great tasks of his life. Here
we have the right to inquire into the circumstances which
brought this about. The earliest of these great works, in
which the essential intention of the later ones is already
implicit (Brussels Museum), was commissioned by Alber
and Isabella for the high altar of the Carmelites at Brussel
(Pl. 30); the Archduke, however, had spent many years in
Rome and Italy. It is highly probable that it was this superl
production that first awakened the urgent demand for more
pictures of the Assumption, and it was very likely not long
after that various compositions by Rubens, or perhaps ever
the preliminary sketches for them, were spread far and wide in
large engravings. But while the theme was in a certain sense
Italian, a perfectly new conception of it was created by Ruben
without a single reminiscence of Titian's tremendous picture
which Rubens must have known intimately,[99] and even quite
independently of the Carraccis, whom he so far surpasses. He
need not have seen the 'Assunta' of Agostino (Bologna
Pinacoteca) and those of Annibale must have served him
rather as a warning how not to treat the subject. He left Italy
too early to have seen Guido's 'Assumption' in S. Ambrogio
Genoa, which is great and beautiful, if exceedingly academic in
parts, nor his Munich 'Assumption'.

We may pause a moment over this latter picture, which
shows only the group poised in the air, without the sarcophagus and the Apostles. Guido Reni, probably the mos
gifted of Rubens's Italian contemporaries, is unequal to him

XIV. Detail from 'The Three Graces'. (Plate 119)

XV. THE RAPE OF THE DAUGHTERS OF LEUCIPPUS
About 1619. Munich, Alte Pinakothek

ot only in colouring, but in the vivacity of his action, and
any of his most attractive figures come into the picture not
ecause they are necessary to it, but because the artist wished
 have them there, while it is Rubens's habit to subordinate
very individual figure to the living whole. This 'Assunta'
 Guido's, however, while the execution is mediocre (and
e state of preservation defective) is inspired by a great
alian spirituality, and the principal figure, in setting, pose
d contour, is greater in power than any of the Flemish
tist's Assuntas. (I am just ignoring the derogatory remarks
 Herr von Schack.)

 There is a further preliminary remark to be made on the
uthful female figures accompanying the Apostles at the
pulchre. Rubens probably added them gladly to enrich the
ctorial effect. They nearly all rank among his loveliest faces [100]
d in their place, they have a wonderful and ever fresh effect.
ut in case of need he could refer to a very ancient legend
cording to which, at the death of the Virgin, not only the
postles appeared, but also three holy maidens whose duty it
as to wash and shroud the body. And further, we find in
ese pictures a habit already noted in the Adorations of the
agi and the Shepherds; the repetition of a very similar, in
rts identical, group of persons, each time in a fresh arrange-
ent, and St. John and St. Peter, for instance, are recognizably
e same throughout these works.

 A special problem, however, namely the Assumption with
e smallest possible number of figures and the most compact
sign, would seem to underlie the picture which exists in the
unich Pinakothek but which (according to the recent
talogue) is no longer on show. It is a rather small and,
dging from memory, beautifully executed replica of a large
ork now at Düsseldorf. Here the centre of interest is not
e Virgin floating diagonally upwards out of the picture with
e delicious cherubs, but rather the linen shroud stretched
ut in the foreground with the lilies and roses found upon it,
d the worshipping groups of Apostles and holy women
nking it on each side are fused into unity with a supreme

H

feeling for the moment. With the 'Assunta' of Brussels (Pl. 3
already mentioned, there sets in that torrent of great work
given up to all power and splendour, which are, above a
triumphs of that gradation of light from the earthly light wi
its deep, gleaming colours, firmly localized in space, up in
ethereal brightness. In addition to those named, I can recolle
five other Assumptions; the splendid sketch in the Uffizi; t
picture in the Colonna Gallery in Rome, a copy of an origin
unknown to me; the famous, entirely authentic work in t
Vienna Gallery, from the Jesuit church at Antwerp; the gre
picture of unknown provenance in the Liechtenstein Galler
and the high altar of Antwerp Cathedral. To these we mu
add the numerous engravings which correspond more or le
exactly to some of these works.

Where Rubens appears inadequate in all these pictures is
the figure of the Madonna, not within the limits of the sty
we have once accepted as his, but in relation to the imagin
tive implications of the problem and to the rest of great a
At the risk of appearing most one-sided and unscholarly, an
of judging the master by a standard which was not his, w
must admit as witnesses against him not only Titian's 'Trar
figured Madonna' and Raphael's 'Sistine Madonna', but ev
Guido Reni's Munich 'Assunta' and his altar-pieces of the 'Ho
Conception' (San Girolamo, Forli, and Bridgewater Galler
London). And it is not the spirituality of the features in the
pictures that we should have the right to feel the lack of
Rubens; it is the spirituality of the expression. Once, to jud
by the Uffizi drawing, he may have attempted the highest; t
Virgin, no longer young, but rapt in longing, is kneeling on t
clouds. Everywhere else, Rubens, in an infatuation shared
the Italians (and even by Guido in his great 'Assumption'
S. Ambrogio), shows the Madonna sitting on clouds, wh
the moment absolutely required a standing or floating figu
But in order to suggest the 'upwards' all the same, he giv
her more than once a diagonal movement. Her head sho
that rich, matronly, unreligious modelling of Rubens's oth
Madonnas, and it is only in the Antwerp picture that she tal

n a greater sweetness. Even in the gesture of the raised arms,
ubens, everywhere else so unerring, betrays a certain con-
raint. The dance of the attendant cherubs, however, is rich
d beautiful and fresh in every picture, and in the Viennese
Assunta', the heavenly apparition as a whole forms a regular,
ough beautifully concealed rhomboid. Rubens's great host
f cherubs (cf. p. 44) found as it were new life and inspiration
these Assumptions.

The lower groups of Apostles and holy women, however,
ith their immense variety of arrangement and gesture, would
ffice in themselves to secure to Rubens the admiration of all
me, as we can see as soon as we begin to realize the abundance
dramatic ideas and artistic means they incorporate. The
aterial data are the sarcophagus, wherever it may be in
e picture, then, in a number of pictures, the raised slab and the
hite shroud with the roses; the imaginative data are the
notions stirred by the flowers and the supreme, self-forgetting
loration for the Madonna as she is wafted out of sight, and
ubens has given all this such instantaneity that the gestures
em to change before our very eyes, and such inevitability
at not a figure could be omitted. Nor must we leave out of
count the great secret symmetry of the structure, which takes
the whole picture. In the Liechtenstein Gallery altar-piece,
here the tomb is seen foreshortened in the centre, the
Madonna and the three principal figures kneeling below form
tall pyramid; only then come the standing Apostles on the
ght and another on the left raising the slab; above, surround-
g the Madonna, there are cherubs in most exquisite move-
ent with two superb angels. The sarcophagus appears in all
nds of positions; in the Munich picture only a corner of it is
sible; in another (Brussels) it forms a horizontal right
rough the picture, while in the great work in the Vienna
allery it is absent and a grotto to the left is presumably the
mb. In this 'Assunta', which was Rubens's own favourite, two
oruses have formed, to the left the two men who have rolled
e stone away from the grotto with the holy women, to the
ght the Apostles, one of whom is speaking across to the

women, while the others are looking and pointing upward. I
this picture, however, the two choruses are separated by
deep receding airy space, a lesson Rubens may have learne
from Paolo Veronese. But even the early Brussels pictu
(Pl. 30) produces a wonderful effect with the great, animate
group of Apostles in half-shadow to the right, with Pet
kneeling in the high light in front of them, while to the le
the loveliest women's faces can be seen in the half-light. I
the Uffizi drawing, on the other hand, the Apostles and wome
are assembled in a single group round the sarcophagus, and i
the composition preserved in an engraving by Paul Pontiu
their eyes are again raised in the same rapt contemplatio
though the arrangement is somewhat different. This w.
obviously a rather provisional design (it is recognizable by tl
St. John seen from behind) and would most likely have unde:
gone considerable modification in execution. The latest in da
of these Assumptions, the altar-piece of the high altar
Antwerp Cathedral, is above all a picture of beautiful wome
with the most vigorous of them in front of the shroud and tl
most beautiful behind it, and finally the Holy Virgin, abov
lying exactly in the central axis of the whole; of the Apostle
only St. John shares the high light, since with his upraised arn
he forms almost the only link between the lower and the upp
groups. The Madonna's beauty is very sweet, though qui
unreligious, and the cherubs converge on her in an upwar
sweep. (The upper part of this picture is said to be b
Cornelius Schut.[101])

As is well known, the very emotional seventeenth centur
often transferred to individual saints the central role in a
apotheosis which was almost an Assumption, and on tl
vaulting of S. Ignazio in Rome, with the apotheosis of tl
founder by Andro Pozzo, we see the most brilliant gener.
treatment of such figures. But even in Rubens's entourage, D
Crayer at any rate produced a fine 'Assumption of S
Catherine' (according to the catalogue of the Brussels Museun
where the picture is) with a close-packed company of wo
shipping Saints below.

Those paintings of the Last Judgement, of the Beyond, and
great moments from the Apocalypse which are generally
rouped under the name of Heaven and Hell, could not possi-
y be ignored by Rubens if only because the demand for them
as in the air at the time, and because even here he was able to
ve life to a world of his own, whether it impresses or repels
s. He did not himself take the initiative in this case; he came
it by way of commissions which reached him from the
stant Count Palatine, Wolfgang Wilhelm of Neuburg, and
om that and other sources the largest number and most
portant examples of this world of Rubens's were brought
gether in the Munich Pinakothek.

We find here studio pictures, large and perfunctory in
ecution, though vivid in conception, such as 'The Fall of the
Vicked Angels', with a somewhat posturing St. Michael, or
he Woman of the Apocalypse' side by side with the 'Greater
st Judgement' (1618; Pl. 31). It is customary to draw a
rallel between this picture and Michelangelo's, though in
ing so we should not forget that Rubens, unlike Michel-
gelo, had not been commissioned to paint the most solemn
esco in Europe in the most solemn place, but an altar-piece for
e Jesuit church at Neuburg on the Danube, in the form of an
l painting on canvas. But if there is any question of Italian
fluence, it would have to be sought elsewhere than directly
Michelangelo, whose 'Last Judgement' had long since done
 work of confusion when Rubens arrived in Italy. It was
intoretto who attempted to blend in one whole Michel-
gelo's use of the nude with Venetian naturalism and colour-
g, and there was in his colossal picture in S. Maria dell' Orto
Venice, the so-called *Finimondo* (i.e., the events just preceding
e Last Judgement), a confusion which Rubens, who saw the
ctures still fresh, had to overcome in the name of the eternal
ws of composition and common sense. He may even have
en Tintoretto's great 'Purgatory', now in the Parma Gallery,
ce the central vista into the distance and the dimensions of
e upper heavenly group, and even the style, are recalled to a
rtain extent by the Neuburg 'Last Judgement'. Most of the

latter, it is true, is by the hands of pupils, but the execution
conscientious and the heavenly glory of the blessed of the O
and New Testaments, which too often passes unnoticed,
pure and beautiful, and if, as was admitted above, there is
certain theatricality about the Christ-Jupiter, he is at any ra
not insignificant, like Michelangelo's Judge of the world. T
finest of the nude figures, both among the blessed and t
damned, though they may occasion some ecclesiastical mi
givings, still retain their original beauty, and the Pan-Dev
who is making off with two women, is a detail we c
imagine only in Rubens.

It is only at this point that the master achieves comple
independence in the two pictures with smaller figures, the s
called 'Lesser Last Judgement' (Pl. 69) and, as a kind of sequ
to it, the 'Fall of the Damned into Hell'[102] already mention
(p. 77), both by Rubens's own hand and obviously painte
for his own joy in his perfect mastery. Here Rubens final
closes his account with the real Michelangelo and appears
full advantage beside him, if only by the perfect gradation
light and the completeness of his colour-scheme. He surpass
Michelangelo in the wealth and variety of his detail and by
greater visual richness in the total effect. In place of t
monotony of atmosphere inevitable in the fresco, Rubens tak
in vast distances and variations of light, from the brightest sl
to the gloomy glow of the night of hell and the torrents of t
abyss. He lets the huge happening take its monstrous course
countless figures without the least misgiving, just as the spi
moves him. It is the most appalling instant uttered in countle
ways. Here again is one of those many worlds in whi
Rubens was, if need be, at home.[103]

*   *   *

Yet another of these worlds was that of classical mytholog
which, in the version of the Latin poets, dominated cultur
European minds at the time. In connexion with Rubens, the
might be ground for surprise in the fact that, of the later poe
of the south known to him, Boccaccio and Ariosto appear on

ice and Tasso, to my knowledge, not at all, but even in Italy
iey gave notably few subjects to painting.

A very big commission for mythologies for the hunting
at of Torre de la Parada, most of them subjects from Ovid's
Metamorphoses, has already been mentioned (p. 26), but our
inowledge of it is very incomplete. In addition to these, how-
ver, an enormous number of mythological scenes by Rubens
extant, and some of them represent momentous milestones
i his artistic career. The spectator who expects the mytho-
igical nude to express the classical ideal of form may pass them
y. The life which Rubens represented in figures, colour and
ght, so enchanted him as he created it that there are moments
ihen it became his own expression of the ideal. The art of his
ay was absolutely innocent of the profound hesitations and
eparations which generally accompany the decision to paint
mythological subject in our own time. These subjects were
ill quite natural, and there was as yet no aesthetic to quarrel
ith the style, whether as a whole or in the detail. What the
rtist had to do was to invent felicitously and paint well.

We can also distinguish here between the narrative and the
enre painting, if genre painting can be defined at all as the
epresentation of anonymous figures and their surroundings
nd experiences freely imagined by the artist. There is, of
ourse, no sharp line of demarcation, and even scenes which
erge on allegory cannot be kept quite distinct from mythology.

Rubens's earliest mythological genre paintings belong to his
talian period, though no kind of influence from Italian art,
arly or contemporary, can be traced in his conception. If
Titian must be brought in, it would have to be with his
Bacchus and Ariadne' (National Gallery) on account of a
ew types; it is, however, uncertain whether Rubens was able
o see this picture (then in the possession of the d'Este family
at Modena or Rome) and during his stay in Italy he took
nothing whatever from Titian's 'Bacchanal', now in Madrid.
He is and remains his own lord and master, and he depicts,
either in three-quarter-length or full-length figures—perhaps
specially for banqueting-halls—what he imagines to be the

daily doings of a rabble with which he, a model of sobriety
must have lived on a quite familiar footing in his own mind
Sometimes there is a general feeling of jollity, sometimes ther
is pure farce, for these mythological beings are attended no
only by Moorish men and women, but by goat-footed Pan
and whole Pan families. Even the artists of Hellenistic time
had given a retinue of the kind to the originally solitary shep
herd god,[104] but archaeologists at the time of Rubens believe
that these goat-headed and goat-footed Pans were satyr
namely the famous rout of Dionysus, and what Rubens intend
are actual families of satyrs. Wild beasts and domestic animal
especially hounds, complete the picture. In countless variant
and in every degree of excellence, from the genuine, perfectl
preserved gem to the most perfunctory of studio painting
these pictures exist in every sizeable gallery, and it is quite im
possible to consider them singly here, let alone evaluate thei
artistic merits. They are generally classed under the name c
Bacchanals, but a large number of wealthy patrons wished ther
at the same time to glorify the pleasures of the chase and femal
beauty, and so we find the trains both of Bacchus and Diana
often with very beautiful nymphs, and as they display thei
booty to each other, on the one hand flowers and fruit, on th
other the spoils of the chase, they also represent a higher forr
of the Flemish still life which so often includes both. Th
Bacchic rout often culminates in a Silenus who must, as i
were, take upon himself the drunkenness of the rest, but a
times the satyrs surprise the nymphs, and the picture may tur
into a Rape. The wooded landscapes, where sleeping nymph
are surprised by satyrs, have already been mentioned. Th
putti are of the same playful type, and the general effect c
such pictures may jar at times, especially when female Pan
have collapsed in heavy drunkenness. But the spectato
accepts the fact that Rubens was also 'at home' among suc
creatures because, with his mysterious fire, he is never tediou
and it is only in tediousness that we become aware of the ob
scene. At times he gives us a dramatic action, even in hi
Italian period, such as in that picture, extant in two excellentl

preserved replicas where the drunken Hercules has wandered into the rout (Pl. 23). We see him led by a male and female Pan and mocked by a nymph dancing behind him; a *putto* has taken possession of his club and is galloping along on it in the rear, while looking round at a panther who is groping for the club; on the right a Silenus with the hero's lion skin pulled over his head is furtively sticking out his tongue, and the whole rout moves, as if in mocking triumph, diagonally through the picture.[105]

Mythical and semi-mythical love-scenes, mostly life-size and full length, and in the open air, may be mentioned here. For amorous lovers of the chase, Rubens several times painted Meleager presenting to Atalanta the head of the Calydonian Boar', and the features might be those of a married couple or two lovers; in a richer variant, several *putti* and leaping hounds are added, with a threatening Fury aloft in the air. A shepherd scene in the Munich Pinakothek (Pl. 117) is quite anonymous in character; a half-naked shepherd, his pipes on his back, is in the act of surprising a young woman by a rocky spring.[106] The ease of the treatment and the power of the tonality vouch for its authenticity, and the nature of the incident seems to betray some intimate experience; here too the figures may be portraits, but they are not those of Rubens and one of his wives, if only because the hooked nose was never that of the artist at any time of his life, and it is my opinion that he represented himself and his family either recognizably or not at all. And so, even in the curious and early picture in the Grosvenor Gallery in London, Pausias, the artist, and his beloved Glycera, the wreath-winder, do not bear the features of Rubens and Isabella Brant. Pausias, in a seated pose which still shows some constraint, is holding up with his right hand the portrait of Glycera propped against a rock; his left hand holds her right; to the right of her there are a jar and a basket of flowers. Perhaps only a general echo of the artist's youth.[107]

Water deities and other water creatures Rubens handled with the utmost freedom. A lovely association had bloomed in his mind between oceans, wild rivers and springs, huge animals and naked female beauty, and he troubled little about traditional mythology, but lived in the simple faith that every water-god must have his mate beside him. Even the Tiber-god in the picture of 'Romulus and Remus with the Wolf' (Capitoline Gallery, Pl. 40; cf. p. 45) has caused long and vain research into the name of the fresh and lovely spouse sitting in the reeds with him.[108] Nor need we trouble about the name of the naked goddess in the famous Schönborn picture in the Berlin Museum, for even if legend had never known an Amphitrite or a Libya, Rubens would have painted that figure in that place. We can recognize this work as one of Rubens's earliest in this genre by the profusion of human beings and animals, Neptune with his goddess, tritons, a nereid, a *putto*, a lion, a tiger, a rhinoceros and a crocodile; we have to admit the comic effect of the crocodile in the embrace of the nereid, and it was only later that Rubens realized that such matters should be left to *putti*. Above the reeds on the shore, a mast with a dark sail rises, securing the most beautiful chiaroscuro for the upper parts of the goddess and for Neptune's head. Looking at it from the cosmopolitan point of view, the picture would look well in the state apartment of any wealthy home in a maritime country, and even the land animals, the lion, tiger and so on, are cheerfully given to this peaceful emperor and empress of the waters as mere emblems of far distance. Later, at the height of his powers, Rubens painted the four gods of the great rivers (Vienna Gallery), the Danube, the Ganges, the Nile and the Amazon[109] with their mates, reclining at their ease on a reedy shore, even the goddesses in friendly converse, while in the brightest foreground light, an entirely different kind of intercourse is going on between the crocodile led and fondled with great jubilation by three *putti* and the snarling tigress suckling her four young; the latter however (in Waagen's opinion), is the most perfect animal Rubens ever painted, since those in the Schönborn picture leave a good deal to be desired. We saw above that the type of the huge, herculean water-gods derived from Roman statuary

Splendid nereids and huge tritons dominate the foregrounds of two pictures in the Luxembourg gallery ('The Landing at Marseilles' (Pl. 65), 'The Exchange of Princesses'), and in the 'Quos Ego' in Dresden (cf. Pl. 98) this whole retinue with the sea-horses occupies the ocean foreground and Neptune's shelly chariot, while through the air the wind-gods, threatened by him, swoop past in most daring forms. But when a sea-horse in the rout suddenly throws its leg over that of another, the spectator can no longer doubt that the wild onrush is really taking place. This painting was only part of the decorations for the state entry of the Cardinal Infante, but in his zeal, Rubens laid hand to the work (cf. p. 17) and the whole gives the impression of a most superb improvisation. In the same gallery, the picture of 'Hero and Leander' (Pl. 2) can only find refuge today among the 'Pupils and Imitators of Rubens' and I shall hardly find support for the opinion that we can recognize in it an original work from the beginning of his Italian period, such as only an imagination like his could produce. The nereids, who, according to the notion of the time, end in fish-tails, carry Leander's rigid corpse through the wild tumult and fearsome light of the sea, while Hero casts herself down from her tower into the waves. Waves and clouds mingle with terrible lightning.[110]

*　　*　　*

Of the pictures which tell definite stories from classical mythology, the most important have already been discussed in some detail, and what follows here are more general and supplementary notes.

This whole genre was universally intelligible in Europe and in general demand, yet it was not equally represented in all the schools. The wealthy Fleming who wanted a picture of some size, and could no longer be satisfied with the mythology of such artists as Abraham Bloemart, was doubtless glad to have a Rubens, but in Spain, where the mythological picture was so backward in comparison with the religious picture, it was the royal house which made the greatest move in

Rubens's favour with the commission for Torre de la Parada
as it had done before with commissions to Titian. Italy, on the
other hand, had seen an enormous development of mythological art, which had set in with the early Renaissance and had
at once taken fresco into its service, and by that means had
gained a wide field in all decoration. At the end of the
sixteenth century, with the Carracci, and later with their
disciples, art arose like a giant refreshed in mythology too,
and what it achieved in this field forms a kind of parallel to
Rubens, though in the end, the whole movement culminated
in a kind of competition between him and Guido Reni.
Powers of imagination and execution such as Rubens reveals
in the 'Rape of the Daughters of Leucippus' (Pl. 39) lay quite
beyond Guido's scope, and his 'Four Seasons', for instance, in
the Vienna Gallery, makes an astonishingly poor show in life
and colour beside Rubens's 'River Gods'. A time may, however, be coming which will do greater justice to the formal
beauty of Guido's composition and to the nobility of his forms
in his more carefully painted works, and which will in a general
way revive the respect for the Bolognese school and other
eclectics.

As a landscapist, Rubens was specially equipped for mythological painting, even though the execution of the landscapes
themselves may have been left to Lucas van Uden and Jan
Wildens. Since he must have seen important mythologies by
Titian at an early age, which are at the same time true landscapes (among others, those in the possession of the royal
house of Spain, such as the 'Guilt of Callisto' and 'Diana with
Actaeon'), they must have made some general impression on
him, and he will certainly have carried away a general feeling
for this harmony of near and distant woodland, bubbling
waters, softly clouded air and the most superb nudes, as well
as with purple and fine linen. But now he set out to compete
with Titian in a subject which exists in a whole series of
examples by Titian's own and his successors' hands, 'The
Farewell of Adonis to Venus'. The subject has already been
mentioned as a composition with small figures in a broad

ndscape (Uffizi), and here, enriched by attendant nymphs, *putti* and an Erinys or goddess of Envy swooping down, it as not the true loneliness of the farewell, which it regains a a totally different version (original, Hermitage, replicas nd copies in Dresden, The Hague and elsewhere). Here Venus . not seated as in Titian's and the Uffizi picture; she has started p and is clinging with both her arms round the huntsman's eck, while Cupid, the only *putto* in the scene, clings to him oo, holding him back (cf. Pl. 27).[111]

But where could Rubens have found the idea for his 'Battle f the Amazons' (Pl. 36)? He had seen neither the reliefs of higalia and Halicarnassus, nor Greek vases, but at most koman sarcophagi and some Renaissance work here and there vhich can hardly have been of the golden age, for it is emarkable that at that period, to my knowledge, the theme ppears neither in pictures nor in cartoons for tapestries,[112] nd the form it has found for all time in the Munich picture is olely and entirely Rubens's own in conception, design and olour.

The master has given us his conception of Olympus in the allery of the Luxembourg ('The Government of the Queen') nd here he is infinitely superior to Giulio's frescoes on a milar subject in the Sala dell'Olimpo in the Palazzo di Corte and in the Sala de' Giganti in the Palazzo del Tè at Mantua, though with far less lavish means. There is a Venetian harm in the distribution and depth of the clouds and the varm stream of light, and the natural wealth of beautiful gures is Rubens's very own. The Apollo is the Apollo of the atican transposed into swiftest movement, but among the emale heads the most beautiful is said to represent a Duchesse e Guémenée, though there is no evidence as to which head . meant.

A very famous and frequent Renaissance subject, 'The udgement of Paris', appears in a rich composition attributed o Raphael and engraved by Marcantonio; here, in the general npression, the effect of the finely developed action of the entral group is quite overshadowed by a number of subsidiary

groups of gods on the clouds, on the river-bank and in front o
a wood at the side, and these figures are hardly aware of Paris
It was left to Rubens to discover the peace of Mount Ida and
the visionary quality of the action, though the satyrs in the
treetops and Eris farther off on a cloud are lurking treacher
ously. Differences between the earlier version in Dresden
(c. 1625) and the entirely authentic and simplified version in
the National Gallery (Pl. 103; c. 1636) have already been
referred to. In the first, Paris merely sits dreaming, and it i
Mercury who instructs the goddesses, but in the second
Paris himself, as the judge, holds up the apple; further, no
only have *putti* been omitted, but the goddesses have been
spaced out, i.e., rather more weight is given to the shade o
the woods. In both pictures, Venus takes the centre of the
three goddesses, and since she is presented in profile, she alone
can be seen full face by Paris, which means that she is victorious
but all three, in the later picture at any rate, are among the mos
beautiful nudes of Rubens extant. The colours of the drapery
should be noticed too; the mantle of Juno, who is seen from
behind, is scarlet and furred; the garment which Minerva
seen full face, is about to put on or take off, is linen, but the
mantle of Venus is rendered in deep blue.[113]

A large number of other mythologies by Rubens are scattered
through the galleries, and in the subject lists of his work
practically every theme of the kind familiar to the Renaissance
will be found. And even though infinitely more existed in
Italian series of frescoes and book illustrations (in engraving and
woodcut) Rubens would not be so very far behind with hi
decoration of the entire Torre de la Parada. What matters
however, is not the number of mythologies, nor the priority o
one scene over another, but the inexhaustible freshness and
originality in design and execution that we have grown
accustomed to find throughout Rubens's work. And if at the
same time the subject is new or unusual, so much the better
I cannot remember having found, in any earlier artist, the
scene where the three Daughters of Cecrops discover the
child Erichthonios in a basket as we see it in the superb pictur

y Rubens in the Liechtenstein Gallery (cf. p. 38). Whether
ıe subject is familiar or not, however, we must accept the
ıct that he never wished to narrate, to draw or to paint in the
pirit of classical antiquity, but conjures up a living scene as it
uits his mood and the moment, and thus it may happen that
etails enter in which seem born of his own gaiety, for
ıstance Juno keeping the peacock chariot and her suite wait-
ıg while she suckles the infant Hercules (Madrid Gallery), or
he studio picture (Munich) where the wicked Lycian peasants
re visibly changing into frogs in the presence of Latona.
Ovid's richer stories contain hints for many a beautiful and
oble mythological picture, but the artist who selects the
ery moment of transformation, whatever its end is to be
and after all it is his duty *mutatas dicere formas*), will easily find
imself on the way to the comic in the mingling of forms.
But Rubens could make use of the horrible too, and in the
Fall of the Wicked Angels' (Munich) the angels are com-
letely human beings whose faces are just taking on
estiality; they were beautiful and are turning into horror
ınder our very eyes.

*   *   *

The famous historical pictures, ranging from the earliest days
f Rome to the beginning of the Republic (wars of Porsena
tc.) are radically different from the mythologies, even
hough it was the legendary quality of their poetry that made
hem paintable at all. Rubens had found Italy very rich in
aintings of this kind, especially in frescoes, whether they had
een conceived as moralities or painted merely for the sake of
he fine dramatic situation, and in this double sense they were
till intelligible to Europe. Whenever one of them stimulated
ım, his imagination, always ready to respond to anything
vith the quality of life, was at once at work. We have already
poken of the various pictures of the Rape of the Sabine
Women; these were not only painted as easel pictures, but
ormed part of the eight great Roman compositions which
Rubens designed for the hall of state in the royal palace at

Madrid.[114] In Dresden, however, there exists the most beauti
ful version of the 'Flight of Cloelia and her Companion
through the Tiber', and here Rubens, as he did elsewhere
has transposed in the loveliest fashion a great single event int
an inexhaustible variety of separate and living motifs (pro
bably executed by Diepenbeeck).[115] Here we may recall, as
harmonious echo from far away, Domenichino's 'Huntin
Feast of Diana' (Borghese Gallery. Van Dyck is also said t
have treated the subject).

The world of Greek anecdote (probably first in Valeriu
Maximus V, 4) gave the scene, so often represented at the time
of the captive Cimon suckled and preserved from starvatio
by his daughter, the so-called 'Carità Romana'. Of Rubens'
pictures on this subject, that in the Hamburg Gallery is sai
to be the finest.[116] This will also be a convenient place to con
sider the story of Philemon and Baucis who, in their poverty
received as guests the gods Jupiter and Mercury. The pleasing
peaceful picture in the Vienna Gallery was at one time incom
prehensibly attributed to Jordaens, whose crude composition
on the same theme, preserved in a large engraving, show
clearly how incapable he would have been of producing an
such work. Baucis is just in the act of laying hands on th
goose for the guests' meal (unicus anser erat etc., Ovid, Metam
VIII, 684) and Jupiter is preventing her with a noble gesture
while Philemon is engaged in earnest discourse with Mercury
In later years Rubens did not lose sight of the venerabl
couple, and in the appalling and fantastic landscape of th
Phrygian Deluge (same gallery) we see them again, rescue
from the flood, on a hill with the gods. This impressiv
picture is among the posthumous works and may have bee
one of the last to be painted (Pl. 72).

Both in conception and execution, the six great historic
pictures on the subject of the Consul Publius Decius in th
Samnite Wars are quite different from all these things (Pl
37-8; Liechtenstein Gallery). They are infused with a dee
and genuine feeling for the greatness of Rome, such as Davi
and his successors, for instance, never attained with all thei

XVI. Detail from the 'Rape of the Daughters of Leucippus'. (Figure XV)

hetoric. The intention, however, was that these pictures
hould serve as models for tapestries commissioned by *nobili* of
Genoa, and in May 1618, Rubens delivered them to the looms
t Brussels. It is probably on this occasion, or at any rate no
iter, that Rubens made up his mind to deliver finished oil
aintings as designs for tapestries, in place of the water-colour
artoons which all previous Italian and Flemish artists had pro-
ably used up to that time. For the great colourist, this was
erhaps the natural and the only satisfying thing to do, and
aintings of the kind, whether they remained the property of
he master, the patron or the weaver, retained their intrinsic
alue as paintings, and were copied in huge engravings. Very
w or any of the tapestries, on the other hand, could ever be
oven, they might vanish from men's eyes in far distant lands,
id we cannot, for instance, say whether and where the his-
ries of Decius are still extant in woven form.[117] There is,
owever, no possible doubt that, if these tapestries were
iscovered, the oil paintings would be much preferred to
iem, in spite of their having been mainly executed by pupils.
f the six events represented—The Preparation for Sacrifice,
he Allocution, The Repulse of the Lictors, The Dedication
Death, The Battle and The Triumph of the Dead Consul,
ie three last, in particular, are exceedingly moving. In the
Dedication to Death', the priest is pronouncing the formula
hile laying his left hand on the hero's head, which is almost
itirely veiled by the red drapery. The solemnity of the
oment has overcome the few onlookers and even the waiting
iarger, who seems to foresee the sudden end. An attempt
as made earlier (p. 67) to give a description of the Consul's
eath in the cavalry battle. The veneration of the body is also
grand sight, and its austerity is not sweetened by any gene-
ous regrets. What we see here are victors and Romans; women,
ossibly destined to human sacrifice, are being dragged away
ith their wailing children by their hair and garments.

It is true that the oil-paintings for most of the great series of
pestries can no longer be discovered, and as for the prelim-
ary coloured sketches, which are scattered all over the world

I

(Pls. 41, 73-4, 87-8), not only in galleries, but in the hands o:
hardly identifiable owners, nobody today can claim to have
seen even the majority of them. A series on the history o
Constantine the Great (for Marie de' Medici?) is said to be
still extant in tapestry, and there are at any rate isolated
engravings of it, but the sketches are hidden in private hand
or in English collections (Pl. 41), for instance the eight sketche
for the history of Achilles (for Charles I) also executed, o:
at least designed, for tapestries (Pls. 87-9). Late, arbitrary
engravings are all we have as evidence of them.[118] But al
nine large oil paintings designed for an important series o
tapestries are extant; this is the 'Triumph of Faith' mentioned
above (pp. 26, 35; Pls. 73-4). It will be discussed later.

Rubens, however, knew the value of the cartoons of othe
great masters, and it was he who persuaded Charles I to
acquire Raphael's cartoons of the Acts of the Apostles. When
after Charles's execution, the royal art collection was sold
Cromwell went through it, but stopped in front of thes
cartoons, saying: 'We'll keep these'. And so it came abou
that England has remained in possession of this wonderfu
treasure to this very day.

Allegory, in the widest sense of the word, occupies so larg
a place in Rubens's work that it cannot be avoided in th
galleries; for that reason he is exceedingly vulnerable at thi
point, since he here served a vogue which is now absolutel
obsolete. The first thing that might be said in reply is that, fo
instance, the whole of the monumental sculpture and even, i
certain cases, the monumental painting of our day cannot d
without allegory at any point, and without this 'vogue', i.e
without the constant help of a good deal of abstractior
would be lost. It would, however, be useless to attempt
vindication, a rehabilitation of allegory in the art of past time
All we can do is to realize that Rubens, too, found in this va
premise of all the art of his time a powerful stimulus to displa
living beauty, and that his huge imagination felt quite .
home in it. European culture in Rubens's day was humanisti
and the *Tables* of Cebes, for instance, had long been a scho

ext-book. This was probably a late classical work in which a
1ost of allegorical figures, moral and intellectual, appears,
peaking and acting as if in a large painting. Considering the
ncredibly vast further accumulation of allegory in the course
f the sixteenth century, Rubens cannot in any essential sense
>e regarded as an inventor. What he did was to select, to give
>erfectly fresh life, and in many pictures to create the most
>eautiful effect.

Even at Antwerp he must have grown up with allegory,
nd in Italy it surrounded him on all sides, in past and contem-
>orary art, in poetry and literature, in the splendid decorations
f all pageants; the Doge's palace at Venice of itself presented
iim with a superfluity of it, as the classic home of political
llegory in painting. In detail, as we know, the world of
llegory consisted partly of freely created personifications of
;eneral powers, qualities, impulses, circumstances, localities
nd peoples, in part of the familiar figures of classical gods or
lemons which had long been regarded as representatives of
uch powers, qualities, etc. As we can imagine, the possibilities
f sublime beauty they contained could only unfold in repose.
'aolo Veronese had, for instance, solved this problem with
mperious freedom in the ceiling of the Sala del Collegio
Ducal Palace). But these allegorical figures had been por-
rayed by countless others in mutual or antagonistic motion,
r even emotion, or they had been introduced into the
.oings of historical personages. But having reached this point,
hey showed themselves pre-eminently suited to take over
 leading part in the action, particularly its inward motive,
ts impulse, and on this daring path Rubens had fared
arther, more boldly and more felicitously than any of his
ontemporaries.

We must first mention a number of more general—we
night say more anonymous—allegories which give form to an
dea, a feeling, common to all educated people and easily
ntelligible in the picture, and these might still be called
moralities'. While still in Italy, Rubens began with a subject
vhich is continued in a number of variants of the fine original

example (Dresden); a huge hero in classical armour (not
portrait of Duke Vincenzo of Mantua and not necessarily
portrait at all) is crowned by a winged Victory, whom h
embraces, while Drunkenness, Luxury and Envy sink to th
ground (Pl. 24).[119] There is greater appeal in those pictures (in
several versions) which show human life, hitherto happy an
peaceful, threatened by Mars, or even by Furies, and protecte
by Minerva. But to depict this earthly happiness as a family i
the open air, with stress on the different generations, indee
needed the visionary soul of an artist such as Rubens was
'an almost naked female figure is pressing her infant to he
breast, surrounded by a numerous family, to whom Par
perched in the branches of a tree, is offering fruit'— so run
the short description in the catalogue of the Munich Pina
kothek, but it is very much worth while to look more closel
at this family as a whole and in detail. A very beautifu
variant of it is to be seen in the picture in the National Galler
which Rubens delivered to Charles I in 1630 (Pl. 80), and i
this picture we have the feeling that in the group representin
happy (and in this case rather Bacchic) family life, there ma
be an allusion to definite persons, more particularly in th
retreating Mars. In another place a wonderfully intimat
family group—including even the grandfather—sits watchin
four children dancing to the tambourine, quite unaware tha
up in the air Minerva is preparing to launch a tremendou
blow at a threatening Fury. (This obviously excellent pictur
is only known to me in a photograph.)[120] True, we must no
always expect these allegorical figures to abide by a singl
meaning. Minerva, for instance, who appeared in the pictur
described as the protectress of earthly happiness, also appear
as the personification of the duty of war and of heroism
namely in the authentic picture in the Uffizi which i
erroneously entitled 'Hercules at the Parting of the Ways
(p. 42). A heroic youth is seated beside Venus (or the personi
fication of earthly happiness); Minerva approaches and take
him by the hand, his weapons and a servant with his wai
horse are already waiting; above Venus hovers Cupid, abov

Minerva, Saturn or Time with his scythe, and to the side, farther back, two young female figures stand in suspense. Here
is hardly possible to deny that Venus, and not improbably
the maidens, too, are portraits; above all, the personal relationship comes out in the hero, and Rubens was clearly in the
secret. But even in his last years we have a triumphant proof
that in these pictures, which are now regarded as 'trivial',
he felt the impulse and the obligation to express serious and
profound truths and feelings. This is the superb 'Allegory of
War' in the Pitti Palace, painted in 1638 for the Grand Duke
Ferdinand II of Tuscany (Pl. 111). A circumstantial interpretation is contained in a letter to the artist Justus Sustermans,
a countryman of Rubens's living in Florence, which was
obviously intended to be passed on to the noble patron. Here
Mars and Venus are still spouses in the mythological sense,
but Mars is tearing himself vehemently free of her and her
amorini, and the Alecto with the torch hovering in the air is
tugging at his garment; other Furies, swooping forward,
represent pestilence and famine; Harmony, as a woman with a
lute, and Family Happiness in the guise of a woman with a
child in her arms, are already being trampled to the ground,
but the master-builder already lies dead, his compasses still in
his stiffening hand, for war destroys the beautiful buildings of
peace. To the left, the open Temple of Janus, while in the
centre the view into the distance already shows the battle
beginning. But that distraught figure (the woman with the
walled crown hurrying after Venus) in black garments and
torn veil, despoiled of all her jewels and other ornaments, is
unhappy Europe, which had so long suffered rapine, shame and
misery. Her emblem is the globe with the cross carried by a
child angel or genius, an allusion to the world of Christendom.
We might conclude with the moving words which Waagen
has added to his description: 'This picture, then, is the most
beautiful memorial of his art which Rubens bequeathed to us
not long before the end of his earthly days; it is born of the
deep feeling in his great and noble soul (which, in a long life of
giving and receiving, had known the highest that art and

science have to bestow) for the unutterable misery whi‹
wars had brought down, not only upon his own country, b‹
still more upon unhappy Germany.'[121]

In a friendly postscript, Rubens had expressed the wish th‹
Sustermans should touch up the picture 'wherever chan‹
(damage in transport) or my negligence have made it nece‹
sary'. Fortunately, this miraculous work was and is in a sta‹
of excellent preservation; it is the immortal and unforgettab‹
frontispiece to the Thirty Years' War, painted by the hand ‹
him who was alone, in the highest sense, called to paint it.

*   *   *

Rubens further won particular fame by large historical pain‹
ings in which he not only made use of allegorical figures, b‹
occasionally transposed the whole composition into terms ‹
an idealized form of life, or at any rate a life outside ‹
historical reality. In 1621–5 he painted for the gallery of t‹
Luxembourg Palace, in twenty-one scenes, the transfigur‹
life-story of the Queen Dowager of France, Marie de' Medi‹
(cf. Pls. 61–7; Louvre).

There is no question that our century would have presente‹
the historical painter of Antwerp with a different programm‹
First he would have been expected to paint the whole pa‹
history of Brabant and the rest of the Netherlands, realisticall‹
in historically accurate costume, with the old battles, rebellior‹
festivals and so on, and all that not on account of its artist‹
quality, but in the name of patriotism and even progres‹
since what matters in such things as a rule is not what actu‹
epochs of the past may have felt, but the present-day notic‹
of what they felt, which is, of course, drawn from such boo‹
and other writings of the day as people happen to be readin‹
He would have had to show, not his own world of feelin‹
but that of other people, further, he would have been expec‹
ed to represent incidents, again accurate in costume and settin‹
whose only importance lay in their consequences, althoug‹
those consequences could not possibly enter into the pictur‹
—for instance, public proclamations, more especially

onstitutions, the unrolling of ground-plans for important
uildings, and so on. But quite especially, he would have had
o hint at the intercourse of a certain very famous modern
elgian artist with the great ones of the earth by showing his
redecessors in art in such intercourse, beginning with Jan van
yck as the chamberlain of Philip the Good.[122] Above all, he
ould be expected to illustrate Shakespeare's plays, and finally
o paint Shakespeare himself, perhaps at the moment when he
as composing Hamlet's monologue. We could add any
umber of details to this list. Rubens, however, did not do
hat the prevailing opinion of our day would expect him to
o. He accepted, in perfect freedom, a commission from a
oreign sovereign which he could just as well have refused.
ut it appealed to him, and by far the larger number of paint-
gs in the series show that it appealed to him, since he was,
or the most part, able to suggest and invent them himself.
o that we may in any case be grateful that the gallery of the
uxembourg Palace exists at all.

At many different epochs, and in many different civiliza-
ons, art has been expected or compelled to take upon itself
he representation of all kinds of past events which had in some
ay (perhaps only in their consequences) been of importance
o the ruling power, which conceived this to be the best way
f achieving immortality. Art, as a rule, obeyed, if only
ecause power, on such occasions, tends to be rather more
pen-handed than at other times; besides, those were times
nd conditions when obedience was the rule, and not even the
rtist attempted to evade it. The position of art is especially
erilous when it has to serve a prevailing opinion, patriotic,
olitical or religious, in great historical pictures, and to instil
, as feeling, into the faces and lineaments of the principal
gures. Those opinions, however, are in no case everlasting;
hey are subject to the changes of time, and it may not be
ong before monstrous and overcrowded pictures have be-
ome unintelligible. The gallery of the Luxembourg has
othing to fear now from such mutability. The brilliant
oments of time here depicted are, spiritually and materially,

clearly self-sufficient in the theme and details of each pictur
they move us in themselves without suggesting to the spe
tator that reading-matter on the subject is awaiting him ou
side. Whatever his response may be today to the factu
content of the series, art has still remained art, even in th
kind of royal servitude, and proves that it is of the race of tl
immortals. Since there was little to choose between the quee
and her enemies, while they had not, like her, secured tl
services of Rubens, Marie de' Medici remains before our ey
'unjustly' privileged by a brilliant mythological apotheos
(Pls. 61–7). The humiliations of her life—among other thing
the fall and murder of her closest confidants—have bee
passed over, and in what we are told of her, she is, and remain
in the right. But while the memoirs and lampoons of that da
are read by few (and not for their pleasure), the great series (
pictures is displayed in its splendour before the eyes of all.

Rubens certainly paid his tribute here and there to a secretiv
age, in so far as the interpretation of certain figures was dispute
even at the time, but the responsibility for that might lie wit
the allegorical adviser, who had a voice in the matter. It
instructive that Rubens makes as sparing a use as possible (
the allegories in this series, while in the Roman historie
including Decius, he did not use them at all because th
emotions contained in them, with all their motives, could b
fully represented by human figures and actions. Marie de
Medici, on the other hand, could not take a visible part in th
action. She could only give counsel, decide, submit to cere
monies, come riding along in triumph and perhaps once fle
by night, so that in this case the impulse and resolve to actio
is very often shown by allegorical figures and Roman divinitie
used as allegories. Gallia urges Henri IV to contemplate th
portrait of Marie presented by Amor and Hymen; on th
landing stage at Marseilles, Gallia and Marsilia hasten to mee
her; the infant Louis XIII is held in the arms of the genius (
Health; in the homage after Henri's death we see, besid
Gallia, the figure of the Regency presenting the helm of stat
to the queen; in the negotiations made necessary by th

XVIII. Detail from the 'Sacrifice to Venus'. (Plate 81)

XIX. Detail from the 'Rape of the Sabine Women'. (Plate 101)

fferences between mother and son, Mercury moves quite
ely between two cardinals; Peace in the guise of a huge
oman is extinguishing torches and finally Time, as Saturn,
ises Truth to the bright heights. Rubens is as rich in figures
evil as in figures of virtue. We see, generally in violent
tion, Discord, Envy, Hate, Deception, Rage, Ignorance,
ander and so on, while Rebellion appears as a many-headed
dra. Yet all these figures blend most harmoniously with
ies and gentlemen of the court and the aristocracy, with
gnitaries of various ranks in the picturesque dress of the
ne, with soldiers, servants and so on, and we may wonder
w the same allegories would fare in the company of our
iforms and dresses, especially our black tail-coats. In Rubens,
wever—admitting his and the queen's way of thinking—they
e, for the most part, introduced with unerring propriety.
is true that a really tedious subject appears once in the so-
lled 'Majority of Louis XIII', where mother and son are
anding on the lavishly ornate prow of a ship, the latter
lding the helm, while a number of Virtues have to row or
sy themselves about the sails, and Gallia, rising threateningly
ove the mast with the globe and the sword of flame, is a
arning that other countries must take to heart; up on the
uds, two goddesses of Fame are blowing trumpets and
ckbuts. But how wonderfully 'The Education of the Queen'
conceived in pure allegory! The execution, as far as I remem-
r, is poor and by the hand of a pupil, and as regards the state
preservation of these pictures, two great restorations have
eady done their work, but the idea saves the picture. Sunny
ght and a waterfall—the Castalian spring—stream from above
to a cool ravine; in the shade and half-light, Minerva is
ting, teaching the young princess to write, while the gesture
Mercury, swooping down with his staff, is said to represent
e teaching of eloquence; in the foreground Apollo is playing
viola da gamba. Opposite to this group, on the light side of
e ravine, the three Graces stand in full radiance, the centre
ae presenting a wreath, and it is they that are the source of all
e light that falls on knowledge and learning, and such

K

beautiful, unquestionably conscious symbolism is to be four
nowhere else. In other pictures where a prevailing gener
condition has to be symbolized, the allegorical content is ve
rich, and here we may imagine that the high-spirited queen,
her discussions with the artist, protested most solemnly,
one-sidedly, that the whole world, except for evil men, h
been happy and contented at that time. This is the sense
which we must understand the superb Olympus, which,
the series of pictures, bears the title 'Effects of the Quee
Government', and the later 'Felicity of the Regency' whic
with the exception of the queen enthroned as Justitia, prese
abstract ideas only. Here, incidentally, even the quee
patronage is glorified, Abundance and Prosperity, matu
benevolent women, distributing medals, laurel wreaths and
on to the genii of the Fine Arts, namely three *putti* at the fo
of the throne, with Ignorance, Slander and Envy cowering
the ground at their feet. This picture which, for all its ligh
ness of hand, produces a magnificent effect is, in the symmet
of its design, the secular echo of a religious picture wi
cherub musicians at the foot of an enthroned Madonna. Som
times it may have been almost indifferent whether individu
figures should form part of the court or belong to the id
world; in the important picture where the king is presentin
to the queen the blue globe with the fleur-de-lis emblematic
her regency, she is attended by two beautiful female figur
which for us are obviously Virtues, but were certainly co
ceived originally as court ladies, for on the other side of t
picture, the king is attended by soldiers. In connexion wi
ecclesiastical ceremonies, allegory is reduced to a minimun
while still in Florence, Marie de' Medici is solemnly espouse
with her uncle, Grand Duke Ferdinand, standing proxy, a
only her train-bearer, Hymen, is a cherub; on the other han
there is a symbolic addition to the picture—on the alt
behind the officiating Cardinal Legate, there rises a marl
group of God the Father seated with the body of Christ
his knees. There are in Florence a number of groups of t
kind, one, for instance by Baccio Bandinelli, and for Rube

all probability, this was a sufficient allusion to the city
ich saw the nuptials; it is a symbol of place, like the river-
d Arno, for instance, in another picture. Above the 'Coro-
ion of the Queen' he was content with two hovering spirits
Plenty, and in this solemn picture, one of the most splendid
the world, he gave pride of place to the absolutely personal
of the participants, in the complete freedom of movement
the unconstrained poses of beautiful and expressive faces.
e number of allegorical beings, however, is much larger
the 'Homage to the Queen Regnant after Henri's Death',
we could well dispense with the whole left-hand side of
picture which is given up to them (among other things
the king borne very ungainly aloft by Jupiter and Saturn);
group of courtiers, on the other hand, swearing fealty
strate before the throne, is of the greatest beauty. But
we should wish to demonstrate the possible superiority
allegory over verisimilitude in a general way, we might ask
ether the landing of a young queen on the shores of what is
w to be her country could be more movingly rendered in a
listic setting than Rubens has shown it in the radiantly
autiful 'Reception of Marie de' Medici at Marseilles'. If
arie had been the greatest queen of all time, and she was far
m being that, even the strictest of aesthetes might stand
chanted before this work and declare that allegory is alone
pable and worthy of such marvels.

The second huge commission which would obviously have
en executed in the same historico-allegorical fashion, the
e of Henri IV, was never carried out, as we saw above,
ving to the fall of the Queen Dowager. The two gigantic
etches in the Uffizi showing the 'Battle of Ivry' and the
tate Entry into Paris'[123] (Pls. 78–9) are a supreme testimony
the fullness of power which Rubens would have displayed
this series, and not only art, but France herself, must
terly regret that it was never executed. Instead of France, it
as England that was to be enriched by the life of a king
alized by art, though the commission certainly appealed
less to Rubens, who had a very deep feeling for Henri IV.

The great allegorical apotheosis of James I of England
the ceiling of the Banqueting House of Whitehall (Pls. 90–
commissioned by Charles I, designed in sketches in 1629 a
delivered complete in 1635, are known to me neither in t
original nor in reproductions, and here the reader must
referred to accounts by other hands. The execution, as in t
great ceiling decorations of the Doge's Palace, is probably
oil on very large surfaces of canvas, which were subsequen
fixed in place in some way or other.[124]

It has never been my good fortune to see paintings
Rubens on ceilings or vaultings, and thus to acquire any cor
plete knowledge of his technique in pictures designed to
seen from below. Besides, I find some difficulty in believi
that he, whose composition was so perfect and so absolut
adequate to a vertical surface, can have found great pleasu
in handling these figures, all of which had to be violen
foreshortened. Yet commissions for such things must ha
poured in upon him because of the universal preference for
ideas, composition and style to any other, and the major p
of extant coloured sketches for ceilings on all kinds of subje
and in all stages of execution prove that he actually accepte
large number of commissions of the kind, although he left t
painting to pupils and in all probability never so much
mounted a scaffolding himself. The precedents which he sa
in Italy were of the most haphazard kind, for there everythi
that could be painted at all had long been painted on vaults a
soffits; the very best artists were engaged for pictures design
for long-range effect, and Paolo's 'Venetia Crowned by Glo
on the ceiling of the Sala del Maggior Consiglio will ha
given Rubens plenty of food for thought. Since Ruber
sketches are, as a whole, so widely scattered, only a f
general remarks can be made here.[125]

In the Collection Lacaze, in the Louvre, we see the 'Sacrif
of Isaac', 'Abraham and Melchisedec', 'The Coronation
the Virgin', 'The Raising of the Cross' (Pl. 57), probal
sketches for a church vaulting. The Gallery of the Vien
Academy possesses a number of sketches for soffits, and th

re specially fine ones in the Liechtenstein Gallery, among
thers a masterly sketch of 'Mercury presenting Psyche to
upiter', and, for a longer soffit, 'Apollo and Diana' sweeping
cross a sky filled with other moving figures, and a tondo of
Olympus, seen from below. Sketches for the Whitehall ceiling
n the Hermitage have been very highly praised, and the
National Gallery possesses a roundish sketch, painted with
pirit and mastery, for the apotheosis of James I, or, as some
elieve, of William the Silent, though it does not correspond
o a scene on the ceiling, but to a painting in private ownership
n England; the sovereign is borne aloft by two allegorical
igures. 'The Glory of S. Francesco di Paola' (Dresden, variant
n Munich) was doubtless destined for the vaulting of a church
f the Minorites; the Saint is freely poised in air; at the sides,
n front of elaborate architecture and flights of stairs there are
roups of worshippers, convalescents, of the sick and the
ossessed. In the Dresden variant the whole is carried out in a
revailing yellowish tone with a hint of a few of the future
rincipal colours; even the Munich copy is a 'grisaille
oloured in parts'.[126]

To return to the semi-allegorical histories, we must discuss
y the way a type of portrait not rare at the time, the frame
f which was surrounded by personified virtues, conditions
nd places, all in the over-dramatic taste of the time. The
voodcut had made manifold use of this type, even in the
raming of armorial bearings and title-pages of books. Rubens,
owever, with his half-length portrait of the victor of the
White Mountain, Bucquoy, in a laurel frame with a rich and
rnate setting of mythological and allegorical figures, pro-
ably achieved greater effect than all who came before and
fter him. For the engraver Vorsterman he painted the fully
nished grisaille picture still preserved in the Hermitage.[127]

A later, but very important, opportunity for expression in
llegorical historical form was given by the splendid decora-
ons, triumphal arches, perspectives, etc. (pp. 13, 17) which
vere set up in the streets and squares of Antwerp for the
eception of the Cardinal Infante, known as the Introitus

Ferdinandi (17 April 1635; Pls. 97-8). Rubens's learned friend
Gevartius took charge of the subject-matter; the entire artistic
side was directed by Rubens himself. He even helped in the
execution, and the museums of Antwerp and the Hermitage
possess several examples of his and Van Thulden's oil sketches.
Of the great painted fields forming part of the whole, which
served not only to glorify the chief personage, but also to
express the desires of good patriots, a number are still extant
in other galleries. In Vienna, for instance, there is the meeting
of the two Ferdinands (of Spain and Austria) before the battle
of Nordlingen, in the presence of Danubius who, reclining
quite peacefully in the foreground between two symbolic
female figures (one of which, probably Germania, bears
Helen's features), prophesies the issue. The same gallery has
two heroic single figures from the house of Hapsburg. In
Brussels, the portraits of Albert and Isabella, by Rubens's own
hand. In Dresden the 'Quos Ego' already mentioned, the
threatening of the wind-gods by Neptune, symbolizing the
fact that a storm had subsided during the Cardinal Infante's
voyage on the Mediterranean. A fine central picture, on the
other hand, the mounted Infante accompanied by Victory
consoling the figure of the Netherlands kneeling in supplication before him, is, to my knowledge, only known to us now
in a sketch and the engraving. But all these splendours were
displayed before the whole people for some length of time
and the knowledge of their manner of narration was not, this
time, restricted to people who had access to palaces such as the
Luxembourg or Whitehall.[128]

No wonder that the great ones of the rest of Europe should
wish to have Rubens perpetually at their disposal for this kind
of glorification of their persons, families and countries, that
they hoped, even after the master's death, to find in the studio
of Antwerp an heir to his powers in this field, and that, in one
of those studios, there actually was an artist who imagined he
was that heir.

This was Jacob Jordaens. Twelve years after Rubens's death
he undertook the 'Apotheosis of the Regent Frederick Henry'

who had died five years before, in the central octagonal hall
of the Palace of Orange in the woods near The Hague, while
other Flemish artists took charge of the other surfaces of the
hall,[129] which they covered with pictures of the rest of the life
of the Regent from birth. It is a well-known fact that idealized
composition was not the forte of Flemish art, nor were matters
improved by the heavy-handedness of Flemish learning. It is
further uncertain how far the widow of Frederick, Amalia
von Solms, had a hand in the selection of the scenes. Possibly
the famous Antwerp artist was able to make up for all the rest
by his great central picture. Even today in an excellent state
of preservation, the picture, which measures twenty-four feet
wide by twenty-seven feet high, is said to be extremely
effective in a number of details, as well as in the power of its
colour-scheme and tonality. I have to judge it partly by a
famous coloured sketch in the Brussels Museum and partly by
a large and later engraving.

This picture provides us with the proof that the palette alone
is not enough, even if it is only slightly inferior to Rubens's
own. It is by way of this picture that we might come to realize
once for all the great qualities of Rubens's allegories. A huge
accumulation of pomp is the greatest enemy of artistic effect.
Now Jordaens had obviously tolerated an immense amount of
interference with his work between the sketch and the
finished picture, and overloading has become extreme. The
principal motif is the quadriga approaching the spectator and
drawing the triumphal chariot of the Prince of Orange, but
the chariot is quite overshadowed by the team. And yet
Rubens, in an 'Allegory of the Triumph of the Church' (to be
discussed later), which Jordaens must have seen in the engraving at any rate, knew perfectly well why he sent his quadriga,
driven and ridden by allegorical figures, sideways through the
picture, thus concentrating the majestic principal view on
Ecclesia, enthroned on the chariot. Further, in Rubens, the
master of movement, the figures have really room to move in
space, while in Jordaens the human beings and animals would
trample each other to death. In addition to soldiers and women,

members of the Orange family crowd in on both sides
William II (the son and successor of Frederick Henry, who
was also dead) even on horseback. We can only admire the
wisdom of those who—between the sketch and the finished
picture—have taken refuge to right and left on the pedestals
of the bronze statues of the ancestors. We may add that the
outer horses of the team are being driven by Mars and Hercules, the middle ones—in the sketch—by Mercury and the god
of Time, while in the finished picture a well-nourished youth,
Contentment, has taken his place on one of them. Under the
hoofs lie Envy and Hatred, though in the finished picture Envy
is alone. Two lions in the foreground signify, according to the
printed guide, Generosity and Strength, two dogs, Vigilance
and Loyalty. The *putti* added in the foreground of the picture
personify 'the pleasures of all ages of life' (?). The upper part of
the picture cannot but produce an effect of anarchy; above the
hero there hovers a skeleton with a lance, with a male spirit of
Glory hurtling towards him, blowing a trumpet, and right at
the top, in an oddly wobbly stance, we see a goddess of Peace.
A garland of fruit with hovering *putti* concludes the whole.[18]

*   *   *

It was King Philip IV who took Rubens into his service for
the great religious allegory during the artist's second stay in
Madrid (1628–9), and it was at that time that he painted the
series of nine compositions which were briefly discussed
above (Pls. 73–4). Ever since the Middle Ages, stories from
the Bible had been regarded as allegories, more especially
those from the Old Testament which were to be understood
as presages fulfilled in the New, and so, in this series, 'Abraham
and Melchisedec', the 'Gathering of the Manna' and the
'Miraculous Feeding of Elisha in the Desert' are as indubitable
presages or pre-histories of the sacrament as they are in many
older works of art. Two further pictures contain great saints
brought together in a peculiarly theological sense, and the
four pictures are left which are allegories in the stricter sense
of the word, namely actions by abstract, symbolic figures,
generalized moments of the Church and humanity.

We have no information whatever as to the way the scenes
ere selected, whether by the king alone or with the assistance
Spanish theologians; the present titles of the last four
ctures vary in the galleries and nobody knows what was the
riginal order intended. If the commission was not entrusted
a Spanish artist, it may be because the royal art-lover recog-
zed the supreme artist merely by talking to him. Further,
ubens was well versed in tapestry and could supervise the
ork in the Brussels looms. That the designs were intended
r tapestries becomes probable by the framework alone, the
cidents being shown as if they were already executed in
chly bordered tapestries; further Palomino confirms it and
nally there is proof that tapestries were actually executed
ter some of these pictures. It is believed that designs such as
ubens sketched, probably under the king's eyes, exist in
ngland, and still more in the Madrid Gallery, but it is uncer-
in whether even the latter are by Rubens himself, and while
ne of them corresponds to a replica in Dresden, it merely
ves rise to more misgivings, for the obviously quite secular
resden allegory with the gods of Time and Truth could
nly be inserted in the series with the utmost difficulty. The
aintings, on large canvases in oil, were executed in Antwerp,
oviously in haste and not by first-rate pupils, while Rubens
robably prepared careful drawings or grisailles for the en-
ravings (cf. p. 33), which most likely were nearest his heart.
Meanwhile, at court, the tapestries would seem to have been
ddenly abandoned, and in their place the painted canvases
ent to Madrid. The king, however, now presented them
his all-powerful minister Olivarez for the decoration of
e church of a Carmelite monastery which Olivarez had
dowed not far from the capital. There they remained until
e French invasion under Napoleon, when they were carried
ff by his plundering generals. Two, it is said, are still in place,
'Triumph of the Church' and a 'Victory of Christianity
ver Paganism'. Of the seven others, two (the 'property' of
Maréchal Sébastiani) came in time to the Louvre, a 'Triumph
f the Christian Religion' and 'Elisha Fed by Ravens'. Three

reached the Grosvenor Gallery in London, 'Abraham an
Melchisedec', 'The Four Evangelists' and 'The Gathering
the Manna'. One was exhibited in 1879 at the South Kensin
ton Museum—'The Six Great Doctors of the Church wi
St. Clare of Assisi'. The ninth, a 'Triumph of Charity', ve
much damaged, is believed to have been in private hands
England in our own day.[131]

Now misfortune has willed it that the two by far mo
accessible pictures of the series, those in the Louvre, are n
only among the worst preserved, but that the so-call
'Triumph of Religion' (according to the distinct inscriptio
Fides Catholica) is a particularly crude and unpleasant compo:
tion, namely two angels, certainly with an allegorical signi
cance, drawing the triumphal chariot on which Fides sits wi
the chalice, and Religio kneels, leaning against a cross; there
in addition a particularly large assembly of angels and cherub
two of whom are helping to push the chariot; there a
several allegorical figures and, as an allusion to the missioi
a negro and a Red Indian. On the other hand, the two pictur
at Loeches, widely known in Bolswert's beautiful engraving
are among Rubens's finest works. There is supreme genius
the 'Victory over Paganism', depicted as a ceremony
sacrifice to an idol cast into confusion by a luminous ang
descending from heaven with the chalice. The other pictur
however, already mentioned in connexion with Jordaen
Ecclesia per sanctam eucharistiam triumphans is alive with profus
truly triumphant splendour; the movement of the quadrig
both of the horses and of the Virtues driving and riding the
is superb, and in particular, the Genius with the insignia
the Papacy on the foremost horse is of a totally different ord
from the 'Contentment' in Jordaens's picture in The Hagu
The triumphal chariot, rolling over howling demons ai
driven by a superb *putto*, with fettered pagans being driv
along beside it, bears the beautiful, victorious Ecclesia wi
the monstrance, which is the source of light, while an ang
holds the mitre in the air above her head. An incredibly ri
composition, yet not overloaded and full of room to breath

the 'Gathering of the Manna', I recall the visionary jubila-
n of Moses as the central theme. 'Abraham and Melchi-
lec' is probably to be distinguished from an earlier sketch
the Albertina Gallery (reproduced by Knackfuss) where the
nporal and spiritual rulers with their retinues met, so to
eak, still on an equal footing, while here Abraham bows
fore the priest as if in homage. But in the pictures of 'The
ur Evangelists' and ' The Six Doctors of the Church with
Clare', quite a new note is struck. The figures are great
man beings, who do not merely stand before us as great
rsonages, as if bearing witness to what has been told in the
her pictures; quite in Rubens's way, they seem to be moving
st us. In monasteries and the homes of devout burgesses,
lswert's engravings must have had a considerable influence.
In all Catholic countries, the age of the baroque covered
e vaults of churches and the ceilings of monastery libraries
th allegorical apotheoses of the church, in many cases by
ists of repute. But what painting, in the whole period, can
proach this triumphant creation in artistic power?

*   *   *

first sight, Rubens would seem to have left genre painting
tirely to other Flemish, Belgian and Dutch artists. The
planation seems easy; like all his famous contemporaries in
ly (apart from the naturalists) his temperament was
amatic. First, however, we know that he had a personal
ing for genre pictures, and bought a large number by
lriaen Brouwer for his own collection. For like other really
eat men, he could take pleasure in much that lay outside his
ovince. Given the enormous quantity of work he did in
e greatest of other forms of painting, it would be quite
mprehensible if he had spent his whole strength on them.
it the wealth of his imagination was such that, in the last
ars of his life, he must needs create the most famous of all
ctures of Flemish folk-life, the 'Kermesse', and the most
lendid picture of seventeenth-century society, the 'Garden
Love'. The 'Kermesse' (Pl. 68; Louvre) at one blow

delivered the doings of the peasant from the manner of t
Brueghel workshop, from the imperious rule of the individe
in type and incident. It gives them perfect freedom and varie
of movement, perfect unity of incident, tonality and color
adding only as much of the locality as may serve the to
effect. The picture must have been accessible to the publ
perhaps even in the master's time, and David Teniers t
Younger, whose close personal acquaintance with Rube
like that of his father, David the Elder, can hardly be dispute
must have known it, even though his own peasant dances a
incomparably tamer. In addition to the 'Kermesse', we ha
another quite peculiar work, the 'Country Dance' (Pl. 11
Madrid Museum and Weber Gallery, Hamburg, engravi
by Bolswert).[132] It is only here that supreme unity of effect
achieved; the dance, which in this picture has involved all t
dancers in one and the same frenzy, is just on the point
breaking up on the one side and doubling on the other, t
couples holding up a kerchief for the others to run und
It is the last moment of coherence before the dance dissolv
and the impression of instantaneity and movement is absolute
enchanting. Further, there is that variety of motion in ea
individual figure which every vigorous dance produces. It
interesting to see how Rubens, in a picture which depend
on beauty of appearance, rejected the actual peasant costur
of the men (the 'buttoned' and the 'sewn'); in the same w
as in the figures in a number of landscapes, the clothi
approximates to that of the Italian pastoral, and there is ev
more of the nude. If anyone knows another artist who cou
have created this incomparable scene, I should be glad
know his name.

As the result of long and possibly very varying visions, as o
of the most mature and splendid fruits of an unexampl
artistic career, there follows the 'Garden of Love' (Pl. 99).

In the conversation piece, the main accent varies with soc
tradition and artistic means. In this genre, however, Rube
felt free in all directions, and clearly yielded himself up to t
happiest of moods, for he had the power to transform it in

he loveliest of pictorial forms. Italy in his day had offered him
ittle in this respect; some Venetian half or three-quarter
igures with attendants singing and playing instruments; the
banquets of Paolo Veronese, with their rich and festive figures,
were past, while the last beautiful 'Marriage in Cana' (Pado-
vanino, Venice Academy) was not yet painted when he was
n Italy. It had never occurred to Caravaggio to represent,
n his sombre and daring manner, the people of his time in
ovely, let alone loving, intercourse. Among the Italian
idealists there are, it is true, love-scenes, but only in mytho-
ogical guise. Refined social intercourse existed, but it was not
painted and art had to wait for Berghem and Lingelbach
(perhaps after the model of Agostino Tassi and Neapolitan
maritime painters) to allow patrician figures to wander about
among the people in their seaport views. In the Netherlands,
however, the conversation piece existed as a genre before and
after Rubens. As for Holland, we might already refer here to a
kindred type of painting, the *Regentenstukke*, which were
painted by artists of repute in the sixteenth century, while by
the seventeenth, the representation of society for its own sake
had become the aim of outstanding artists such as Dirk Hals,
Peter Codde, one of the Palamedes and others, who painted
subjects with a large number of figures showing the conversation, dancing, games, even music of men and women in
costly clothing, in stately rooms or gardens, with a semblance
that is not always pleasing. In Antwerp, however, the circle
which figures in the conversation piece was at any rate more
attractive in type and more distinguished in movement; it had
better taste in clothes and the women were ladies. There is a
whole series of such social gatherings in magnificent interiors
painted by the generation preceding Rubens, especially in
the studio of the Francken family (though I lay no claim to
distinguish the different hands) but the true gem of the collection is the court ball in the presence of the archducal
couple, by Frans Pourbus the Younger, 1611, now in the
gallery of The Hague. In Rubens's own time, the high society
of Antwerp, as it really was and moved, in its splendid

interiors and garden, appears in the work of Christophel van Laenen or Laemen, a whole series of which exists in the Mansi Gallery at Lucca (recently made accessible by good photographs). The modelling is moderately good, but the execution is sensitive and careful, if not without repetition in the detail. The true value of these works is for the history of manners.[133]

In Rubens's 'Garden of Love', however, this society, or some select part of it, is raised to a united and blissful life. Even the setting is not a formal garden, but a superbly imagined *plein-air* background; grottoes, a baroque portico, a fountain with a statue of Venus and trees with a vista into the distance. He does not show us the real life of patrician Antwerp, yet a great deal is based on personalities who belonged to it, and one of the central female figures has always been taken to represent Helen Fourment. For all the nobility of its atmosphere, the picture might still look like some social pleasantry; winged *putti*—that is, cupids—are scattered gaily all over it in every kind of movement, as a merry comment. The central group of ladies and gentlemen, one of whom is sitting quite happily on the ground, contains as its central action the impending chastisement of one of the cupids, who has taken refuge in a lady's lap, but she is holding back the hand raised to punish it. Others are coming down the steps from the fountain, others again are seated on the ground caressing each other, or stand embraced.

No wonder that there are repetitions and copies of varying value and size, and Rubens was probably urged to make them, though it was his habit to attack his problem afresh every time. In all probability the earliest picture is that in the possession of Baron Rothschild in Paris, formerly belonging to the Duke de la Pastrana in Madrid, and this is known to us by the excellent studio picture in Dresden and by Jan van Balen's copy in the Vienna Gallery; the latter may even have been painted under the master's supervision. The version in the Madrid Museum, however, is presumably later and was regarded by Rubens as superior; here the figures were on a larger scale and the space proportionally more restricted, so that the portico

irned out lower and the Venus on the fountain was reduced
) a *Vénus accroupie*. (Original only known to me by a photo-
raph; Pl. 99.) Probably because the fame of the picture had
pread in the meantime, Rubens sketched the principal scenes
)r Jegher the woodcutter in very free association, adding
nother charmingly playful action in the middle distance.[134]

Subsequent Flemish painters, who owed so much to Rubens's
nethods, did not, however, adopt the tone of the 'Garden of
ove'. This is true even of Teniers in his pictures of high
)ciety and of Tilborgh, Gonzales Coques, Siberechts and
thers. But we cannot explain the half-Flemish Watteau,
vith all his French successors, except on the basis of a know-
dge, direct or indirect, of the 'Garden of Love'.

It may seem surprising that this chapter should close with a
eference to a New Testament parable. Rubens, too, once paid
is tribute to the immortal story of the Prodigal Son. For a
)ng time nothing was known of this picture but the masterly
ngraving by Bolswert. The picture itself, which had passed
om one private owner to another, was at last acquired for
ie Antwerp Museum in 1894 (Pl. 50). How are we to regard
? Is it a genre, animal or architectural painting, or a still life
ith every possible kind of tool? Rubens, who would simply
ave smiled at all this terminology, painted first of all as the
pirit moved him, and a whole of the strangest kind came
ito being. This farm shed, with rafters through which
ie distance is seen, may have been part of the farmstead on
is estate of Steen, and what he has painted here so lovingly
vere his own plough-horses, groomed by busy farmhands,
is own oxen, his own sows at the trough with their young;[135]
is only in the last third of the picture that we see a poor
rodigal on his knees, with a maid and a farmhand watching
im in astonishment; but they are not cruel, they will not
oint the finger of scorn at him, he has fallen among kindly
olk. It may well be that the great artist, possibly the master of
iis farm, who describes here the nobility of deep repentance,
'as once witness to a scene of this kind in these surroundings.

*   *   *

It is the generally accepted opinion that, in portrait, Ruben
was overshadowed by his great pupil Van Dyck, and
recent times so acute and profound a critic as Fromentin h
criticized him severely at this point, both in the whole an
in the detail. A few scattered notes may be permitted here.

This genre is the only one in which Rubens found a grea
purely Flemish tradition before him, for the Flemish man
nerists, not excepting Frans Floris, left excellent portrai
behind them. Further, in Italy he saw the works of Titian an
the other Venetians, and he himself, as we saw above, w
almost on the point of becoming the great portraitist of Geno
and it may be of Italy. From the time he returned home, I
not only painted portraits as long as he lived, but all the rest
his work, even of remote or idealized subjects, presuppos
that ceaseless study of the living person without which ev
the greatest master, with the most brilliant memory, mu
degenerate in time into vain repetition. Further, portraits wer
of course, expected of him, at any rate in the principal figure
In addition to all this there is a vast number of portraits
princes and nobles, of men of distinction and fame, of clo
friends and finally of the family, of his two wives and the
children.

The earliest of these family portraits, however, must probab
be refused to Rubens, though it certainly represents him wi
his first wife, Isabella Brant, still young, sitting in a hone
suckle arbour; this is the very charming picture in the Muni
Pinakothek (frontispiece). In the present writer's opinio
Rubens once took a day off and sat for his portrait to a c
league and friend, perhaps Cornelis de Vos; it is, howeve
unnecessary to give reasons for that opinion here. [136]

Every other attribution must be left to special researc
which has seen so great a development in our time. Whoev
would have believed that that most exquisite young lady in t
Dresden Gallery with the roses in her left hand is only
studio picture? It is, however, interesting from the standpoi
of the history of costume. It was the moment of transitic
since the stiff, high, pleated ruff was yielding to the coll

xx. Detail from 'Quos Ego'. (Plate 98)

ther turned down or open in front. Now in our picture the
uff is still there, but it is wide open in the middle so that the
neck with its coral necklace is exposed.[137]

Of late years, several portraits have been disputed between
Rubens and Van Dyck. With others, again, we are in doubt
as to the identity of the sitter. Helen Fourment, whose
features we know without possibility of doubt in several
pictures in Munich alone, had to give her name at one time to
other portraits, for instance, the same young lady with the
roses and (also in Dresden) the charming widow with the
pearl necklace. The result is that these two have lost their
names for ever. That miracle of youthful charm in the most
radiant chiaroscuro, the so-called 'Chapeau de Paille' (actually
Chapeau de Poil) in the National Gallery[138] (Pl. 59) is now
believed to be a Mademoiselle de Lunden; the patrician lady
with the very big eyes in the Louvre was a member of the
Boonen family. A large number of other female portraits—
including the royal sitters—with a distinct echo not only of
Rubens's manner but of his social environment too, is scattered
through the galleries, even in Italy, and those among the sitters
who are no longer young still show considerable traces of
former beauty; their expression ranges from the mocking to
the passionate, though the latter is quite different from the
expression of yearning in the idealized figures of Guido Reni.
Fromentin has examined the *air de famille* among these ladies
and has, in this connexion, given a brilliant discussion of
invention in the conception of the portrait in a later generation, namely that of the great ladies of the court and time of
Louis XIV.[139]

In all these portraits, especially those of Helen, it remains an
open question whether the costumes, which are not only
splendid but extremely beautiful and varied, together with
their strange appropriateness to the individual sitter, are a
mere feat of Antwerp fashion, the fruit of feminine taste in
Antwerp, or whether they were, in their essentials, created by
Rubens. Van Dyck often gives rise to the same doubts, for
instance, in his 'Luisa de Tassis' (Liechtenstein Gallery), a

L

creation of similar splendour, though the tones of the materi
are softer. The most ravishing of Helen's portraits, howev
according to those who have seen it, is the full-length standi
figure in the Hermitage (Pl. 86).[140]

As regards Rubens's self-portraits, we cannot name with c
tainty those early ones, formerly regarded as certainly authent
that handsome, vivid face was familiar far and wide in repli
and copies. (I am informed that the Windsor exam
(Pl. 120) is now regarded as the original.) In the later pictu
which can be dated with certainty, there is a sharp discrepan
between the Munich 'Walk in the Garden' (Pl. 84; *c.* 163
and the portrait in the Vienna Gallery (1635); in the fir
Rubens is still in the fresh vigour of the prime of life; in t
second, we see him already in physical decline and with
touch of suffering, but with a far deeper appeal than before.

It is generally recognized that the family groups, all w
the same beautiful unconstraint in the design, reach perfecti
in the picture which was once in the possession of the Duke
Marlborough (now Baron Rothschild, Paris). In front o
magnificent open hall, Rubens and Helen, in stately costur
are strolling with a child in leading-strings. We can only rep
that, if nothing else by Rubens had survived, these portr
alone would win him fame as an absolute artist and assure
of his perfect family happiness.[141]

But when the artist and his family are identified in religio
historical and mythological pictures, the resemblance is, in 1
opinion, fortuitous; such resemblances come about of the
selves in the work of other artists, and they must have done
more than ever in Rubens, who was so preoccupied, as
artist, with his own enchantingly beautiful family. It is furt
not at all rare that something of the master's own personali
his features and figure, should appear in the male figures of ri
years in religious or secular histories. This may even be trac
in Rubens's type of Christ; on the other hand, it must
denied in many other cases. Thus, in particular, I can
understand how Rubens can be recognized in every
George, indeed in every Roman captain (for instance, in

russels 'Bearing of the Cross', in the 'Coup de lance' in the
ntwerp Museum). All these faces differ widely from each
ther, even in the predominant features. Above all, it can
ever be admitted that Rubens made an intentional, but con-
ealed, allusion to himself and his family by means of a vague
semblance. Later times, it is true, imagined that greater
alue was conferred on a picture by such assumptions.[142] It
ounds very well to say of the altar-piece over his tomb in
Jacques (Pl. 105) that Rubens wished to have all his family
ound him in this picture; unfortunately it is simply not true
f. p. 91).

Of the other portrait groups, that of the Arundel family in
e Munich Pinakothek (Pl. 58) is specially designed so as to
oncentrate the fullness of pomp on the central figure, the
ountess; her retinue includes, first, the huge hound, then
e fool, then her husband to the right, with the page or dwarf
front of him with the hawk; the rest of the picture is a
urtain with armorial bearings, a splendid building with
visted columns and a carpet with a rich pattern. The spectator
ay judge for himself whether and how far Rubens may have
garded his masterpiece with ironic condescension (including
e hands, this time so strongly stressed). It was with a far
eper feeling of sympathy that Rubens painted in London a
llow-citizen of Antwerp surrounded by his large family,
mely his wife and nine lovely children. (Windsor.) This was
althasar Gerbier, a man who enjoyed the full confidence of
harles I, an artist himself, and, like Rubens, entrusted with
plomatic business. Rubens, therefore, must have felt in every
ay at home in this picture. The setting and costumes are, as
ual, distinguished, but what stands out above all else is the
genuousness of the design and the beauty of the whole
mily. The patron, however, who had one Fleming painted
another, was Charles I himself.[143]

A group of quite a different character, painted quite early
d probably on Rubens's first visit to Rome, is the so-called
our Philosophers' (Pitti; Pl. 21) sitting round a table with
oks, above to the right in a niche a classical marble bust of

the type once believed to represent Seneca (now regarded
Philetas of Cos). The sitters are Rubens and his brother Phili
then, as the principal figure, an old, perhaps Italian schol
(erroneously believed to be Justus Lipsius) and another frien
from the Netherlands (quite erroneously identified wi
Hugo Grotius). The movements of the hands of the o
scholar and Philip are not well combined and some ha
believed this to be the result of a beginner's awkwardness. T
picture, on the other hand, does not seem to have been painte
of the master's own free will.[144]

As for male portraits, in view of all the other work Rube
took upon himself, their number is amazing, and if eve
able-bodied Fleming had not been a born portraitist—whi
the contemporary Italians were assuredly not—this wou
not be so. All the same, it was probably a great favour to
painted by Rubens, and we have throughout the impression
privileged and choice sitters. He painted them for the mo
part completely at rest, and shows them as normally cons
tuted as himself. There is nothing transitory or obtrusi
about them; character and mind speak with full force. If th
have become more interesting in the portrait than they we
in real life, that comes of the mysterious superiority of gr
art over nature and of the beauty of the artistic means. Tho
would be no sense in enumerating them here; they impr
the spectator without any such assistance, and descriptions
words are quite particularly powerless at this point. T
spectator should simply make friends with the Gevartius
the Antwerp Museum, the Des Cordes in the Brussels Museu
the De Vicq in the Louvre, the superb Dr. van Thulden in t
Munich Pinakothek, the man with the curling forelock
Dresden (of late given to Van Dyck). He should not overlo
this or that half-length portrait of a monk, called as a r
'Rubens's Father Confessor'. Michael Ophovius (Pl. 2
Hague Gallery), the Dominican priest, was an importa
person, and Rubens probably had good reasons for painti
his portrait. In a general way these are quite different peo
from the sitters of the Dutch Van Mierevelt and his ma

uccessors. Time, property, occupation and mentality had
lready had time to give the Dutchman and even the Dutch-
woman a distinct type and expression.[145]

Rubens began very early with royal portraits. While we
hould have difficulty in tracing other pictures of the Mantuan
ourt than that of the kneeling woman in the altar-piece of the
Trinity (Mantua; Pl. 5), this scarcity may be accounted for
by the dispersal of the Mantuan art collection, due in the first
place to sales by the first Duke of the new line, Charles
Gonzaga-Nevers (accession 1627), but completed by the
rightful plundering and ravage of the town, the notorious
sacco di Mantova (18–21 July 1630). Rubens must have known
ll about these atrocities, which certainly did not spare works
by his own hand.[146]

It was, however, the house of Hapsburg which, between
Titian in the past and Velazquez in the future, availed itself
bundantly of Rubens's art. At the Spanish court, where the
portraiture of such men as Alonso Coello and his pupil
Pantoja, with its faithful and diligent, but arid likeness, had
been highly appreciated, Rubens may have well carried off a
definite victory with Philip III and the Duke of Lerma (Pl. 7)
during his first stay in 1603 by the freedom of his manner of
portraiture. After his return to Antwerp (1609) the Regents,
Albert and Isabella, most likely made a start with an important
commission, the 'Altar-piece of St. Ildefonso' (cf. p. 8), with
themselves kneeling in reverence under the protection of their
patron saints on the side-panels (Pls. 94–5). Some doubt, however, has been cast of late on the early date of this work (or at
ny rate of its completion). In the figure of the Archduke, here
and in other pictures, the insignificant and presumably rather
flaccid forms are enlivened, ennobled and combined with a
truly princely bearing. The Infanta, Isabella Clara Eugenia,
born in 1566, who appears as a child in Schiller's *Don Carlos*,
is still depicted in the altar-piece with rather sharp, very vivacious features, corresponding to an age of little over forty, so
that this panel of the altar-piece must have been one of the first
parts to be completed. Ten years later, when she was already

a widow, and wore, as a rule, the habit of a Clarisse, she was
often painted by Van Dyck, and in these portraits Isabella is all
spirit and character. Finally, however, Rubens painted her
again, two years after her death, *post fata atque funera*, when, in
the Introitus Ferdinandi, he had to show Albert and Isabella
standing behind balustrades over the central portal of the
triumphal arch, and each of these portraits is said to have been
finished in a day (now in the Brussels Museum). He transposed them into an earlier time of brilliance such as they had
never known, and the figure of the Infanta, radiant with
vigour and life, is the enthusiastic homage not only of the
great master, but of the devoted and trusted servant. In our
day, it is loyalty 'to principles' that is appreciated, not loyalty
to persons. But Rubens may have gathered together in this
portrait his finest memories of a long association.[147]

As for the other portraits of this house (I have by no mean
seen them all) there would seem to be some hesitation here
and there in the names given by the galleries which is no
fault of Rubens. For instance, Philip IV (born in 1605) i
confused with his brother the Cardinal Infante Ferdinand
(born in 1609). The christening of Philip IV's first wife
Elizabeth of France, is still uncertain; she can be distinguishe
from her sister, Henrietta Maria of England, but not alway
with absolute certainty from her other sister, Christina o
Savoy. The attribution to Rubens or Van Dyck is also dispute

One example of difficult and contradictory attribution
particularly instructive. Every visitor to the Uffizi in Florenc
knows the great equestrian portrait of Philip IV which ha
long borne the name of Velazquez. Further, it was said to b
a repetition (*réplique*) of a Velazquez in Madrid.[148] Anyor
who only knows Velazquez outside of Spain will be chary o
expressing an opinion of the resources of his artistic manne
but when we come to the invention, the accessories have alwa
given rise to doubt. These are the helmet-bearer hurryir
after the king and the figures in the clouds, namely the tw
putti with the globe, the goddess of Peace with the cross ar
laurel-wreath and the goddess with the thunderbolt; here

was impossible not to feel the *ambiance* of Rubens's allegory.
Now Rubens's name had already been mixed up in the matter
by a misunderstanding on Baldinucci's part; a repetition of an
equestrian portrait of Philip IV, which is actually Velazquez's
work and is still said to be in Madrid, was sent to Florence for
the famous sculptor Tacca, who was to model the bronze
equestrian statue of the king; it was this replica (now in the
Pitti Palace) that Baldinucci believed to be Rubens's work. It
is, however, improbable from the mere standpoint of chrono-
logy that Rubens, who cannot possibly have been in Spain
later than 1630, should have copied an artist so much younger
than himself as Velazquez, and quite apart from that, nobody
will recognize his hand in the picture in the Pitti Palace, which
is rather to be taken as an excellent replica from Velazquez's
own studio.[149] It already shows the king older than Rubens
had known and painted him at the age of 24–5, for instance,
in the three-quarter-length portrait in the Hermitage (according to a reproduction) and that in the Pinakothek. Among the
portraits of the king at that age, however, there was actually
a famous equestrian portrait by Rubens (1629); this, however,
cannot be the Uffizi picture, which was destroyed by fire.
Here the equestrian portrait of the Cardinal Infante in armour
comes in; in the Munich Pinakothek picture from Rubens's
studio, we see the Infante in the atmosphere of late evening
galloping on a fiery brown charger, to the left a clump of
trees, in the distance a battle and a wide horizon. We might
have passed over this picture if it had not been for an engraving
by Paulus Pontius in which the war goddess in the air is an
obvious repetition of the same figure in the Uffizi Philip IV,
though in this version she is accompanied by an eagle. Both
engraving and picture may have been executed either immediately after the victory of Nordlingen (1634), or at the state
entry into the Netherlands in 1635, and we may be sure that
Pontius would not have added Bellona without Rubens's
approval; but whoever permitted this borrowing from the
picture of the royal brother must have had some kind of
right to it. Meanwhile the Flemish touch came to be more and

more clearly recognized in the Uffizi picture and the name of
Gaspard de Crayer was put forward (I cannot say by whom
in the first place) as its author. Moreover there is an equestrian
portrait by De Crayer, not of the king, but most likely of the
Cardinal Infante (Prado), galloping leftwards, bare-headed, in
armour, with scarf and field-marshal's baton, as in Rubens. A
further consequence was that the Uffizi picture was also assumed
to represent, not the king, but his brother, the Cardinal
Infante. Yet this line, too, was abandoned and the latest opinion
tends to the view that the Uffizi picture is a copy by a Spaniard,
perhaps Juan Carenno, of the famous lost equestrian portrait
by Rubens. Carenno (1614–85), who first knew the king in
later years, will have given the king the more mature features
he knew in place of the youthfulness he must have had in
Rubens. In this roundabout way, justice would at last be done
to Rubens. We may, however, draw a further conclusion; if a
Medicean Grand Duke, perhaps after Rubens's death, wished
and asked for a copy of his Don Philip IV, the original must
have been a most famous and admired picture.[150]

*   *   *

Of the historical personages in the gallery of the Luxembourg,
we may assume that Queen Marie de' Medici is painted as
flatteringly as was compatible with likeness (Pls. 61–7). All the
same, her features, which are familiar to us from other sources
were of such a cast that they could be rendered with a certain
magnificence, whether in private or on state occasions. In-
creasing years are hinted at with the utmost discretion. Rubens
preferred to lend her a certain maturity in youth (for instance
in the picture of the marriage by proxy) so that he could make
up for it by giving her more youth in her later years. Her
camarilla was of an extremely dubious kind, but in all the royal
functions which belonged to her public life, she had been able
to acquire that indubitable look of majesty which we see in
other portraits of her. I am not referring here to the hastily
painted additions to the gallery of the Luxembourg, where
she masquerades as Minerva or Bellona and so on, but the

rtraits in the galleries of Madrid and Vienna. In the first,
judge by the reproduction, she is enthroned in great
idowed dignity, in the latter, a pupil's work, though excel-
nt, we see her in the voluptuous grandeur she probably
ished all her later portraits to show. There are two full-
ngth portraits of her consort, Henri IV, in the Luxembourg
f. Pl. 63); in one he is contemplating her portrait, in the other
: is conferring the regency on her, and these two portraits,
hich were those mainly used by later artists, made a decisive
ntribution to the greatness of his memory.[151] The little
ortraits by Frans Pourbus the Younger (Louvre) could have
one little in that direction; even in Cherubino's engraving,
d still more in the large engraving by Goltzius, Henri, for
l his vivacity and spirit, looks scrawny and odd, and in his
st years he is said to have looked shaken. Whether or when
ubens saw the king is quite unknown. If he did so, it was in
l probability on the journey either to or from Italy (1600
: 1609). He shows the king tall in stature and with an exhila-
ting magnificence, and since that time it is this idea of him
at has prevailed. The transfiguring power of supreme art has
ndered a great service to the whole royal house descended
om Henri. A third countenance in the series which is of great
istorical interest is, in the 'Coronation of the Queen', the royal
dy standing in the midst of her own suite (cf. Pl. 61); it is
beautiful face, though the contours are a little thickened by
ge. This is a historical curiosity, for it is Henri's first, divorced
ife, who was present at the ceremony, walking in her
iccessor's train because she was the last of the house of Valois
d a sister of three preceding kings, and without her the
ourt would, so to speak, have been incomplete. For the older
eneration she was still Marguerite de Valois, who had been
o enchantingly lovely in her youth, and we cannot say whether
ere exists (apart from insignificant engravings) an undisputed
rly portrait of her. She is, moreover, indispensable to the
istorian of France by her lively memoirs.[152] Names have
en given to a large number of other distinguished personages
these pictures which are regarded as certain and, when the

series was completed in 1625, there were still so many people
alive who could judge of their resemblance that we may, on
the whole, accept them as faithful portraits.

*   *   *

In animal painting, Rubens stands at the cross-roads of time as
the greatest master; there is one kind before him and another
after him. He united the two essential qualities of the animal
painter, a strong desire to study and paint formidable beasts and
supreme delight in all movement. There may be beauty and
dignity in an animal at rest, but it is only the animal in free
powerful movement that can fully reveal its own peculiar
life. The gifted and predestined animal painter finds his
stimulus everywhere, and any detailed calculation of influence
is a risky matter. What Rubens inherited from earlier Flemish
art and from German engravings and woodcuts was little
enough, and not a line of it, for instance, is to be seen in his
horses. In Mantua, however, there were two great impressions
he could hardly avoid; in animal painting, Mantegna'
'Triumph of Caesar', and in reality, the famous ducal stables
whose finest horses were, as a rule, splendidly recorded in the
Sala de' Cavalli (Palazzo del Tè). As a cavalier of Vincenzo
Gonzaga, he even accompanied a presentation to the court of
Philip III at Valladolid, consisting of horses and a chariot of
state, and there he at once set to work on a great equestrial
portrait of the Duke of Lerma, then at the height of his power
(Pl. 7). As regards classical Italy, it was probably the galloping
horses in the Battles of the Amazons and the Celts on superb
sarcophagi that appealed to him most, with here and there a
fine marble lion, but the Renaissance—apart perhaps from the
bronze equestrian statues of Donatello and Verrocchio—made
at any rate a deep and lasting impression on him. He was able
to see a drawing of the 'Battle of the Standard' from Leonardo
da Vinci's Florentine battle cartoons by or after Leonardo
himself, and his copy of that drawing is the only documentary
evidence we have on this vast subject (Louvre, drawing;
also the engraving by Edelinck). We are entirely ignorant of

hether he had any further acquaintance with Leonardo's
udies of horses, or with any of his sketches for the equestrian
atue of Francesco Sforza on a galloping horse. As for
Iichelangelo, he cannot have failed to see the fresco of the
Conversion of St. Paul' in the Cappella Paolina in the
atican, with the wildly but stiffly galloping horse. The
st of Michelangelo's world of animals, however, is
otably uniform—the front part of the centaur's body in the
lief in the Palazzo Buonarroti, the fish in the fresco of
onas', the half pack-animal in the 'Deluge' (Sistine Chapel)
ad the partially visible ram in the 'Sagrificio' (also Sistine
hapel). Raphael had found much greater inspiration in the
orse (in 'Heliodorus', 'Attila' and the 'Battle of Constan-
ne', for which there must have been a very exact cartoon by
is own hand) and they are so powerfully conceived and
xecuted that they at any rate play a worthy part in the drama-
c moments which are the subjects of these pictures. On the
ther hand it would appear that the assistants were given far
oo much licence in the fairly numerous animals of various
inds in the Vatican loggias.[153]

Nor did Rubens owe much, if anything, to the Venetians
a his animal painting. He may have seen, though in a bad
ate of preservation, Giorgione's fresco of 'Horsemen between
Colonnades' on the Fondaco de' Tedeschi, which is men-
oned as late as Ridolfi (I, p. 87). Titian painted animals well
o long as they posed for him, for instance, whole herds of
heep at a distance, or St. John's lamb, or the rabbit in the
Vierge au Lapin' (Louvre). The movement of his horses is
efective, and the galloping and falling horses in his 'Battle of
he Bridge' (so-called 'Battle of Cadore'), which Rubens can
a any case only have seen in the uncertain copies still extant
oday, are extremely conventional in modelling. Probably his
est animal painting is the excellent hound in the portrait of
he 'Gentleman in Red' (Cassel Gallery); here and there, there
re fine little spaniels, but only at rest, never in movement,
ince spaniels in movement hardly appear till Rubens and Van
Dyck. It was, however, the lion which came off worst in

Venice. We should expect to find only noble pictures of the lion in a city which saw so much of the sea-transport of wild animals and had St. Mark as its patron saint, yet even in Titian the lion of St. Jerome, for instance (Brera), is quite conventionally rendered and as for the lion in the votive picture of the Doge Grimani with the Fides (Doge's Palace) we can only hope that it is not by the hand of Titian himself. In Tintoretto and Paolo, the lions are utterly mean creatures, as if painted from memory and against the grain, and in later artists, the lion often turns out ridiculously sentimental. Tintoretto's horses are pitiable, and Paolo really only managed with more skill, but without greater love for the creature. Of all earlier Italian artists, he may be said to render the heads best, and in the equestrian wings to his pictures, i.e., the equestrian groups flanking certain compositions, we may admit that even Rubens learned from him. But as soon as the horse has to be presented in profile, even partially, convention reappears and predominates ('Bearing of the Cross', Dresden) while rearing horses, though intended to convey the impression of swift movement, produce a most dubious effect. (In S Sebastiano, Venice, one of the oval soffits from the story of Esther; in the Sala del Maggior Consiglio in the Doge' Palace, the two officers' horses in the lower part of 'Venetia crowned by Glory'.) But if we wish to have further proof of Paolo's carelessness in animal painting, we must compare the head of the bull in the three variants of the 'Rape of Europa' (Anticollegio Hall, Doge's Palace; Capitoline Gallery National Gallery). It is only in Paolo's dogs that we get the impression of animals painted of the artist's own accord and for the sake of their beauty, especially the unforgettable cream-coloured dog which recurs so often, and here Rubens too, learned how life and grace can be given to the middle foreground in great historical scenes by a group of noble dogs. But Rubens made no use of the monkeys which seem to have been favourite pets in distinguished Venetian households and were introduced by Paolo even into sacred pictures such as the 'Banquet of Gregory the Great' (Monte Berico).[1]

is quite true that he found in Jacopo Bassano (1510–92)
a abundance of animals, true to life and beautifully har-
onized with light and colour to form pictures. They were
ot, however, animals that could appeal to him, but sheep,
oats, oxen, asses, sheep-dogs and so on. On the other hand,
is true that the Florentine artist Antonio Tempesta had
·corded in his engravings, besides other animals, the wild
easts of the wilderness, lions, tigers, elephants and so on, and
hen Rubens arrived in Italy, he had just published a book
f drawings of supposedly savage fights between them. Most
f them, however, look like hearsay animals, and even
empesta's domestic animals are weak, including the horses
·hich he uses so freely in a large number of historical composi-
ons for engraving. Indeed, we might say of horses in general
nat, with the exception of Leonardo, all Italian artists fought
ther shy of the noble creature, even though they had to
nake great use of it in battle-pieces and triumphs. Good animal
aintings by Annibale Carracci were mentioned above (p. 49).
he horses of the Bologna School are nowhere significant in
nodelling, although the team drawing Apollo's chariot in
uido's 'Aurora' have a very fine contour.

It is possible that Rubens had ridden from boyhood. Later,
a the service of Mantua, he acquired a perfect connoisseurship
f fine horses, in Antwerp he possessed superb Andalusians
nd would 'ride through the town like other cavaliers and
entlemen with a golden chain round his neck' (Bellori, Le
'ite etc., p. 248). European taste has, of course, changed
adically since that time, and now prefers the slender build of
he racehorse, obtained by crossing with Arab, and later with
inglish stock. Yet we may be glad to have the picture of the
oble horse of that time, which was first painted by Rubens,
ot, as we should expect, in a historical picture, but simply as
mount. This is the picture in the Berlin Museum (not now
xhibited); three gentlemen in an open landscape are exer-
ising their horses, one at the walk, one at the trot and the
hird at the gallop.[155] It seems that Rubens never saw war; he
id not, like Bourguignon after him, follow the camps for

years, yet he paints, as no one did before him, the horse sharii
in the general tumult and, already swift and wild, bearing i
rider into battle. He knows the creature in danger and in rag
and it is to the horse that he gives the expression of great ar
terrible moments in the conflicts of men or beasts. The indiv
dual spectator will find his own response to the higher divin
tion which must have guided the artist in the creation of tl
'Battle of the Amazons', the 'Death of Decius', the 'Host
Sennacherib'. Rubens could never have achieved those frigh
ful foreshortenings by study alone. But one thing must nev
be forgotten—the light that passed from Leonardo to Ruber

Something like predestination governed the equestria
portrait (a number of which have already been discussed).
was not by chance that this genre, which had been rare
practised in painting up to that time, should have sudden
found so great a representative as Rubens at the dawn of tl
warlike seventeenth century, with his Lerma (1603), his Arcl
duke Albert (1621? Windsor), his Philip IV (c. 1629). He
also said to have painted equestrian portraits of previous king
during his first or second stay in Spain, namely Philip II
possibly from life, and Philip II 'in an idealized concep
tion' after his death.[156] Princesses on horseback had lon
figured in the decorations of state entries, marriages, etc., b
the gallery of the Luxembourg contains, as a remembrance
the captive of Pont-de-Cé (in the war of the court parties
Marie de' Medici riding in triumph towards the spectator on
graceful white horse with the field-marshal's baton hel
against her side and Victoria, Fama and Fortitudo hoverin
round her. I cannot remember a commission of the kind eve
having been executed with such splendid effect. Further, it
interesting to observe how equestrian portraits of princes
generals, painted or engraved, became customary from th
Thirty Years' War on. In Rubens, however, we shall alway
turn back from the horses of ceremony to those freely ima
gined, the horses of the battles of the beasts and of Deciu
(Pl. 38), the magnificent black and white horses in the 'Rap
of the Daughters of Leucippus' (Pl. 39), or in the 'Martyrdoi

'St. Lievin' (Pl. 104), the rearing horse, seen in profile, which
s thrown its rider, or, in quieter mood, the good nag
the rider who, leaning back in the saddle, listens to the
lpless beggar and cuts off a piece of his cloak for him. This
cture (in Windsor) must be mentioned in any discussion of
ibens (even if only a photograph is available) because it was
e more vigorous model for a picture, chiefly famous for its
bject, by Van Dyck (in the church of Saventhem), which is
ways erroneously regarded as Van Dyck's invention—
e 'Charity of St. Martin'.[157]

Elsewhere this greatest of pupils takes his place beside his
aster with a whole series of equestrian portraits of distin-
uished and royal persons which, scattered from Rome,
enoa, and Turin as far as Paris and London, are regarded by
the galleries as their finest treasures. But who shall say how
r Rubens's influence was carried by paintings and engravings?
Holland, in addition to a great wealth of animal painting in
neral, Philip Wouwerman in particular glorified the horse
nes without number. Belgium attached war-artists, that is,
uestrian painters, such as Snayers, Van der Meulen and
hers, to all kinds of armies,[158] while in Italy, a huge number
battle-pieces were painted by Neapolitans and cosmopolitan
tists from the north. All this, it is true, was characteristic of
e epoch, but a good deal depends on who gives the sign. In
ese battle-pieces there is a great deal of perfunctory work and
great deal of plagiarism, but there was at least life and truth to
ture. The horses of the mannerists of the sixteenth century,
ith their conventional movements, had by this time died out,
d it was Rubens, we may say, who signed their death-warrant.
Further, Rubens conquered another field for painting,
mely that of the bigger wild animals, whether in the train of
ds, or in the life of the wilderness (as in the great picture
lions and tigers in Dresden), and in their frightful conflicts
ith human beings, who are as a rule mounted. It was a high
ctate of his nature; from time to time he had to fare forth on
e wildest sea of action, and neither other artists nor spectators
n be expected to follow him. Yet once, it would seem, there

had to be such a man. And he was so powerful and so fortun
that he was able to find and train one worthy companion a
helper: Frans Snyders of Antwerp (1579–1657), who came
him from the workshops of Brueghel and Van Balen, as th
said 'to be, not his disciple, but his collaborator'. But tha
a mere quibble. Snyders had to be entirely trained by Rub
in order to be able to help him in this and in so many oth
kinds of painting.

Even his actual pupils, however, learned to work brillian
with colour, form and light after the master's designs. For t
hugest fighting-scenes of this kind, the great 'Lion Hu
(Dresden), like that in the Munich Pinakothek (Pl. 34), wou
unquestionably pass for the master's own work if research h
not proved the contrary. The suddenness, the riot of mome
of the fight, already past or still to come, here reach th
culmination. It is well known that Rubens kept a lion for
considerable time, and it might be possible to recognize t
animal in the beautiful lion of St. Mark which strides
patiently in the picture of the 'Four Evangelists' (series
allegories for Philip IV, p. 124). He must have made full use
every opportunity for studying the tiger, but such oppo
tunities were open to other artists too, and no one else cou
have painted the wonderful tigress snarling at the crocodile
the 'Four Rivers' (Vienna Gallery). Not only was the fame
these pictures, especially the fights, spread far and wide by h
engravers, especially Bolswert and Soutmans, but from th
time on, a genre could seriously be spoken of. Even the bo
and bear hunts of Snyders can take an honourable plac
beside the master's pictures, and the Pinakothek in Munich h
his two young lions pursuing a roebuck, 'a work astonishin
in its vividness and excellently composed'. Yet among t
boar hunts, Rubens's own original in Dresden (Pl. 49) w
always bear the palm—a very rich, dramatic scene with smal
scale figures in a superb woodland glade; it is, so to speak,
'morality' of the inevitability of fate, for the huge an
dangerous old beast is meeting its end at the hands of hunt
men, horsemen and peasants. Yet it lay in Rubens's nature t

XXII. Detail from the 'Battle of the Amazons'. (Plate 36)

XXIII. Detail from 'Adam and Eve' (Plate 60), showing the work of
Jan Brueghel

w, even here, the struggle not yet decided, and in a stag
t (Berlin Museum) the stag has turned at bay on the hounds.
ong the wolf hunts, that formerly in the possession of
d Ashburton (London) is said to be very early and entirely
entic, and to contain among the mounted huntsmen
ens and his first wife (Pl. 33). We know by an engraving a
opotamus and crocodile hunt by Moors on horseback and
foot, and even here, where there can be no question of
-hand observation, the animals are rendered with impres-
verisimilitude and their huge shapes are so placed and
oreshortened that they conceal as little as possible. We
t not, however, forget that Rubens's imagination had
dy taken possession of the world of wild animals in the
f of Romulus and Remus (Pl. 40).[159]

Ve have already spoken in passing of Rubens's dogs. Apart
n breed and shape, this animal has at times a special artistic
tion. Leaping dogs, accompanying a very animated scene
as the 'Country Dance', for instance (Pl. 110), can very
h enhance the impression of instantaneity. The hunting
nd in Rubens is defined as a 'wolf greyhound', but we also
slender setters and even the mastiff. After 1630 we make
acquaintance of Rubens's house-dog, with his peacocks
turkeys, in the delightful family group in the Munich
kothek, the 'Walk in the Garden' (Pl. 84). He shows the
p-dog in the 'Adorations of the Shepherds'. As a rule,
ers find it unnecessary to mention the fact that this whole
of creatures, which mean so much to man, was first
d to its high place in painting by Rubens. As for the ass,
ch is indispensable in the 'Adorations of the Shepherds and
i', and in the 'Flight into Egypt', a considerable study by
ens has recently become known.[160] The cat Rubens left
ordaens, who painted it excellently.

*   *   *

e grand total of Rubens's work, his landscapes speak quite
uliar language, and also stand in quite a peculiar relation-
to their author.

Here the Antwerp tradition was not without importa
In paintings and engravings, some of considerable size, by
immediate predecessors, the Brueghels, Vinckeboons,
Rubens was early familiar with pictures of sacred and my
logical stories and figures which had, as it were, me
provided a humble occasion for vast, fantastic, and gener
overloaded landscapes. In Italy, where Flemish influence
landscape cannot be quite excluded from the very begin
of the Renaissance, a similar style of fantasy to that
Flanders arose towards the end of the sixteenth century. T
was also in Italy a monumental use of landscape in fresco,
the Roman history painters of the mannerist epoch c
called in Flemings for their landscapes. Yet a change
already taken place when Rubens appeared in Rome. A
bale Carracci and, it is believed, under his influence a
countryman of Rubens's, Paul Bril, had abandoned the fan
tic and overloaded landscape in favour of simplification
fewer and more vigorous figures, and a greater verisimili
in the vegetation. Rubens must have met Bril in Rome, an
was probably closely associated with another leading re
sentative of the finer landscape, Adam Elsheimer of Frank
whose name was suggested above in connexion with the 'F
into Egypt' (p. 81). The landscape of the Venetian schoo
the other hand, appealed very little to Rubens, though
cannot deny a certain reminiscence of the landscape settin
Titian's mythologies which comes out in the proportion
in the harmony with the figures, and also Tintoretto may
given him some ideas with his fantastic light effects
volumes. Rubens painted no definite landscape view in
and took nothing but the luxurious Italian vegetation in
pictures. The only real view by him is that of the Escori
which several copies exist, though probably only by p
This may have been a fruit of his first visit to Spain.
Dresden copy, it seems to have been painted very freel
from memory; throughout the picture there are glea
sunshine between deep, sagging clouds, and a faint bea
light falls immediately behind the great building.[161]

As everyone knows, we find a totally different sky in
ibens's subject pictures; it is that soft, magnificent, moist
mosphere with the beautifully shaped clouds, and it would
pear as if he had painted it in with his own hand to give the
neral tone even in big pictures which had been mainly
ecuted by pupils. If any Italian predecessor made any im-
ession at all on him in this direction, it can only have been
olo Veronese, in whom he found a similar harmony of story
d sky to that which became his own.

After his return home to Antwerp, he again met his friend Jan
ueghel, called the Velvet Brueghel (1568–1625). Brueghel
d himself spent some time in Italy, but not to learn from
lian art. His position was that of a *Fiamingo* much admired
r his fantasy and delicate workmanship. Since his return to
ntwerp he had taken a highly honourable, and even great,
nsitional position in the landscape with many figures, which
e in some cases biblical, in others Flemish folk-groups. In
oth respects he overcame the fantastic and the glaring, and his
ly link with earlier artists is a general overcrowding. For a
t time, Jan Brueghel summarized very brilliantly the art of
e multitudinous, the small, the separate, while with Rubens
eatness was on the way. In landscape he is a very considerable
et and the last great man of the older style. Of his figures in
dscape, the latest in particular are wonderfully vivid, espe-
lly that of the travellers with carriages and horses which
metimes make their appearance in whole caravans. Further,
never abandoned his early training in flower-painting. In
eal, and especially mythological subjects, he willingly colla-
rated with others, as he did with Rubens, in priceless pictures
inted after his return. All that need be enumerated here are
the Munich Pinakothek: the 'Sleeping Diana with Nymphs'
d the 'Resting Diana with her Train' (the figures in the first
e by Rubens) have landscapes and animals by Brueghel;
und the famous 'Madonna and Child' he painted the garland
flowers with the eleven hovering cherubs after which the
cture is now called. Here, where we would prefer a garland
roses in the great painterly style of Daniel Seghers, the

good fellowship of the artists went perhaps too far, f
Brueghel's splendidly rich choice of flowers still belongs to th
conscientious, rather miniaturesque older style, but each
these two great artists simply wished to leave the other fr
to express himself. In the splendid 'Paradise' (main examp
in the Hague Gallery; Pl. 60), where Adam and Eve are I
Rubens, Brueghel, who undertook the landscape and the ma
animals, was allowed to decorate the foreground with a
kinds of beautiful single flowers. The strangest example of th
collaboration, however, is to be seen in the picture of Flo
with *putti* and nymphs (also Munich Pinakothek), whe
Brueghel even seems to take the lead with his rich and splend
flowery thicket in a glade with ruins.[162]

Elsewhere, Rubens dealt with the landscape in his subje
pictures himself and, at any rate in the big pictures, gave
along with the foreground terrain and the accessories, chief
to Lucas van Uden and Jan Wildens. The landscape bac
grounds, especially those painted by himself, will often I
found more important on closer consideration than at fi
sight. The 'Rape of the Daughters of Leucippus', the 'Judg
ment of Paris', the 'Garden of Love' (Pls. 39, 99, 103) reve
a prodigious landscapist, capable of introducing the effe
of great, untamed nature into his story in masterly fashic
and pressing light and atmosphere, vegetation and distan
into his service. Even the landscape distances in the galle
of the Luxembourg (where, in addition to the assistants alrea
named, he also employed Jodocus de Momper), howev
little they seem to signify, take on an uncommonly poet
effect on closer acquaintance. Of the hunting scenes, the sm;
'Boar Hunt' in Dresden (original; Pl. 49) takes place at t
edge of a wonderful wood; the trees are most carefully ar
individually characterized and we can see in this early pictu
what he owed, not only to hunting and riding, but to qui
different studies.[163]

In the landscapes proper, however, we see the man of t
north who has not yet lost his power to dream dreams whic
demand expression in landscape, and who has the strength a

desire to express them thus in spite of vast work in other
res. What nature said to him, at times, we may be sure, in
ispers, was transmuted within him into moving visions of
own soul, and thus he gave it back to the world. That is
y, so far as my knowledge goes, the landscapes are all
nplete pictures painted with a full palette, and no mere
tches or provisional studies. They were done at various
ments in this great career—some even in Italy. By far the
ger number, however, belong to his last years, and, given
ir moderate or even small size, they were certainly wel-
ne easel work for the artist who was already plagued with
it, and probably spent the intervals between the attacks on
large works for altars and palaces mentioned above. He
uld appear to have painted most of the landscapes for his
n pleasure, and even though a large number of them are
raved, that was done at a time when his immense fame and
demand for any works by his hand had reached their
ght. The engravers themselves may have wished it, and
swert especially was perfectly capable of entering into the
ter's intentions. Of some fifty recognized landscapes,
ty-six are said to have been engraved.

ubens seems never to have had any misgivings about the
and importance of the figures, and the question whether
figures in a landscape should present a whole incident, and
it should be their scale, would have seemed simply odd to
. It may be that, in the sunset picture of the 'Tourney in
Moat' (Pl. 108; Louvre), the threefold tourney of armed
s of horsemen with heralds and knights was only added on
nd thoughts, but it turned the picture into a tragic genre-
ating, a tournament. And who is going to set up precise
sifications when rural occupations in magnificently living
ups of men and animals fill the foregrounds almost as far
e picture-frame? Further, the fine oxen, horses, sheep, etc.,
certainly not by Snyders's hand but by the master's own,
they may have belonged to his own estate. Note, for
ince, the Munich 'Landscape with the Rainbow', and in
same gallery the 'Cows at Pasture', and add to these the

'Evening Return from the Fields at Mowing Time' in
Pitti Palace. Incidentally, this last picture also gives us a h
of locality, for the tall steeple in the far distance can hardly
anything but that of the Cathedral of St. Rombaud at Malin
and that is the region of Steen, the manor which Rubens h
acquired in 1635. We see this Château de Steen (Lond
Pl. 107) in a spreading, radiant landscape in the morn
light. The Château, a building of moderate size, rises to
left among the trees; the only figure is a huntsman stalk
partridge, while a market cart approaches from the Châte
Here Rubens knows every hedge and every ridge, every rov
willows, every group of birches and every brooklet. I
similar way to Philips Koninck and even Ruysdael, he has
to place the viewpoint artificially high in order to take in
vast, almost flat plain to its farthest distance. The wh
however, is treated with that joyousness which speaks
deepest sympathy, and the atmosphere itself (in so far as it
remained untouched) is one of the finest Rubens ever pain
In other pictures, too, his distances are a whole tract of cour
with woodland, villages, country houses, meadows, fields
waters, and his sunshines are wide and splendid. Surround
woods appear here and there, for instance, according
Bolswert's engraving, in a picture with a hunting scene w
derfully suffused with evening sunshine. Otherwise the ma
shows a predilection for the edge of the wood, and this set
of trees is given supreme charm by the way the light p
trates it. Other rural scenes which are at the same time fan
landscapes must be enumerated here at second hand: in
Hermitage, 'La Charrette Embourbée', with sunset and moon
and at Windsor the so-called 'Laeken Meadows'.[164]

In addition to the 'Tourney', the Louvre possesses his h
known pastoral, a picture which spread far and wide in be
ful, even authentic variants and several engravings (Pl. 1
Men, herds of sheep and landscape are bathed in the p
evening peace. Of the shepherds, some in free classical drap
one couple is just approaching from the left, under a tree t
sits another singing in loud delight with Pan's pipes in

hands; beside him a young woman, resting in the grass, looks
up to the approaching couple; but in the middle of the foreground there is a charming love-scene taken direct from the
patrician world of the 'Garden of Love' into this shepherd's life
—it may indicate the same date of composition. The landscape
with clumps of trees to the left, with the contours of the
terrain made clear to the eye by patches of sunlight, stretches
from the centre of the picture into an impressive, rich and
beautifully gradated distance, above which the clouds of a
past thunderstorm are rolling away. The little 'Landscape with
the Birdcatcher', also in the Louvre, is a very curious piece
(Pl. 109); unfortunately, like the foregoing picture, it is not in
a perfect state of preservation. Here Rubens was, above all,
painting, for his own pleasure, what he painted in other
pictures—the sun struggling through the haze; to the right, a
brook with a little bridge, farther off, a windmill, a steeple and
rolling hills; to the left, above a kind of sunk lane, a fowler has
spread a large net, and three men, seated on the ground, are
watching him. There is no question that the picture is highly
original in its effect, but we shall never cease to wonder how it
came to be created out of such everyday material. Once again
this picture brings home to us that what the landscapist paints
is far less important than his love for what he paints.

A great deal more could be added from the engravings, and
we can see again and again what simple things in the lie of the
land could inspire Rubens. Yet even here the edge of the wood
was most sublimely rendered when Bolswert created for him
that engraving in which a high wooded hill is bounded by
waters, while a shepherd watches his flock below.[165]

Rubens always took liberties of many kinds; we must make
allowances for his frequent use of rainbows, while admitting
that at any rate nobody solved the problem better than he.
And how remarkable it is that he can make the light, even
strong sunshine, fall from two opposite sources without
confusion. But the magic that is always his lies in the variation
of cloud-shadow and patches of sunshine. As a rule, such patches
rest mainly on the foreground figures, men and sheep, but

even footpaths, little bridges, felled tree-trunks, hedges, and
meandering brooklets take on an intrinsic value, in themselves
and in the picture space, because Rubens's light and shade have
befriended them. Nor must we forget that most wonderful
gradation of tones towards the middle distance, or even a quite
modest distance, and the beauty of all his water surfaces. The
horizon is not set so low as in most Flemish art, but rather
about the middle of the picture. The buildings, only beginning
in the middle distance, farmsteads, churches, etc., lay no special
claim to attention. The ruling power is always the effect of light

Yet from time to time the spirit moved Rubens to paint the
meteoric catastrophe. From the Third Book of the *Aeneid* he
took 'Aeneas's Shipwreck on the Strophades' (Pl. 71; Hope
Gallery, London and, it appears, a corresponding engraving)
The ship has dashed against a cliff on which a lighthouse stands
we see the rescued in flight, and in the distance a compact
seaport; 'a glowing dawn illuminates the black storm-clouds
and the tempestuous sea' (Waagen). The most amazing
of these pictures, however, is the 'Phrygian Deluge'
(Vienna; Pl. 72) mentioned above in connexion with Philemon and Baucis; a broad mountain valley dreadfully inun-
dated with the flood, which is already bearing away drowned
animals; in the air a mass of fire and water, in all the clouds
lightning, flashing in on every hand, and to the left, below, a
rainbow; the water-levels are impossible and contradictory,
but all the same it is a work of the highest order. It seems to
find its counterpart in Bolswert's great engraving, where not
only the heavens appear enraged to the point of a cloud-burst,
and the precipice against the background of inky clouds is
illuminated by ghastly lightning, but the sea itself is driven
into the land by a hurricane, towards a many-steepled town
and a wooded tract of country with a church nearer the spectator. A title in two distichs warns the spectator to comprehend
this battle of the elements as emblematic of discord on earth.[16]

Finally, however, in one of the most splendid pictures in the
Pitti Palace (Pl. 83), the storm-clouds over the sea are depart-
ing and in the heights, a distant, ethereal apparition, we see

as in supplication before Jove; soft, warm morning atmo-
ere occupies the rest of the horizon, and in the most magical
ht, a mountain rises steeply, with waterfalls, castles and a
den set with terraces and beautiful buildings. These are the
dens of Alcinous, king of the Phaeacians, whose seaport
visible in the distance. In the foreground, we see the ship-
ecked Ulysses, a naked suppliant, for whom Pallas has been
erceding with Jupiter, while the king's daughter, whose
ids had taken flight before him, quietly orders them to give
n help and clothing. It is Nausicaa.

And so they meet, the Ionian and the Fleming, the two
atest story-tellers our earth has ever borne—Homer and
bens.

NOTES

NOTES

Notes marked by an asterisk have been added by the present editor.
The other notes are by Burckhardt.

Joachim von Sandrart states (*Teutsche Akademie*, ed. Peltzer, 1925, 156) that Rubens entered the service of Archduke Albert already before his journey to Italy (possibly upon the recommendation of Otto van Veen). The statement is not confirmed by any other source.

We follow here the generally accepted dating, but cannot decide whether it is correct. Others believe this 'Last Supper' to have been painted only after the arrival at Antwerp. *The dating then generally accepted is wrong. The 'Last Supper' (in Milan) was painted about 1620; it was placed in the church of St. Romuald at Malines in 1632. The pictures mentioned in the text further below were likewise painted after the return from Italy: the 'St. Sebastian' in Berlin about 1612, the 'St. Jerome' in Dresden and the 'St. Francis' in the Palazzo Pitti about 1615 and the 'Romulus and Remus' in the Capitoline Gallery about 1618. The 'Three Graces' (Uffizi), the 'Hero crowned by Virtue' and the 'Drunken Hercules' are also to be dated later, see Notes 105 and 119 below.

We add a few further notes on the paintings of the Italian period. The 'St. Sebastian' in the Corsini Gallery, Rome, was for a long time attributed erroneously to Van Dyck, but has recently been vindicated (G. Glück, *Rubens, van Dijck und ihr Kreis*, 1933, p. 18). The 'Gonzaga family adoring the Trinity' (cut up in 1797, fragments in Mantua, Vienna and elsewhere), together with the huge 'Baptism of Christ' in Antwerp and the 'Transfiguration of Christ' in Nancy, adorned the walls around the high altar of the church Santa Trinità in Mantua. The pictures were unveiled in 1605 (see Note 146 below). The 'Apotheosis of Gregory the Great' in Grenoble was originally intended for the high altar of Santa Maria in Vallicella in Rome, but owing to the bad lighting Rubens substituted for it another triptych, which is still there. See Rubens's letters on pp. 195–8 below. The sketch for the 'Circumcision' in Genoa is preserved in the Vienna Academy (No. 97). That the 'Miracles of St. Ignatius' (Genoa, about 1620) should have been commissioned at such an early date is most improbable.

These magnificent portraits of the Genoese period were rediscovered only a very short time ago (cf. L. Burchard in *Jahrbuch der preussischen Kunstsammlungen* 50, 1929, 341; R. Longhi in *Annuaire des Musées royaux de Belgique* 2, 1939, 123, and G. Glück in *Jahrbu* *der kunsthistor. Sammlungen in Wien* 6, 1932, 157). G. F. Waage however, knew already the portraits in the Bankes collection Kingston Lacy; see Note 19.

4* The portrait of the Duke of Lerma is now in the Conde Valdel grana collection in Madrid; two preliminary drawings in Paris ar Weimar correspond well in their composition with the finishe picture, but Rubens used a bearded stable lad as model instead of th duke. (G. Glück, op. cit., pp. 30 and 377; H. G. Evers, *Rubens und se Werk*, 1943, p. 105.) The copy after Titian's 'Adam and Eve' w painted during the second journey to Spain, 1628–9. The series Apostles in the Casino Rospigliosi in Rome is a repetition by pupils the original series by Rubens, in Madrid. The figure of Christ missing there. See Note 63 and Rubens's letter on p. 207 below.

5 Of Titian's works which Rubens saw in Italy, the Madonna Casa Pesaro in the Frari church at Venice may have made the stronge impression on him. I do not refer here to later copies after Titian, f which see below. *For Titian's importance for Rubens see above a Th. Hetzer, *Tizian, Geschichte seiner Farbe*, 1935, p. 215, and : Kieser in *Münchner Jahrbuch der bildenden Kunst* 8, 1931, 281. See al our Notes 14 and 54. Burckhardt's criticism of Tintoretto and adm ration for Paolo Veronese are very characteristic for his attitu towards the influences on Rubens's art. Censure of the former ar praise of the latter artist are repeated in ever new variations (s pp. 61, 64, 70, 74, 76, 97). We cannot say which 'Adoratio Burckhardt had in mind further below 'which might be attribut either to Rubens or to Paolo Veronese'. It is strange that there a drawings in existence which are attributed sometimes to Verone and sometimes to Rubens (cf. *Burlington Magazine* 76, 1940, 199).

6* The 'Triumph of Caesar' was not painted until 1629. At that tim Rubens was staying in London, where Mantegna's cartoons had ju been brought. See also H. Kauffmann, 'Rubens und Mantegna' *Koeln und der Nordwesten*, 1941, p. 99.

7* The drawings after Leonardo's 'Battle for the Standard' are no in the Louvre and in the collection of the Queen of Holland. Rube: made a further copy after the same work (London). His copies aft Michelangelo's Prophets and Sibyls in the Sistine Chapel are also pr served in the Louvre (Glück-Haberditzl Nos. 12–21). He also sketch the figure of 'Night' in the Medici Chapel at Florence (ib. No. 22

Cf. Glück-Haberditzl, *Die Handzeichnungen von Peter Paul Rubens*, 1928, and J. Q. van Regteren Altena in *Burlington Magazine* 76, 1940, 194.

8* The small copy of Caravaggio's 'Entombment' was painted, strange to say, not until after the return to Antwerp, though it is no doubt based on drawings, now lost, which Rubens must have prepared in Italy. Caravaggio's picture was in Santa Maria in Vallicella, the same church for which Rubens painted the high altar triptych (see Note 2). Caravaggio's importance for Rubens has recently been stressed again by R. Oldenbourg in *Peter Paul Rubens*, 1922, p. 63, and by L. Burchard in *Pinacoteca* I, 1928, I. See also the following Note.

9* The painting in the Hermitage is now considered to be a copy after a lost early 'Crucifixion of St. Peter' by Caravaggio. The similarity of the pictures of Rubens and those of Caravaggio has been observed already by Waagen (*Die Gemäldesammlung in St. Petersburg*, 1870, p. 82). At the same time, about 1602, Guido Reni painted his naturalistic 'Crucifixion' for San Paolo alle tre Fontane, a picture that Rubens no doubt admired more than the 'academic' composition which Burckhardt mentions a little earlier (cf. W. Friedländer in *Journal of the Warburg and Courtauld Institutes* 8, 1945, 152).

10 According to recent research, the actual execution, or at any rate the completion, of this picture would have to be dated considerably earlier. *The work was commissioned in 1629 by the Fraternity of St. Ildefonso for their chapel in the church of S. Jacques on the Coudenberg at Brussels; it was dedicated in 1632. The costs were defrayed by the duchess, who had lost her husband ten years before. Rubens painted the archducal couple in the full splendour of their state robes. In point of fact, the duchess, after her husband's death wore always the garb of the Franciscan nuns. See also Note 95.

11* The engraver Lucas Vorsterman had designs on Rubens's life, but his motives and other details are not known. It is not even clear whether this was a serious threat; see H. Hymans, *Lucas Vorsterman*, 1893, p. 28; F. van den Wijngaert in *De Gulden Passer* 23, 1945, 159. Cf. Rubens's letter on p. 219 below.

12* The 'Martyrdom of St. Lievin' dates from the master's last period, about 1635. A coloured sketch is in the Van Beuningen collection at Vierhouten, Holland. See Note 88.

13 Further details, in part differing from those given here, in Waagen's text to his Rubens Album. For the three large altar drawings saved from the fire, and now in the Vienna Gallery, see below.

*Many oil sketches for the ceiling decorations destroyed by fire in 1718 have been preserved and are now scattered over many collections. Three of them are illustrated in Plates 55–7. Some drawings of decorative elements and arrangements are also still in existence. In 1718 the Dutch painter Jacob de Wit copied all paintings of the ceiling and his drawings were engraved and published by Jan Punt 1751. Another publication appeared in 1735. We have thus a great deal of information about the appearance of this large decoration (cf. Leo van Puyvelde, *The Sketches of Rubens*, 1947, pp. 26–8, and Glück-Haberditzl, *Die Handzeichnungen von Peter Paul Rubens*, Nos. 128–32).

14 It was at this time in Madrid that Rubens made those copies after Titian which Palomino (chapter 129) declares to have surpassed the originals. The Spaniard who here pronounces judgement between the Italian and the Fleming was probably voicing the general opinion of his time, about 1700. *It is most unlikely that the Infanta sent Rubens again to Spain after his return from London. The story of this third Spanish journey goes probably back to a misunderstanding in R. de Piles's *Dissertation sur les ouvrages des plus fameux peintres*, 1681. See H. Riegel, *Beiträge zur niederländischen Kunstgeschichte* 1, 1882, 311. See also Note 34.

15* The altar-piece of St. Roch for the church at Alost was painted in 1623.

16 cf. Passeri, *Vite de' Pittori* etc., Rome 1772, pp. 284, 285, 288. *Ed.* Jacob Hess, 1934, p. 260.

17* H. G. Evers (*Peter Paul Rubens*, 1942, p. 248) has recently shown in detail that the famous 'Kermesse' was painted in the early twenties. Most scholars had assumed a date in the middle thirties.

18* The 'St. Francis' at Cologne was painted already about 1615, and was engraved by Lucas Vorsterman in 1620. During the year before, Rubens sought to obtain the privileges of the Dutch States-General. In the list attached to a letter addressed by Rubens to Pieter van Veen, he describes the engraving as 'St. Francis receiving the stigmata'. See his letter on p. 214 ff. below.

19* Gustav Friedrich Waagen's essay on Rubens, to which Burckhardt refers repeatedly, appeared in 1864 as text to a Rubens Album. At that time Waagen had not seen the paintings in Spain. He visited that country later as an old man and published his observations on the Rubens paintings there in *Zahns Jahrbücher für Kunstwissenschaft* 1,

8, 89. Waagen, mainly a connoisseur, was appointed director of
newly founded Berlin Gallery in 1830. He wrote excellent guides
the art collections of Europe; his *Treasures of Art in Great Britain*
e become world-famous (1854-7). In questions of dating, Burck-
dt generally follows Waagen, even in cases where Waagen was
staken (e.g. the Ildefonso altar-piece and the copy of Mantegna's
iumph of Caesar'). See A. Woltmann, *Kleine Schriften von G. F.*
agen, 1875 (which includes the Rubens essay), and W. Waetzoldt,
utsche Kunsthistoriker 2, 1924, p. 29. See Note 31.

Les maîtres d'autrefois, p. 133. *English edition, 1948, p. 76.
e painter Eugène Fromentin (1820-76) was a very gifted writer
art and a great admirer of Rubens.

Geschichte des Barockstils, II, p. 20 ff. *Since Gurlitt's time, little
v material has been published on the subject of Rubens's abilities
an architect. Modern critics are inclined to dispute his authorship
architectural designs. The Jesuit church, for instance, was built by
ns Aguilon and Pieter Huyssens, though Rubens may have given
vice upon the arrangement of the façade and above all for the
apel of the Holy Virgin. See J. Plantegna, *L'art religieux du*
bant au 17e siècle, 1925, p. 101; *Verzamelde opstellen* 1926, p. 54,
d in *Heemschut* 1934; Martin Konrad in *Belgische Kunstdenkmäler* 2,
3, 204; Stan Leurs, *Barockkerken te Antwerpen* 1935; Oda van de
styne in *Revue belge d'art et d'archéologie* 1, 1931, 103. See also the
lowing Note.

* It is almost generally agreed that Rubens took an active part in
signing his own house. After Rubens's death, the buildings were
fortunately allowed to decay, and the restoration, which was
mpleted in 1945, has led to many differences of opinion (cf. Max
oses, *Het huis van Rubens*, 1910; A. J. J. Delen, *Het huis van Peter*
uwel Rubens, 1933 and 1940; F. Clymans, *Rondom den wederopbouw*
i het Rubenshuis, 1941, and *Wederopbouw van Rubens woon- en*
rkhuis, 1946).

* Burckhardt got to know this collection of architectural sketches
ough H. v. Geymüller (cf. *Burckhardt's Briefwechsel mit H. v.*
ymüller, edited by C. Neumann, 1914, p. 143). They are now in
ningrad; some of them are reproduced in the book by Clymans
ed in the preceding Note. But these sketches, in respect of which
ymüller already made 'les reserves que vous et moi connaissez',
ve never been referred to since by art historians.

N

24* In the opinion of Schlosser, G. B. Bellori (*Vite de' Pittori, Scultori et Architetti moderni*, 1672) is the most important European art historiographer in the seventeenth century. His 'vita' of Rubens is one of the twelve biographies in his book.

25* Giuseppe Cesari, called Cavaliere d'Arpino, 1568–1640, was a Roman artist who enjoyed great renown and influence during his lifetime. He is no longer regarded as of any importance.

26 On 22 April 1629, he wrote to the Queen from Susa: 'Madame j'ai creu que Votre Majesté n'auroit pas désagréable que je lui dise que j'estime qu'il seroit à propos qu'elle fit peindre la galerie de son palai [namely the second] par Josepin [Arpino] qui ne désire que d'avoir l'honneur de la servir et d'entreprendre et parachever cet ouvrage pour le prix que Rebens a eu de l'autre galerie qu'il a peinte.' The writer might at least have spelt Rubens's name correctly, for it certainly means as much to the world today as his own. *The Cardinal all the same owned some paintings by Rubens. See also G. Hanatau in *Sur les chemins de l'histoire* 1, 1924, 264, and O. G. von Simson 'Richelieu and Rubens' in *Review of Politics* 6, 1944, 422.

27 I do not know whether or where information respecting the exhibitions of the day was ever collected, more particularly as regards St Joseph's day, March 19, which was the day of exhibitions both in Italy and in other countries. There is a good deal of scattered information about art dealing in Italy, and more particularly in Holland. In the seventeenth century we find a number of saints' days connected with art exhibitions, especially in Rome and Naples, for instance in De' Dominici. *Vite de' Pittori . . Napoletani*, Naples 1742. For conditions in the Netherlands cf. H. Floercke, *Studien zur niederländischen Kunst- und Kulturgeschichte*, 1905, and J. Denucé, *Bronnen voor geschiedenis van de Vlaamsche kunst*, I-II, 1931–2.

28 A large altar-piece which the present writer always regrets having missed in St. Paul's and knows only from Lafenestre, *La Belgique* p. 272, and a few vague remarks in Bellori, p. 223, shows the Fathers of the Church and other Doctors assembled in front of a half-cupola with columns, with an altar and monstrance in the middle. Since even Bellori mentions 'i quattro dottori che parlano del divino pane' and the picture is called to this day 'La Dispute du Saint-Sacrement' it is possible that the Fathers of St. Paul's, having received news of, perhaps even seen, what was at that time erroneously interpreted Raphael's Vatican fresco, may have wished to have a 'Disputa' in

ıbens. The picture was one of the earliest to be painted after Rubens's
:urn from Italy (1609) and in spite of a certain constraint in the
inting, shows extreme care in the execution. *Reproduced on
. 12. About the acquisition of Caravaggio's 'Rose-garland
adonna' see pp. 7–8.

In addition to the 'Great Last Judgement' he accepted commis-
ns from Neuburg for the 'Great Fall of the Wicked Angels', the
doration of the Shepherds' and the 'Pentecost', and for the cathe-
al of Freising the 'Woman of the Apocalypse', all of which are
w in the Munich Pinakothek. The same gallery also contains the
ion Hunt' painted for Duke Maximilian of Bavaria in 1618, for
bens was becoming as famous for his secular as for his religious
ork. *See Pls. 31, 34, 69, and letter on p. 207.

Passeri, *Vite de' Pittori etc.*, Rome 1772, p. 272, Vita di Mitelli.
Ed. Jacob Hess, 1934, p. 283.

Cf. Waagen, Text to Rubens's Album, p. 25. *Kleine Schriften
n G. F. Waagen*, ed. Woltmann, p. 265.

The series of wall tapestries of the 'Triumph of the Eucharist',
hich consisted originally of fifteen pieces, was commissioned by the
fanta Isabella for the convent of the barefoot Carmelite nuns in
Iadrid; it was completed when Rubens went to Spain for the second
ne. It was only later that Philip IV acquired the painted designs.
part from these large cartoons (now in the Louvre and elsewhere),
me sketches have been preserved (Madrid, Cambridge, Chicago,
d private collections). See L. van Puyvelde, *The Sketches of Rubens*,
. 32–5, and E. Tormo in *Archivo Español de Arte* 15, 1942, 294;
oris-Held, *Rubens in Amerika*, 1947, p. 57. See also pp. 35, 124.

Thus Bellori, p. 233. *See also Note 24 above.

* Antonio Palomino (mentioned also in Note 14 above), was the
thor of *El Museo Pictorico* (1715), a work in three volumes dealing
ith aesthetics and art history. The last part contains interesting infor-
ation about Spanish art history. The 'Judgement of Paris' in
Iadrid does not belong to the series of decorations for the Torre de
Parada. Many of these paintings were executed by pupils and are
gned with their names. The magnificent sketches, however, are
ubens's own; they are now scattered over many collections. See
. van Puyvelde, *The Sketches of Rubens*, pp. 41–3.

35* 'Latona with the Lycian Peasants' (Munich, No. 307) is a workshop production of about 1620; it does not therefore belong to the Torre de la Parada decorations. The 'Diana with the Nymphs' (Dresden, No. 1000) is said to have come from Spain, but is a work of J. Boeckhorst.

36 There would have been nothing new in the idea of such a series. For the great series of tapestries composed by Jan Vermaeyen, an actual eye-witness of the Tunis campaign, and commissioned by Charles V, cf. Engerth's *Catalogue of the Vienna Gallery*, Vol. II, p. 522 ff., where details will be found of the large gouache cartoons now part of the Vienna Gallery as well as on the small sketches and the two extant tapestries. Rubens must certainly have seen the tapestry series in Madrid, but his mind worked on other lines from that of the good Vermaeyen. The sketch in Berlin is memorable especially for the group round a Tunisian leader who is falling head down from his rearing charger, while a Spanish officer is striking down at him

37* The correspondence between Rubens and Sir Dudley Carleton was published in 1859 by W. Noël Sainsbury (*Original unpublished papers . . . of Sir Peter Paul Rubens*). The letters to which Burckhard refers are printed below on pp. 205–9. Sir Dudley Carleton (1573–1631) was English Ambassador to the States-General from 1615 to 1625, and a great connoisseur and collector. He gave Rubens some Roman antiquities which he had collected at Venice, in exchange for some of the painter's works.

38* The part which assistants may have played in painting the Luxembourg Gallery can indeed not be traced with any certainty. In his letter of 3 July 1625, there is only a Justus (of Egmont) mentioned as a pupil working in Paris. It is, however, unlikely that Rubens should have done this enormous work without any help. See also Note 16: Pieter van Mol was born in 1599 and not 'as early as 1580'.

39* The 'Flight of Cloelia' (Dresden No. 1016A) is probably by follower of Rubens; whether it is by van Diepenbeeck is not certain. Other repetitions exist in the Louvre and on the art market. Another composition exists in two repetitions, in Woerlitz Castle near Dessau and in the Kaiser-Friedrich Museum, Berlin.

40 For further details of the techniques which can be demonstrated in Rubens's works, see Von Frimmel, *Handbuch der Gemäldekunde*, p. 52 f. *The technique of Rubens's sketches has recently been

vestigated more closely. L. Burchard, in particular, has pointed out
e sketch-like character of the 'modello' (*Sitzungsberichte der Berliner
nstwissenschaftlichen Gesellschaft*, 1926-7, p. 1). Old copies after
etches are also in existence (id. ib. 1930-1, p. 7). See also Exhibition
quisses de Rubens, Brussels, 1937; L. van Puyvelde, *The Sketches of
ibens*, 1947; and M. Delacre in *Bulletin de l'Académie royale de
lgique*, Classe des Beaux-Arts, 1937, 51 and 81.

* The sketches concerned are those for the cycle on the life of
arie de' Medici. Sixteen of them are preserved in Munich and some
hers in Copenhagen, Leningrad and Paris (L. van Puyvelde, op. cit.,
. 30-2). These sketches were not intended as models for possible
llaborators. See Note 38 above.

For all questions of publishing and business, other writers must
consulted. For a general survey of Rubens's engravers cf. Woer-
ann, *Geschichte der Malerei*, III, p. 340. *Further literature: G. Voor-
lm Schneevoogt, *Catalogue des estampes gravées d'après Rubens*, 1873;
Rosenberg, *Der Kupferstich in der Schule und unter dem Einfluss des
ibens*, 1898; F. van den Wijngaert, *Inventaris der Rubeniaansche
entkunst*, 1940; L. Lebeer, *Rubens et l'art de la gravure*, 1942; (J. C.
binge Wubben) *Catalogus van de tentoonstelling de prentkunst rondom
ibens*, Rotterdam, Museum Boymans, 1942-3. See also the literature
oted in Note 11 above. Rubens complained repeatedly about
e difficulty in finding competent engravers, and also about the
igthy procedure to obtain and renew the necessary privileges. See
letters on p. 214 f. below.

* For the 'Raising of Lazarus' see Note 71 below. The first state of
e 'Virgin with the parrot' (Antwerp), about 1616, can be seen in
e engraving by Michel Lasne. It was only in the early thirties that
ibens himself enlarged the painting to its present size (cf. L.
irchard in G. Glück, *Rubens, van Dijck und ihr Kreis*, p. 393).

* The woodcut of Christoffel Jegher (who, incidentally, was born
Antwerp) is a free reproduction of a Rubens painting in Madrid
l. 99). The woodcut was made, as were the others, under the per-
nal supervision of Rubens, who, moreover, re-drew the Madrid
mposition specially for the purpose and made corrections to the
oofs. The 'Boar Hunt' of Soutman is based on the painting in
arseille.

* As mentioned in Note 2 above, and explained repeatedly by
Glück (*Rubens, van Dijck und ihr Kreis*, pp. 18, 155, 275, 409), the

'St. Sebastian' in the Corsini Gallery dates from Rubens's Itali
period. Kauffmann, on the other hand (in his edition of J. Burc
hardt's *Erinnerungen aus Rubens*, 1928, p. 193), assumes a date after t
master's return to Antwerp, which is certainly correct for the '
Sebastian' in the Berlin Museum.

46★ The 'Susanna' in Munich dates from Rubens's last years, but l
suffered badly owing to restorations and overpainting (by Rube
himself?) The 'Antiope' in Antwerp—the subject is, in fact, Ver
and a Satyr—is dated 1614.

47 Rubens may have seen Titian's 'Girl in the Fur Cloak', now in t
Vienna Gallery. Charles I of England had 'bought it in Spain', pr
bably before 1630, and in that case it cannot possibly have been wit
held from Rubens. He would also see it in such integrity as it m
have had before it passed through the Vienna 'Stallburg', when t
most important pictures were cut down for the sake of symmet
The stance of Rubens's 'pelsken' is different, but the kinship remai
and in both pictures the right arm is bent towards the left should
★'Het pelske' may be dated about 1638 (cf. G. Glück, *Rubens, 1
Dijck und ihr Kreis*, p. 125; H. G. Evers, *Peter Paul Rubens*, p. 451).

48★ The 'Farewell of Adonis' in the Uffizi is attributed to F. Wout
by G. Glück (*Rubens, van Dijck und ihr Kreis*, p. 168). The 'Th
Sleeping Nymphs' is a workshop production (Munich No. 73
according to G. Glück (op. cit., p. 356) by J. Boeckhorst in col
boration with Jan Brueghel.

49★ The 'Judgement of Paris' in London dates from the first half
the thirties. The latest version, however, is that in Madrid (No. 16
which Burckhardt, strange to say, mentions only briefly in anot
connexion (see p. 27 and Note 34). The earliest version of t
subject is also in Madrid (No. 1731); it was rediscovered by
Burchard (*Pinacoteca* 1, 1928, 14), after it had been attributed
many years to Jordaens and others.

50★ 'Hercules at the Cross-roads' is no longer given to Rube
Oldenbourg and G. Glück (op. cit., p. 184) have attributed it t
Boeckhorst. On the iconography of the picture cf. E. Panofs
(*Herkules am Scheidewege*, 1930, p. 113), who suggests an attribut
to Th. van Thulden. A translation of the letter mentioned
Burckhardt in the following sentence is given on p. 244 f. below

* Burckhardt means probably H. Witdoek's engraving of 1638; e corresponding picture is in the Prado (No. 1643). Another nmaus composition by Rubens with six visible hands was engraved early as 1611 by W. Swanenburg; two corresponding paintings in e collection of the Duke of Alba, Madrid, and in the church of nt Eustache in Paris.

* 'Romulus and Remus' was painted at Antwerp as late as 1618, d the St. Ildefonso altar even as late as 1629–32. See Notes 2 and 10.

The number eleven might be prophetic of the future apostles, cluding Judas. There is probably a reminiscence, too, of the old resentations of the so-called 'Holy Kinsfolk', where the Apostles ure as children.

Though we cannot deny a kinship of atmosphere with the so-led 'Garden of Love', which seems to find here, as it were, a ythical echo. *The copy after Titian's 'Children's Festival' is now Stockholm (No. 599), Pl. 81. It is, however, not impossible that ubens worked after a different version; there are some small dif-ences and the Rubens copy appears to have been painted after 1628.

* The painting in Dresden is probably only a copy. L. Burchard ahrbuch der preussischen Kunstsammlungen 49, 1928, 63) calls the ture in London only 'a finer variant' of that in Dresden.

Les maîtres d'autrefois, p. 147.

It would be well to restrict this whole discussion to what is known be authentic. Even the most magnificent studio pictures ('Holy mily', etc.), which pass for originals in the galleries, generally tray the hands of pupils by their greater sentimentality and inferior wer of characterization.

I lack full information about the portraits of older women who e called 'Rubens's Mother' in certain galleries. *The Antwerp ture was probably painted with the help of pupils. The sketch, the odello', was exhibited in Vienna in 1930 (No. 97, Messrs. N. chmann).

For the expression and modelling of the heads in general, I grate-ly refer the reader to what Woermann says (Geschichte der Malerei, , p. 410): 'The bold arch of the foreheads, the powerful curve of e brows, the large eyes, the full, fleshy cheeks, the well-marked lips. e individual features contrast more strongly than in the Italian types; the faces as a whole look more vigorous and self-willed.' For the flesh in Rubens, we may recall Guido Reni's question on seeing one of his pictures: 'Does this man mix blood with his colours?'

60★ The 'Holy Family' in Turin is a copy after the Madrid version (No. 1639), whose authenticity is sometimes doubted. Of this composition there exists also an early full-length version and two later variants derived from it, with the addition of St. Francis (in Windsor —a copy?—and in New York). See R. Oldenbourg, *P. P. Rubens*, 1922, p. 162.

61★ The 'Annunciation' in Vienna has recently been dated, in my opinion correctly, from the first years after the Italian journey, about 1609. (K. Bauch in *Jahrbuch der preussischen Kunstsammlungen* 45, 1924, 185.)

62★ The famous painting by Titian came to the Dresden Gallery in 1746, from the Ducal collection of Modena.

63★ The 'Apostles' in Madrid may certainly also be regarded a single half-length figures with a purely expressive function (see Note 4). The half-length 'Christ' in the National Gallery of Ottawa also belongs to this series (repetition in the Schottenstift). Cf. R. R. Tatlock in *Burlington Magazine* 50, 1927, 233, and E. Greindl in *Pantheon* 29, 1942, 42.

64★ Of this composition there exist several, slightly different variants (Bordeaux; Philadelphia, Johnson Collection; London, Wallace Collection, and elsewhere). The version in Antwerp (No. 313) is certainly not one of the best. The composition was engraved by Paulus Pontius, and a preliminary drawing is in the Boymans Museum, Rotterdam.

65 Fromentin's paean in *Les maîtres d'autrefois* concludes with the words: 'Il faut pour aujourd'hui quitter le Musée'. ★See English edition 1948, p. 59.

66★ The original of Titian's 'Battle of Cadore' was destroyed in the fire of 1577. That Rubens's recollection of the composition was based on an engraving (e.g. that by Fontana) is made probable also by the fact that his composition is reversed left to right, as can be seen by comparison with a painted copy of Titian's picture in Florence. A drawing by Rubens after this composition is in Antwerp (A. J. Delen in *Old Master Drawings* 7, 1932, 31).

67 For the 'Dispute du Saint-Sacrement' in St. Paul's, Antwerp, see Note 28 above, ★and Plate 12.

This must not be taken to mean that he painted slowly; there is
umentary evidence for the amazingly small number of days in
ich certain very famous pictures were painted. A further proof of
complete maturing of the inward vision which preceded work,
well as of the reliability of the pupils, without whose help this
idity of execution could not be imagined, even if the master's
sical powers had been unlimited.

The authenticity of the coloured drawings in the Louvre has
n disputed by G. Glück (op. cit., p. 70) and others. There exists,
wever, a very good oil sketch (reproduced ib., p. 66) in the L.
uchez collection, and two sketches in Dulwich College for the
sides of the wings, as well as some drawings for details. See also
sketch in the Toronto Art Gallery, engraved by J. Witdoek
ris-Held No. A 57: studio work).

This St. John, running about in Daniele's picture, recalls the
atest work of a Flemish artist who must be mentioned in any work
Rubens: the industrious and conscientious Philippe de Champaigne
Brussels (1602–74), who was so important for portraiture. The
ture is the 'Lamentation for the Death of Abel' in the Vienna
llery, painted in 1656 for the Archduke Leopold Wilhelm, a work
great academic perfection and large size, in which, however, the
e dramatic impulse gives way to mere calculation. We have but
see how Adam runs about in the picture, wringing his hands, to
lize how unimaginable such a figure would be in Rubens.

It is very unlikely that the engraving by Boetius à Bolswert
roduces a preliminary composition of Rubens's painting in Berlin:
painting dates from about 1620, the engraving from 1629–31, the
he years in which Bolswert engraved other works by Rubens.
sides, the engraving does not carry Rubens's privilege, which sug-
ts that the master did not wish to assume the responsibility for the
nges made to his composition.

The presence of children only became a beautiful and poetic
stulate of modern art. Livy (I, 13) only allows the children to be
ken of by the wives.

According to Oldenbourg (*Klassiker der Kunst, Rubens,* p. 461,
No. 171), the sketch in the Vienna Academy is not authentic. Van
ck's collaboration may be assumed for the painting in Leningrad.
o

74★ About the relation between the painting of the 'Raising
Lazarus' and the engraving, see Note 71 above. For the two versio
of the 'Judgement of Paris', see Note 55 above.

75★ The engraving by Paulus Pontius (1620) reproduces the painti
in the Boston Museum (formerly Earl of Darnley and Earl of Ha
wood), with the addition of some embellishments. The version in t
Louvre is probably to be dated a little earlier. See C. C. Cunningha
in *Bulletin of the Museum of Fine Arts, Boston*, 39, 1941, 35.

76★ In a letter of 1614 to the Archduke Albert, Rubens compla
that the successor of the Bishop of Ghent who had commission
this painting for the high altar of St. Bavo refused to adopt Ruber
original design for the altar (see the translation of the letter on p. 2
below). But the Archduke does not seem to have had much influe
in this matter, for Rubens's altar-piece was not erected until 16
under another bishop. A coloured drawing, probably a first sket
for the centre panel and the wings is in the National Gallery, Lond
(No. 57). I disagree with G. Glück (op. cit. p. 198), who attribu
this sketch, which has since been cleaned and restored, to F. Franck
See also H. G. Evers, *Rubens und sein Werk*, 1943, p. 145.

77 Was Rubens perhaps the first to introduce Joseph as Mar
travelling companion? He is not mentioned in Luke I, 39.

78★ In addition to Pieter de Jode's engraving after the 'Visitation'
the wing of the 'Descent from the Cross' in Antwerp, there
further variants and preliminary studies of this composition
Strasbourg, Borghese Gallery, Rome (according to G. Glück by T
van Thulden) and in the former Giovanelli collection (Rub
exhibition, Amsterdam 1933, No. 2).

79★ The 'Last Supper' in the Brera dates only from 1620. See Not
above.

80 Caravaggio's influence might be defined in the sense that Ruben
picture, in the whole and the detail, would probably have spoke
rather different language if Caravaggio had never lived.

81 His extreme and very eminent achievement in dramatic painti
may probably be seen in the magnificently painted picture of t
Brussels Museum, 'St. Martin healing the possessed slave of the no
and still pagan Roman' (the vir proconsularis Tatradius, cf. Sulpic
Severus, *Vita Sancti Martini*, c. 16); the Roman, who was converted
a result of the healing, is portrayed—in a manner, of course, qu

erent from Rubens—in the man watching from the upper arch.
e same gallery possesses the mythological picture recognized as
daens's finest, 'La félicité'. Cassel has his excellent family group.
e great allegory of the 'Triumph of the House of Orange' in
sch, near The Hague, will be discussed later.

* The 'St. Ignatius' in San Ambrogio, Genoa, was commissioned
Niccolo Pallavicini, painted in 1619 and delivered in 1620. There is
reason for assuming that it was promised already in 1606 (see
te 2 above). The two large altar-panels for the Jesuit church at
twerp, the 'Miracles of St. Francis' and the 'Miracles of St.
ıatius', were completed as early as 1619. Thus Burckhardt was
ite right concerning the chronological sequence of these inter-
ated compositions.

* Nowadays many experts attribute the study of the negro heads in
ussels (Cat. No. 389) to Van Dyck, particularly since it has become
own that in older catalogues it was always listed under Van Dyck's
me. L. van Puyvelde, however, still gives it to Rubens. See G.
ück, Klassiker der Kunst, A. van Dijck, 1931, p. 14, and L. Burchard
G. Glück, Rubens, van Dijck und ihr Kreis, p. 390.

* The statement that Rubens painted exactly ten 'Adorations of the
ngs' was taken over by Burckhardt from Waagen, who in turn
sed himself on John Smith's catalogue raisonné.

* Rubens was deeply moved by the death of his friend Elsheimer.
ıe letter which he wrote to a common friend in Rome on this
:lancholy occasion is printed on p. 201 below.

* The engraving corresponds to a painting in the Metropolitan
useum, New York, which is, however, only a pupil's work.

* Around the 'Bearing of the Cross' in the Brussels Museum, there
n be grouped, apart from the engraving by Pontius, which is dated
32, several sketches (in Amsterdam, Copenhagen, Vienna Academy,
'arsaw), whose chronological sequence and authenticity have not
t been established. See H. G. Evers, P. P. Rubens, p. 360 and note
4, with references to literature.

* The completed sketch for this painting is in the Van Beuningen
llection, Vierhouten, Holland. See also Note 12 above.

* In Rubens's earliest version of this subject (in the A. Neuerburg
llection, Hamburg; engraved by J. Matham) the hero is also asleep.
ıe Munich version has been attributed variously to Rubens or to

Van Dyck, while the sketch for the composition, in Chicago,
generally acknowledged to be by Rubens. Van Dyck also painted t
subject in his early years (Dulwich Gallery; about 1618–20). S
L. Burchard in G. Glück, op. cit., pp. 382 and 395, and H. G. Eve
op. cit., p. 158.

90* The original of the 'Tribute Money', now in the M.H.de You
Memorial Museum, San Francisco, dates from about 1613–14. It v
engraved by L. Vorsterman in 1621.

91* P. de Jode's engraving reproduces the painting intended for t
tomb of Pieter Brueghel the Elder. It was last heard of in the Nem
collection and exhibited in Vienna in 1930 (Cat. No. 7).

92* 'Christ and the Woman taken in adultery', of the same size a
same date as the 'Tribute Money' (about 1612), is now in the Bruss
Museum (No. 381).

93* The sketch is probably not authentic.

94 In the choir of a convent at Fosaldanna, not far from Valladol
Palomino also saw (chapter 70) a huge and magnificent picture
Rubens, perhaps the biggest picture in the whole of Spain. He do
not say, and we can only guess, that it was a 'Madonna with Saint
and the picture is mentioned here only to draw the reader's attenti
to Palomino's statement. Since Rubens in all probability visit
Valladolid on his first journey to Spain in 1603, the picture must ha
been painted then. *It was an 'Assumption of the Virgin' and is no
in the Valladolid Museum. Carl Justi (*Velasquez und sein Jahrhunde*
ed. L. Goldscheider, 1933, p. 245) also praises the 'masterly drawir
in this picture. Rooses considers it a pupil's work.

95 We consult the catalogue in vain for the names of the four h
women, which it should be possible to discover in the archives of t
community that commissioned the picture. The Archduke's patr
saint depicted as a cardinal on the wings is neither St. Jerome nor :
Bonaventure, but the cardinal St. Albert of the House of Braba
who was murdered at Rheims in 1192. The patron saint of the Infa
would appear to be St. Clare of Assisi, but might also be interpreted
St. Elizabeth of Hungary, Countess of Thuringia, who would
represented as a widow in the habit of the Dominicans, in which c
the roses on the book in her hands would have to be interpreted as
allusion to the famous miracle of the roses.

96* For these two works cf. p. 137 and Notes 2 and 10 above.

From Lafenestre, *La Belgique*, p. 289. *In addition to many copies, re is a preliminary drawing of the composition in Stockholm, and o oil studies in Frankfurt and Berlin (Glück-Haberditzl, *Die ndzeichnungen des Rubens*, No. 172, and L. van Puyvelde, *The etches of Rubens*, Nos. 57-8).

The 'Assunta' nevertheless appears in the ecclesiastical sculpture l painting of the north. A very curious old Flemish triptych in the ussels Museum has as its central picture, below, the Apostles at the en tomb, in the air, the Holy Virgin among angels, borne aloft by rist and the Holy Ghost (not by two saints as the catalogue has it), th God the Father in benediction at the extreme top. *The old mish triptych in the Brussels Museum (No. 534) is one of the ncipal works of Albert Bouts.

Had Rubens seen Andrea del Sarto's 'Assuntas'? This is as doubt- as the other cases of apparent or real echoes of del Sarto. Rubens k little from Paolo Veronese's 'Assunta' in the Venice Academy.

In the 'Assunta' of the Munich Pinakothek, mentioned just ow, one of these figures belongs absolutely to Rubens's well- own type of the Magdalen.

1* The following additional information may be given regarding e various compositions of the 'Assumption of the Virgin' discussed Burckhardt: the Munich painting has been removed to Schleiss- im; it is only a school work, and differs not inconsiderably from e large picture in Düsseldorf. The latter was painted about 1618-20 the high altar of Notre Dame de la Chapelle in Brussels, and was d to Johan Wilhelm, Elector of the Palatinate, in 1711. The sketch the Uffizi corresponds with the Liechtenstein version and may have en used for the engraving of J. Witdoek (not listed by Glück- berditzl). The painting in Vienna dates from about 1620, that in twerp Cathedral from about 1625. The latest version is not that in twerp, but that of the Liechtenstein Gallery, which was painted ut 1630-5. The statement that the upper part of the Antwerp high ar was painted by Cornelis Schut is due to a misunderstanding: e frame for this altar-piece was ordered from one Adriaen Schut, a binet-maker.

2 The former picture is 6 ft. high by 4 ft. wide, the latter 9 ft. 6 in. h by 7 ft. 6 in. wide. The former has three-fifths daylight and two- hs light of hell and night.

103 The engravers seem to have made use of parts of these pictures
their variants, e.g. Soutman, 'The Fall of the Damned' in his 'Lap
Draconis'. A St. Michael above an immensely animated tangle
fallen angels, in an engraving by Vorsterman, was dedicated
Rubens to King Philip IV (hence after 1621). A 'Fall of the Wick
Angels' (possibly this composition) was destroyed in the fire of
Jesuit church at Antwerp. The 'Rise of the Blessed to Heaven'
the Munich Pinakothek, doubtless invented by Rubens, is rat
alien to his manner in the somewhat slender modelling of the figu
and in the whole treatment. *A 'St. Michael', which is now in
Detroit Museum, has been attributed by J. Held (Goris-Held, *Rub
in America*, No. A70) to a follower of Rubens. The 'Rise of
Blessed', now in Erlangen, was still highly praised by Waagen,
modern opinion has followed Burckhardt in rejecting it. R. Old
bourg thinks that it is an unfinished sketch by Rubens overpain
and enlarged by Jan Boeckhorst (*Peter Paul Rubens*, 1922, p. 178).

104 Cf. Preller, *Griechische Mythologie*. Child Pans also in Pompe
paintings.

105* The two excellently preserved repetitions of the 'Drunk
Hercules' to which Burckhardt refers are presumably the pictures
Dresden and Cassel. The original has since been found and is now
Dresden (No. 987; formerly it belonged to the royal House
Saxony). It is a pendant to the 'Hero crowned by Virtue' in Mun
(No. 997). Both pictures, however, were painted only after
return from Italy (cf. Note 2 above and 119 below). See E. Hensler
Kunstchronik und Kunstmarkt 59, 1925–6, 662; L. Burchard, ib., p. 7
and E. Hensler in *Festschrift Paul Clemen*, 1926, p. 435.

106* This painting is described in Rubens's estate as 'Silvia'. G. Gl
(op. cit. p. 95) assumes that it represents the lovers Silvia and Ami
from Tasso's pastoral play *Aminta*.

107* 'Pausias and Glycera', formerly in the collection of the Duke
Westminster, is now in the John and Mabel Ringling Museum of *
Sarasota. It was painted, in collaboration with Jan Brueghel, ab
1618.

108 If it is not, after all, Rhea Silvia (cf. Preller, *Griechische Mytholog*

109 It is permissible to wonder whether the picture has retained
original dimensions or has been cut. Under Charles VI it suffered
fate of the major part of the Imperial collection; it was hung in

Stallburg', where the pictures were symmetrically distributed to form a wall decoration. Some mild details of the appalling operations, which were inflicted at that time upon a large number of pictures can be found in the large (new) catalogue, vol. I, p. xlviii of the introduction, and in the text vol. II, p. 134. *Old reproductions show that the painting was in fact originally somewhat larger.

10* Burckhardt was, in fact, entirely right on this point: the 'Leander' in Dresden is an authentic work of Rubens's Italian period. Another version was some years ago on the Swedish art market.

11* The picture in Leningrad is not the original. All copies and workshop repetitions are probably based on the painting in Düsseldorf, which was painted shortly after the return from Italy. See R. Oldenbourg, op. cit., pp. 73 and 148.

12 What Giulio Romano painted as the 'Battle of the Amazons' in the Palazzo del Tè in Mantua probably left Rubens completely unmoved.

13* That the variant in Dresden is probably a copy was mentioned in Note 55 above.

14 The execution in full size, doubtless on canvas, was completed with the help of pupils in Antwerp. For two sketches made in Madrid, now in the possession of Lord Ashburton in London, cf. Waagen, *Rubens Album*, p.25. *Kleine Schriften von G. F. Waagen*, ed. Woltmann, p. 25. The sketches were lately in the A. de Rothschild Collection (Rooses, Nos. 804–5).

15* See Note 39 above.

16* The original of this composition seems to have been lost. The picture in the former Weber collection and the version in Amsterdam are workshop productions.

17* Several pieces of this tapestry series have been preserved; the rest is said to be in the possession of Fürst Schwarzenberg in Heiligenberg Castle, Bohemia.

18* It was mentioned above (Note 40) that the interest both of collectors and of art historians has lately concentrated upon the sketches of Rubens. Six sketches for the 'Story of Achilles' were purchased by the Boymans Museum, Rotterdam, at the Lord Barrymore sale in 1933.

119 A rather unattractive variant, actually a still life with hero
figures, with the hero and Victoria sitting on the corpses of the slain
while the whole of the rest of the picture is filled with weapons and
other engines of war, is in the Munich Pinakothek. Studio picture.
Also in the Vienna Gallery, a victor, crowned by Victoria and
accompanied by Minerva, sitting in the same crude fashion on corpses
with his right foot resting on the shoulder of one of them, this time
an excellent and authentic picture. In an important picture by Rubens'
own hand in Cassel (Pl. 25), the corpses can at any rate be interpreted as allegories of Envy and Discord. In a variant (in private
hands in Paris), a cupid is furtively drawing the hero's sword out of
its sheath. *The original of the 'Hero Crowned by Virtue' is in
Munich (No. 997), the oblong version in Dresden being a repetition.
The painting dates from about 1612 and is the pendant to the
'Drunken Hercules', for which see Note 105 above, with references to
literature. The 'variant' in Munich (Cat. 1886 No. 756) is, according to Burchard, the original of a composition at Tours. The picture
in Vienna (No. 835) is a sketch, reworked later (by Rubens himself?)
for the famous painting in Cassel (No. 91). See G. Glück, op. cit.,
p. 160.

120* Not known today.

121* See the letter printed on p. 244 below.

122* The allusion is to Nicaise de Keyser, an artist very celebrated in
his time, whose colossal allegories of the Antwerp schools of painter
(1864–6) were placed in the entrance hall of the Antwerp Museum.

123 In these amazing productions, Rubens, with his main motive
secure, seems once more ready to abandon and transform the rest.
We see him here in the heat of battle with his own creation. For the
time being he paints everything himself, nor can we imagine how
pupils could be called in for the execution. Later research should be
consulted for a divergent sketch for the 'Entry into Paris' as well as
for sketches said to relate to other pictures of the series. *Recent
literature: Rooses, Œuvres de Rubens, Nos. 755–62; L. van Puyvelde,
The Sketches of Rubens, pp. 35–6; G. Glück in Jahrbuch der kunst-
historischen Sammlungen, Vienna, 11, 1937, 176; H. G. Evers, Rubens
und sein Werk, Neue Forschungen, p. 306.

124* The large canvas sheets were taken down in 1948 and are being
carefully restored.

25 All that matters about the former vaulting decorations of the
suit church at Antwerp has been said above on p. 10 as well as
out the story of Psyche painted on the ceiling of a bedchamber in
reenwich Palace (p. 28).

26* The sketches in the Louvre and the Vienna Academy are studies
r the ceiling of the Jesuit church at Antwerp, those in the Liechten-
ein collection belong to the cycle of Henry IV. The sketch for the
Apotheosis of the Duke of Buckingham' (not of James I) in the
ational Gallery (No. 187) is a study for a ceiling decoration now in
e possession of the Earl of Jersey in Osterley Park. The finished
icture of the 'Glory of San Francesco di Paolo' has been lost;
etches are in Dresden and Munich.

27 I owe the knowledge and impression of this portrait to the
xcellent and fully illustrated biography of Rubens by Knackfuss in
e *Künstlermonographien*, which has been useful to me in many ways.
The portrait of Charles de Longueval, Count of Bucquoi, is in the
eningrad Gallery. It was engraved by L. Vorsterman; his preliminary
udy is in the British Museum.

28* The large canvas pictures of this festive decoration were mostly
xecuted by pupils and other Antwerp contemporaries; the studies,
owever, are by Rubens himself. See Pls. 97–8. The 'two heroic
ngle figures from the House of Habsburg' in Vienna (Nos. 849 and
51), namely Ferdinand of Hungary and Cardinal-Infante Ferdinand,
e from the so-called Arch of Ferdinand, a work entrusted to Gasper
d Jan van der Hecke. 'The Meeting of the two Ferdinands' (No.
56) is, like its pendant, the 'Quos ego' in Dresden, a pupil's work
etouched by the master. The portraits of Albert and Isabella in
russels are likewise not by Rubens's own hand, but—according to
lück—by Cornelis de Vos; they come from the Arch of Philip,
hich was decorated by de Vos and Jacob Jordaens and which was
other part of the festive decoration.

29 Theodor van Thulden also painted a number of scenes; born at
ertogenbosch in Holland, he was one of Rubens's most important
ounger pupils and his chief assistant in the Introitus Ferdinandi. We
ay suppose that his manner of composition was distinguished, to its
wn advantage, from that of Jordaens. *Van Thulden's pictures are,
fact, not the worst of this series. Others who collaborated were
. Honthorst, P. de Grebber, P. Soutman, Th. Willeboirts-
osschaert, S. de Bray, J. Lievens, C. van Everdingen.

130★ Jordaens's own commentary on his allegory is reprinted by M
Rooses in *Jordaens, sa vie et son œuvre*, p. 169. Sketches to the gigant
picture are in Brussels, Antwerp and Warsaw.

131★ For the commissioning and the sketches of this cartoon se
Note 32.

132★ The 'Country Dance' of the former Weber Gallery is only
copy after the fine painting in Madrid (No. 1691), which was er
graved by Schelte à Bolswert.

133★ The 'Court Ball' in The Hague (No. 244) is by Frans Franke
and Frans Pourbus the Younger; the latter painted only seven of th
heads.

134 A similar social sphere was depicted by Rubens in that sketch i
the Vienna Gallery which is there called 'The Castle Park' and show
a castle in a lake with a few very animated figures in the foregroun
engaged in some kind of game of catch. ★The Prado version of th
'Garden of Love' is probably the only original of this compositio
About the numerous variants cf. G. Glück, op. cit., p. 108, and I
Burchard ib. p. 386. The painting in the Rothschild collection is ver
little known and has not been exhibited for some years past.

135 There are some grounds for this assumption. The building, wit
all its odd furniture, must really have existed, and it is difficult
imagine Rubens undertaking such patient studies on anyone else
estate. A picture in Windsor Castle is akin in subject, if not in feelin
(according to *Klassischer Bilderschatz*, Pl. 1162), also an open she
with human beings and animals, known as 'Winter' on account
the whirling snowflakes outside. We do not know whether a who
series of Seasons by Rubens existed. ★The 'Winter' in Windsor an
the 'Prodigal Son' in Antwerp do, in fact, date from about the san
period, between 1618 and 1620. But the Steen estate was not acquire
by Rubens until 1635.

136★ It would have been interesting to learn Burckhardt's reasons fc
this erroneous opinion. But he has never discussed this point again.

137★ The original of the Dresden portrait is in the collection c
Baron G. Rothschild, Paris.

138 Painted with unparalleled swiftness and lightness in the mc
transparent tones, this half-length figure makes an unforgettable im
pression with its great dark-blue eyes and the charmingly folde
hands against a background of blue atmosphere and clouds. Was

bens himself who later added the dark brushstrokes to the eye-
shes and brows? *In a letter from London, dated 6 August 1879,
urckhardt describes his impressions to a friend: 'Besides, I have seen
r the first time Rubens's wonder picture, "Le chapeau de paille";
it it is a plumed felt hat and its correct name is "Chapeau de poil",
hich was misunderstood by some drunken English art lover. Under
e felt hat lives Rubens's second wife, Hélène Fourment, probably
inted when she was betrothed to him. Everything apart from the
ght cheek is in the shadow of the wide hat, but at the same time in
e fullest blond light, the devil knows how and the whole lit up by
vo quite magnificent dark-blue eyes.' (Jacob Burckhardt, *Briefe an
nen Architekten*, 1913, p. 93.) It is a portrait of the master's sister-in-
w, Susanna Fourment, who had married one Arnold Lunden in
522. The old name 'Chapeau de paille' (the hat is made of felt) has
:ver been satisfactorily explained. H. G. Evers (*Rubens und sein Werk*,
943, p. 275) assumes that the name was given to the picture by
ubens himself and that *paille* is used in the sense of the old French
esle (baldachin) and refers to the sitter's new high station.

89 *Les maîtres d'autrefois.* *English edition 1948, p. 64. Though the
ortrait in the Louvre comes from the Boonen collection, there is
othing to prove that the sitter was a member of that family.

40* Now in the National Gallery, London (Gulbenkian loan); also
portrait of Susanna Fourment.

41* The fine group portrait of the Edouard de Rothschild collection
xhibited in Paris, 1946, No. 46) may have been painted during the
:cond half of the thirties. Its authenticity was doubted, without
ty reason, by R. Oldenbourg (*Rubens*, Klassiker der Kunst, 1921,
447); cf. also L. Burchard in *Rubens, van Dijck und ihr Kreis*, p. 387.
he 'Walk in the Garden' in Munich may, however, be the work of a
upil.

42 For the alleged representation of Rubens and his two wives in the
uise of mythological lovers, cf. p. 101 above.

43* The Gerbier family portrait was not painted all at once. The
entre part may date from Rubens's visit to London 1629–30. It was
ilarged by Rubens himself and the patron's figure was added on this
:casion. At Rubens's death the picture was still unfinished. See
. Burchard in *Catalogue of the Exhibition of the King's Pictures*,
946–7, No. 103.

144* The group portrait of Rubens with his Roman friends w
painted only after the artist's return to Antwerp. The sitters ar
Rubens and his brother, Justus Lipsius (died in 1606, painted after
portrait by A. Janssens) and Jan Woverius.

145* The portrait of a priest in Munich represents Hendrik va
Thulden (1580–1617) and was painted about 1616. The two portrai
in the Brussels Museum, Jean-Charles de Cordes and Jacqueline d
Caestre, are by Van Dyck. Of these portraits copies have been found i
Warsaw, which show the original state before they were cut dow
See P. Lambotte in *Apollo* 21, 1935, 231; G. Glück, *A. van Dijck*
Klassiker der Kunst, 1931, pp. 84–5.

146* Another fragment, the portrait of Prince Vincenzo II Gonzag
has since been found and was acquired by the Vienna Museum i
1915. Two further fragments, one of them in L. Burchard's colle
tion, must also be extant, but have not yet been published. S
G. Glück, *Rubens, van Dijck und ihr Kreis*, pp. 1 and 373–4. See als
Note 2 above.

147* For the late date of the Ildefonso altar, see Note 10 above.

148 And again, recently, in Lafenestre, *Florence*, p. 83.

149 This picture has nothing more in common with that in the Uffi
than two galloping horsemen in fine armour cannot help having.
the Uffizi picture was painted after an equestrian portrait of the kin
by Velazquez in Madrid, it must have been totally different from tl
original of the picture in the Pitti Palace. We might in this connexio
venture the suggestion that Velazquez first felt the impulse and tl
capacity to paint equestrian portraits through the examples by Ruber
which were in Spain, from that of the Duke of Lerma (1603) on.
must, of course, have seen Titian's 'Charles V' (cf. Woerman
Geschichte der Malerei) which is regarded as the most miraculous of
portraits, but Rubens's galloping horses move quite differently fro
that of the Emperor, which seems to have cost Titian so mu
trouble. Muentz (*La fin de la Renaissance*, p. 142) is of the opinio
that Titian's lack of knowledge of the structure of the horse was ev
prejudicial to the rider: 'on dirait Don Quichotte sur Rosinante'.

150* The equestrian portrait of Philip IV in the Uffizi is a Spanis
copy after the portrait painted by Rubens in Spain in 1628 (see tl
letter on p. 228 below), which was destroyed by fire. This was recog
nized already by Carl Justi (*Velazquez*, Phaidon ed. 1933, p. 444, an

iscellaneen II, 1908, 259). The portrait of the Cardinal-Infante in
Munich is a copy after the equestrian original in the Prado (No. 1687).

1 I have omitted from this consideration the portraits of Henri in
the two huge sketches in the Uffizi, since they are unfinished, and we
may also leave out of account here his somewhat strange apotheosis
the gallery of the Luxembourg. But would it not be useful and
structive, both from the artistic and the historical point of view, to
collect, with the help of a few photographs, all that we know of the
changes in the tradition of the king's appearance? He would certainly
be a worthier subject of a work of this kind than his grandson,
Louis XIV. But how did Rubens come by his deep feeling for Henri
IV and his desire to transfigure him?

2 She lived in Paris (until 1615) in a great palace with a splendid
garden on the Rive gauche.

3* J. Q. van Regteren Altena (*Burlington Magazine* 76, 1940, 173)
points to a large number of Rubens's sketches after Raphael. See
also Note 7 above.

4 With the exception perhaps, of the picture of Cimone from the
story of Boccaccio (Vienna Gallery), where there is a monkey eating
fruit.

5* This sketch dates probably from shortly after the return from
Italy. Rubens sketched the horse in three different views. G. Glück
and L. Burchard (*Rubens, van Dijck und ihr Kreis*, p. 32) have shown
that the little picture was often copied, either as a whole or in parts.

6* The magnificent portrait of the Duke of Lerma is discussed on
p. 4, 142 above (see Note 4). The 'Man on a White Horse' at Windsor
(he position of the horse is identical with that on the left study of the
sketch in Berlin) is certainly not the Archduke Albert, whose equestrian portrait has been lost. Its type is known to us only from copies
and repetitions in the Liechtenstein Gallery, Vienna, and Longford
Castle. For literature see the previous Note. The equestrian portrait
of Philip IV is likewise known only through a copy (Uffizi); see
Note 150. Rubens's equestrian portrait of Philip II is in the Prado
(No. 1686). The portrait of Philip III is known only through P. de
Jodes's engraving; but it is not on horseback.

7* Both the picture in Windsor and that in Saventhem are youthful
works of Van Dyck. See L. van Puyvelde in *Burlington Magazine*
?, 1940, 37 and A. van de Put, ib. 78, 1941, 32.

158 For the whole series of Antwerp battle painters of the seventeen century, cf. especially Woermann, *Geschichte der Malerei*, III, p. 491 *R. Oldenbourg, *Die flämische Malerei des 17. Jahrhunderts*, 192 p. 167.

159* The 'Wolf Hunt' from the Lord Ashburton collection, whi is now in the Metropolitan Museum, New York, was painted abo 1616. The 'Hippopotamus and Crocodile Hunt' which Burckhar knew only from an engraving, is now in Munich (No. 4797; former Augsburg); it was painted about the same time, probably with t help of pupils. See also letters, p. 208 f.

160* The 'considerable study' is probably the picture reproduced the *Klassischer Bilderschatz* as No. 880. It is certainly not by Rube probably not even from his workshop.

161* The Escorial landscape is not by Rubens's own hand. In a let to Gerbier written in 1640, he states clearly that 'la peinture de Laurens en Escurial' was painted by one Peter Verhulst and 'achev selon la capacité du Maistre avec mon advis'. It was painted afte sketch by Rubens, which he made probably during his first visit Spain. See his letter on p. 248 below. H. Hermann believes Verhuls painting to be identical with one in the collection of the Earl Radnor, Salisbury. Repetitions in the Dresden Gallery and in Lo Leconfield's collection, Petworth. See H. Hermann in *Arch Español* 1933, p. 237; id. *Untersuchungen über die Landschaftsgemälde* Peter Paul Rubens, 1936, p. 29; E. Kieser in *Münchner Jahrbuch* bildenden Kunst 8, 1931, 286. For the landscape paintings of Rube see G. Glück, *Die Landschaften von P.P. Rubens*, 1945. Contrary Burckhardt's belief (p. 153 above), no landscapes are known fro the master's Italian period. It is true that Bolswert's engraving af the Palatine landscape in the Louvre is inscribed 'Peter Paul Rube pinxit Romae', but considerations of style have led modern crit (Leo van Puyvelde excepted) to reject this early date.

162* Other examples of this collaboration are: 'Flora and Zephyr in Mosigkau near Dessau; the 'Three Graces' in the Vienna Acaden the same subject in Stockholm (according to Oldenbourg, a cop 'Diana going to the Hunt' at Augsburg, No. 2463 (a school wo sold some time ago); 'Flora' (Madrid, No. 1675); 'Nature atti by the Three Graces' (Museum in Glasgow); 'Achelous and These (New York); and finally the 'Madonna in a Garland of Flowers a Landscape' in Paris (No. 2079), Berlin (No. 912), Munich (No. 1) and Madrid (No. 1418). See also p. 46 and Notes 48 and 107 ove. Further examples from contemporary documents in J. Denucé, *ieven en documenten betreffende Jan Breugel, I en II*, 1934.

3* It is not known that Jodocus de Momper collaborated on the xembourg cycle (cf. Note 38 above). The magnificent early 'Boar unt' in Dresden is discussed on p. 148. Two preliminary drawings r this picture were published by F. Lugt (*Gazette des Beaux-Arts* 12, 1925, 194–5).

4 From personal observation I might add: in the National Gallery o small pictures: a slope rising gently towards the distant edge of a ood with splendid clumps of trees, in the right foreground a cart rning towards a ford, and a glorious sunset with a small manor use; the horizon above the middle of the picture (Pl. XII). Baring allery (Lord Northbrook), an exquisite little landscape with a cart iving into water in the foreground. Bridgewater Gallery, London, picture whose attribution may remain in question, with four ndentives from the Farnesina above, and below a brilliant landscape ith mountains, water, islands and towns, almost in the manner of ul Bril. Dudley House, a moonlit landscape with trees, water flecting the moon and no great distance, a horse grazing in the fore- ound. Grosvenor Gallery, a delicately executed picture, alleged to ve been painted before Rubens left Antwerp for Italy; on a height the right windmills, to the left a steep valley with a castle, park and id-distance, and a hint of the sea. Peasants are returning from the lds, coming down the hill in a cart. (Notes taken in 1879.) *For the ke of clearness, we give below references to the illustrations in ück, in the same order in which the landscapes are described by rckhardt: 'The Tourney' in the Louvre, Glück No. 36; 'The inbow' in Munich, Glück No. 29 (another, larger, and certainly chentic version in the Wallace Collection); 'Cows at Pasture' in unich, Glück No. 6; 'Return from the Fields', Pitti, Glück No. 22; teen Castle', National Gallery, Glück No. 30; 'A Wood', engraved Schelte à Bolswert, sketch Glück No. 28; 'La Charrette embour- e', Glück No. 7; 'Laeken Meadows' in Windsor, Glück No. 2; dge of the Wood' in the National Gallery (No. 948), only a ool work; 'Sunset' in the National Gallery, Glück No. 31; 'Cart in e Water', Lord Northbrook (now Van Beuningen Collection, erhouten), Glück No. 32; the original of the picture in Lord Elles- ere's Collection at Bridgewater House is now lost; there are replicas

in Budapest, Sanssouci and elsewhere (see L. Burchard in the *San*
souci Catalogue, 1930, No. 102); the landscape of the Dudley collecti
now belongs to Count Seilern, London, Glück No. 38; th
landscape from Grosvenor House (Duke of Westminster) is, to judg
from reproductions, not by Rubens, but rather by Jan Brueghel.

165* The corresponding painting was acquired by the Nation
Gallery in 1913 (Glück No. 4). The same landscape motif was used b
Rubens in a larger painting, which is also in the National Galler
(Glück No. 5), cf. Neil MacLaren, *Rubens, The Château de Stee*
Gallery Books No. 11, p. 6.

166* 'Aeneas's Shipwreck' is now in the Kaiser-Friedrich Museu
in Berlin; it was engraved by Schelte à Bolswert (Glück No. 19
'The Phrygian Deluge', Vienna, Glück No. 12. The original sketc
of its 'counterpart' also engraved by Bolswert (Glück No. 1
belongs to the Stichting Nederl. Kunstbezit (lent to the Boyma
Museum). 'Pallas before Jupiter', Pitti Palace, Glück No. 18.

SELECTED LETTERS
OF RUBENS

SELECTED LETTERS OF RUBENS

PAINSTAKING scholar has estimated that Rubens wrote about 8,000
ters; of these about 230 are known. We mention this as a warning
ainst the temptation to draw hasty conclusions from the character of
ose letters that happen to be extant. All family papers have been lost
d are thought to have been destroyed by fire.

Rubens preferred to write in Italian, even when his correspondents
re English, French or Dutch. The letters printed below are translated
m that language unless the contrary is stated.

The standard edition of Rubens's letters, together with some letters
dressed to him or referring to him, was published, with a full commen-
y, by Ch. Ruelens and M. Rooses half a century ago (*Correspondance de
bens*, 6 vols., 1887–1909). Since then only inconsiderable additions have
en discovered. English translations of our letters IX–XIV,XVII–XVIII,
XVIII, XXXIV–XXXVI appeared in W. N. Sainsbury's *Original Unpub-
hed Papers illustrative of the Life of Sir P. P. Rubens*, 1589. These
nslations have been adapted for the present edition.

I. TO ANNIBALE CHIEPPIO

Valladolid, 24 May 1603

my most illustrious and honoured patron Annibale Chieppio,
cretary to His Most Serene Highness of Mantua.

OST ILLUSTRIOUS SIR,

Malign fate is too envious of my content and does not fail to vex
e with some displeasure, sometimes finding the means of doing an
ury where human foresight is of no avail and does not even suspect
sfortune, as now with the paintings, packed with all possible care
ith my own hands in the presence of the Duke, then examined in
icante at the instance of the excisemen and again found to be in
rfect condition; but now, when unpacked in the house of Signor
nnibale Iberti, they appear to have rotted to such a degree that I
ellnigh despair of being able to repair them; for the damage is not
erely on the surface, such as mould or stains which could be
moved, but the canvas itself (though protected by metal plates and
o layers of wax-cloth in addition to the wooden case) is completely
cayed and destroyed, owing perhaps to continuous rain for twenty-
e days, a thing incredible in Spain. The colours have faded and by
sorption of much humidity are swollen and protruding, so that in
any places there is no remedy but scraping them away with the

knife and laying them on afresh. Such is (and would it were not s
the damage, nor am I exaggerating the damage to enhance the labo
of restoration to which I shall not fail to devote myself in every w
since it has pleased His Serene Highness to make me custodian a
conductor of the works of others, without adding to them one stro
of my own brush. I speak thus, not because I resent it, but beca
Signor Iberti wishes me to do quickly many pictures with the aid
the Spanish painters, a desire which I will obey rather than appro
considering the shortness of time and the impediment of the spoi
pictures—in addition to the incredible insufficiency and carelessn
of those painters, and (which is very important) their manner
wholly different from mine (may God preserve me from resembli
them in any way). In short, *pergimus pugnantia secum cornibus adve*
componere.[1] Moreover, the affair is bound to come to light through
indiscretion of the assistants themselves, for they will either scorn
help and retouching or else they will usurp it and proclaim that i
all their own, for it will be easy enough for them to perceive that
pictures are for the service of the Duke of Lerma and intended fo
public gallery. This is of little import to me and I will gladly ma
them a present of the honour; but I am certain that (on account
the freshness of the colours alone) it will of necessity be discove
that the work has been done here either by them or by myself (wh
I shall never allow, having always made it a precept not to let
work be taken for that of any other man, however great), or b
combination of one and the other, and I shall remain dishonoured
a vile business unworthy of my fame, which is not unknown he
If this, however, had been the Duke's commission, I could, with m
honour to him and to myself, have given much greater satisfaction
the Duke of Lerma, who is not without knowledge of what is go
for it has been his great pleasure and custom to see so many fine wo
by Titian, Raphael and others, which have astounded me by th
number and quality, in the King's palace, in the Escurial and el
where, whereas by modern painters there is nothing here of wort
declare frankly that my only aim at this Court is the constant serv
of His Serene Highness, to which I have devoted myself since the v
first day I saw him. He may command me, he may dispose of m
this and every other matter, and he may be sure that I shall not ov
step his instructions in any way. Similarly, Signor Iberti has (
indirectly) the same authority over me, for I know well that it is o

[1] We go on to set together, face to face, things that fight one another.

s sincere desire to do better which makes him reject my opinion, and
e shall be obeyed. I do not write this to find fault with him, but
lely to show how loth I am to make myself known, unless it be in
atters worthy of myself and of my illustrious Master, who will, I do
ot doubt, through your good offices interpret these reflections of
ine aright.

> Your most humble servant,
> PIETRO PAULO RUEBENS

his letter and the next tell of Rubens's journey to Spain, in the ser-
ce of Vincenzo Gonzaga of Mantua. The Duke had decided to send
deputation with valuable presents to the Court of Philip III of Spain,
d Rubens was chosen to accompany this deputation as envoy extra-
dinary. He left Mantua on 5 March 1603 and the first letters to
nnibale Chieppio, the Duke's secretary, tell of setbacks on the journey
-misunderstandings at the embarkation, heavy expenses, delay in
orence and so forth. Valladolid was not reached until 13 May, three
eeks after the landing at Alicante. At Valladolid a new disappointment
as in store: the entire court was away on a hunting expedition. It was
cessary to wait for the return of the court, because the presents—a
ate-coach with six horses for the king, paintings and other works of
t for the Duke of Lerma, the all-powerful chancellor, and other gifts
r the remaining officials—were so valuable or bulky that it was
ipossible to think of setting out again in pursuit of the court. In this
tter Rubens tells of the damage to the pictures, which were copies
ter compositions of Raphael in Rome, painted by the Mantuan court
inter Pietro Facchietti. We learn also that Rubens had visited during
is journey the royal art collections in Madrid and in the Escurial. In
alladolid he was already at work on new commissions for the Duke of
erma.

II. TO ANNIBALE CHIEPPIO

Valladolid, (?) October 1603

o my most illustrious and honoured patron, Mr. Annibale Chieppio,
irst Secretary to His Most Serene Highness, in Mantua.

It would seem from your last letter that His Serene Highness persists
a the instructions given before my departure, that I should go to
rance, concerning which may I be allowed to give my opinion of
ay fitness for such a mission, if the Duke has, as I believe, no other
urpose in mind than those portraits. Now I am somewhat con-
ounded that he so urges my return in his many letters to Signor
erti as do you in your letter of 1 October, since the business is of no
rgency, and moreover, orders of that kind have always a thousand

inevitable consequences. I have in mind my visits to Spain and Rom
when the weeks foreseen for my stay were prolonged into so ma
months. Signor Iberti knows well what necessity compelled him a
me *ad jus usurpandum*.[1] You may be assured that the French are seco
to none in curiosity; principally because their King and Queen a
not averse to this art, as witness the great works now interrupt
inopia operariorum.[2] I have had detailed reports concerning the dilige
enquiries they have made for men of talent in Flanders, in Floren
and even, since they were misinformed, in Savoy and Spain. I shou
not reveal this information to you (I say this with the assurance
your pardon) if I had not chosen the Duke for my patron, so long
he will permit me to call Mantua my adopted country. Though the
portraits are hardly a worthy commission, I would have been conte
to look upon them as a prelude to higher things, were it not that wh
I consider the cost of the journey, I cannot imagine that the Duke I
nothing else in mind beyond giving Their Majesties some idea of n
It would, I think, be safer and quicker if M. de la Brosse or Sign
Carlo Rossi were to commission the portraits from some experienc
painter at the court who already has such a collection at his hou
Why should I waste time, journeys, expenses and salaries (whicl
should have to do in spite of His Highness's generosity) on wor
which I think ignoble and which any painter can execute to I
Highness's satisfaction? Nevertheless, as a good servant, I shall subn
myself entirely to my master's slightest desire, but I implore him
make use of my services, whether at home or abroad, in matters mc
in keeping with my gifts, and for the works I have already begun.
this favour I shall feel assured if you will be pleased to intercede w
the Duke my master in my behalf, and trusting to your benevolen
I kiss your hand with humble respect.

> Your most humble servant,
> PIETRO PAULO RUEBE

During July the presents were at last handed over and in two lette
one to the Duke of Mantua and the other to Chieppio, Rubens repo
proudly, how delighted the Duke of Lerma was with the pictures, wh
had been painted over by him. In the meantime Rubens had finish
for that connoisseur the 'Heraclitus' and the 'Democritus' (now
Madrid) and some portraits, including the fine equestrian portrait
the Duke. The visit to Spain was nearing its end. The Duke of Man
had ordered the painter to go to Paris and paint some of the beauties

[1] To assume authority.   [2] For lack of workmen.

e French court for the ducal portrait gallery. Rubens, however, dis-
ked a commission which he thought beneath his dignity and Chieppio,
ho enjoyed the painter's full confidence, succeeded in dissuading the
uke from that project. We know from other letters also that the Duke's
cretary and the court painter assisted one another frequently. The
Mantuan agent in Spain, however, a certain Annibale Iberti, whose
ame is mentioned repeatedly in the letters of that period, was less
elpful; in fact, he regarded the painter as a rival and tried to keep him
way from the high officials of the Court. Rubens returned to Mantua
a June 1604.

Towards the end of 1605 Rubens was in Rome, for the second time in
is life. The Duke and his family had gone away and the painter was not
eeded in Mantua. It is not quite clear what Rubens did when he first
rrived in Rome; he may have copied certain famous paintings for the
Duke. In any case he continued to draw his salary, though very irregu-
rly. On 29 July 1606 he asks for the outstanding arrears in order that
e may be able to 'continuare li miei studij senza procurar altronde
ell'utile che non mi mancarebbe in Roma'. The following letter shows
aat this was not an empty threat.

III. TO ANNIBALE CHIEPPIO

Rome, 2 December 1606

o my most illustrious and honoured patron, Mr. Annibale Chieppio,
ouncillor and First Secretary of His Most Serene Highness, in Mantua.

MY ILLUSTRIOUS SIR AND MOST HONOURED PATRON,

I am much embarrassed by His Highness's unexpected decision
oncerning my return to Mantua in so short a time, necessity having
orced me to accept certain commissions of importance, which will
ot allow me to leave Rome so soon. To tell you the true reason,
aving devoted the whole summer to the study of art, I found myself
nable to furnish becomingly and maintain my house in Rome with
vo servants, for a full year, on a mere 140 scudi, which is all I have
eceived from Mantua since my departure. And when the finest and
aost superb opportunity in the whole of Rome presented itself, I was
rompted also by ambition to avail myself of my good fortune. This
the high altar of the Chiesa Nuova of the priests of the Oratory,
alled S. Maria in Vallicella, today without doubt the most celebrated
nd most frequented church in Rome, being situated in the very
entre of the city and decorated in competition by the foremost
ainters of Italy, so that, although I have not yet begun the work, it

has aroused the interest of persons of such high standing that it woul
do me little honour to abandon an enterprise which I have secured s
gloriously against the pretensions of the first painters in Rome. More
over, I should thereby wrong my patrons, who would be most di
appointed, for when I alluded to my obligations at Mantua, the
offered to intercede for me with the Duke, should any such obstacle
arise, urging that it should be most welcome to His Highness that on
of his servants should do him such credit here in Rome. I know tha
Cardinal Borghese, among others, would not fail to speak in m
favour; but for the moment I feel I need turn to none but you, fo
you alone will suffice and are, in fact, better able to persuade the Duk
how great my interest is, both in the honour and in the benefits o
this work. I do not doubt that your efficacious intercession, togethe
with the benignity of the Duke, will not disappoint my hopes. Never
theless, if the immediate service of His Highness is so pressing that
does not admit delay, I shall always place it above all else in the worl
and will return thither at once, in which case I would entreat H
Highness to give me his word as a prince that next spring he wi
consent to my returning for three months to fulfil my obligation
towards these gentlemen in Rome. Let my return now be postpone
for three months or let me be granted permission to return in th
spring for three months to Rome: either would be the highest favou
I could hope to receive from His Highness and yourself. Such, i
short, is my request, which I recommend to you, with my usual tru
in your kindness. Forgive me if I dare to hope for too much; you
courtesy and benevolence encourage me to trouble you in th
manner. I can but hope that Divine Majesty will grant you suc
favours as you have shown me and in this spirit I humbly kiss you
hands.

Your very devoted servant,

PIETRO PAOLO RUBENI

The Duke granted the painter's request and on 13 December 1606 k
wrote to Chieppio that Rubens 'se ne stia a suo comodo per questi t
mesi, ma che per Pasqua di Resuretione infalibilimente egli se ne venga
Mantova'. Until then he might stay in Rome, for the Duke preferre
'to fall in with Rubens's wishes rather than to follow his own'. But
the beginning of the following June the painter was still in Rome, and i
the middle of that month he accompanied the Duke on a visit t
Genoa. After his return from Genoa in September 1607, Rubens on
more returned to Rome to finish the altar-painting for Santa Maria i
Vallicella.

IV. TO ANNIBALE CHIEPPIO

Rome, 2 February 1608

> my most illustrious and honoured patron, Mr. Annibale Chieppio,
cretary and Councillor of His Most Serene Highness, in Mantua.

OST ILLUSTRIOUS SIR,

You have always shown such affection for me and such interest in
y affairs that I feel it incumbent upon me to acquaint you with an
traordinary accident that has befallen me. I do so the more readily
I am convinced that my ill-fortune may be turned to the advantage
His Highness. My painting for the high altar of the Chiesa Nuova
s turned out extremely well and has given the greatest satisfaction,
t only to the Fathers, but also—and this is unusual—to all others
ho have seen it, but so wretched is the light above the altar that the
ures can barely be discerned, nor is it possible to appreciate the
quisite colouring and the delicacy of the heads and draperies,
odelled from nature with great care, which, as all agree, have turned
t very well. Seeing now this good work thrown away and being
able to reap the honour due to my labours if the picture cannot be
n, it is my intention not to unveil it, but to remove it from here and
d a better light for it, notwithstanding that the price has been fixed
800 scudi. But the Fathers will not consent to its removal unless I
dertake to make a copy for the same altar by my own hand, either
stone or on some other material which will absorb the colours, so
at they will not receive lustre from that perverse light, and I con-
er it ill-becoming to my honour that there should be in Rome two
e paintings by my hand. Remembering that His Highness and the
uchess have often said that they would like a picture by me for
eir gallery, I confess that it would delight me if Their Highnesses,
ce they wish to do me this honour, were to make use of this work,
hich is beyond doubt the best picture I have painted. I shall not
sily bring myself a second time to employ all my skill in such an
ort; and if I did, I might not succeed so well. Moreover, there
uld be no place more suitable for this work than a gallery animated
the competition and jealousy of so many able men.

As regards the price (though it was fixed and agreed at 800 scudi),
e valuation made here in Rome shall be no obstacle and I shall leave
to the discretion of His Highness, who may pay me at his con-
nience. I would merely ask now for 100 or 200 scudi, which I shall
ed while I am at work on the copy. This can be dispatched very

soon, at the most in a couple of months, as I do not need to study t
subject again, so that I shall be back in Mantua before Easter witho
fail. If you will be pleased to favour me by putting my propos
before the Duke, you will, though my obligations towards you ca
not be further increased, renew them all in one. I beg that you w
inform me of His Highness's decision as soon as possible, for I sh
keep the painting covered and leave the matter in abeyance un
then. Should His Highness accept the offer, I shall take down t
picture immediately and exhibit it publicly in the same church ir
better light, to my own satisfaction and to that of Rome. The co
does not demand so much care and finish, for it will never be possi
fully to enjoy it. But that you may be informed of everything, y
must know that the composition is very fine indeed owing to t
number, the size and the variety of the figures—old men, youths a
richly clad women, and although they are all saints, they have
attributes or qualities that would not fit any other saint of the sa
rank. The picture is narrow and high, and not of such huge dimensic
that it will occupy much room. In short, I have no doubt that Th
Highnesses will be as completely satisfied as all those who have se
it here in Rome. Forgive me for troubling you with this bagatel
which, I know, does not compare in importance with your oth
affairs. I am, I admit, abusing your courtesy, but the matter is of su
moment to me that I beg you to make it your concern. Be assur
that none can appreciate your favours more than I do; I humbly k
your hands.

Your most devoted servant,

PIETRO PAULO RUBEN

The Duke did not accept the altar-piece and by Easter 1608 Rubens h
not yet returned to Mantua. It seems that relations between the a
loving Duke and the painter had cooled; besides, Rubens had found
Rome many new and distinguished patrons and friends.

In the autumn he had to leave very hurriedly. 'Salendo a cavallo'
the famous words he wrote in the margin of the letter in which he ask
for permission after he had decided to go; but his mother had die
week earlier.

V. TO ANNIBALE CHIEPPIO

Rome, 28 October 16

MY ILLUSTRIOUS SIR,

I feel it my duty, although the Duke has not yet returned
Mantua, to inform you that I am forced to commit almost an i
pertinence, namely, to add to so long an absence yet another, thou

hope a short one, in more distant countries. The reason is that, two
days ago, I received very bad news concerning the health of my
mother, who is seriously ill, which, in addition to the asthma which
afflicts her and the fact that she is 72 years old, makes it impossible to
hope for any other end than that which is the common lot of us all.
will be hard for me to go and see such a distressing spectacle and
equally hard to go without my illustrious master's leave. I have,
therefore, consulted Signor Magni and have agreed with him that it
would be best if I could meet His Highness on the way; during my
journey I shall hear of his movements and I will choose my route
accordingly. It is some comfort to me that, during His Highness's
stay at Antwerp, my kindred had already requested that I should
come home, and had fully informed Signor Filippo Persia and Signor
Annibale Iberti of the necessity of my presence. From these two
gentlemen they received assurances of His Highness's compassion in
such an event; but as the illness had not then reached such a desperate
stage, they did not make every effort, as they do now, to secure my
presence. I beseech you to inform the Duchess of my distress and to
forgive me if, in order to save time in meeting His Highness, I shall
not pass through Mantua, but take the direct route with all speed.
Concerning my return I will say only that every wish of my Serene
Master will be carried out and observed by me as an inviolable law in
all places and at all times. Here in Rome, my work on the three large
pictures in the Chiesa Nuova is finished, and if I am not mistaken,
they have turned out better than anything I have ever done. Nevertheless I leave Rome without unveiling them—the marble ornaments are
still unfinished—as I must not lose a moment. The work as such will
not thereby be affected, being painted in public, at the place for which
it is destined, and upon stone. I shall thus be able, when I return from
Flanders, to go straight to Mantua, which I am very glad to do for
countless reasons, particularly to put myself in person at your service.
I kiss your hands and pray I may continue to enjoy your favour and
that of my Most Serene Masters.

Mounting my horse).   Your most devoted servant,
                                PIETRO PAUOLO RUBENIO

VI. TO JAN FABER

Antwerp, 10 April 1609

To the very illustrious and excellent Mr. Jan Faber, herbalist to His
Holiness and lecturer at the 'Sapienza' and doctor of medicine, in
Rome.

MOST ILLUSTRIOUS AND EXCELLENT SIR,

Your kindness deserves a more regular correspondence on my pa
and I should be hard put to it to excuse my dilatoriness, if the tru
did not speak for itself. My brother's wedding embroiled us in su
manner that we could attend to nothing except serving the ladies,
as bridegroom and I as groomsman. If you should doubt that such
affair is so intricate, ask your Signor Martellano to tell you his e
perience and I am certain you will then agree that my excuse
legitimate. In short, my brother has been favoured by Venus, t
Cupids, Juno and all the gods, for his mistress is beautiful, wis
gracious, wealthy, and of good family, and alone would confute t
entire sixth Satire of Juvenal. It was indeed his lucky day when he la
aside the scholar's gown and dedicated himself to the service of Cupi
but I would not dare to follow his example because his choice was
good that I cannot hope to rival it, nor would I have him find
bride ugly when he compared her with his own. It is therefo
Martellano's turn to boast of serving the most beautiful lady in t
world and you may tell him to be quick and not to worry about
age; if he feels himself touched to the quick and spurred on by t
encouragement of Don Giovanni and Alfonso as well as by that of t
old man, let him make that good and fervent resolve, though I can s
only one danger, if he delays, namely that the old man may die, whi
might prejudice Martellano's hopes, for he it was who introduc
him into that house and won for him the esteem of the whole fami

I know from experience that such matters must be pursued
coolly, but with great fervour; my brother also, who had pined
vain for two years, changed his style after my arrival. To turn
my own affairs, I have still not made up my mind whether
remain in my native country or to return for always to Rome, wh
I have been offered very tempting conditions. But here, too, eve
effort is being made to retain me with all manner of complimen
The Archduke and the Most Serene Infanta have caused letters to
written urging me to remain in their service. Their offers are genero
enough, but I have little inclination to become once more a court
and would be content with Antwerp and its citizens, if I could
farewell to Rome. We may count upon peace, or rather a truce,
many years to come and our countries will thereby prosper aga
It is thought that peace will be declared throughout the Provinces
the course of next week.

Signor Schioppio has favoured me with letters from time to time, but of late I have had no news from him and believe he is engaged upon important business. I hear that Scaliger has joined the great majority and now awaits consecration and his entry *inter deos*[1] after the custom of Holland. When Schioppio heard from my brother that Scaliger had fallen ill, he replied with a line from Menander: *Vivus mortuusque vapulabit malus*,[2] with many threats to continue their controversy *etiam si ad genitorem imas erebi descenderit umbras*.[3]

I entreat you to recommend me to the favour of Signor Schioppio, when he returns to Rome, and to that of my colleague Signor Adamo, of Signor Enrico, and of the other good friends. My heart will often pine for Rome when I think of their pleasant conversation. But let us have patience: *non cuivis homini contingit*,[4] etc. . . . I kiss your hands with all my heart, and my brother also, who tells me he would serve you likewise if his Juno would give him leave. Vale.

> Your very affectionate servant,
> PIETRO PAUOLO RUBENS

VII. TO JAN FABER

> Antwerp, 14 January 1611

To my most honoured and illustrious Mr. Jan Faber, doctor of medicine and herbalist of His Holiness, in Rome.

MY ILLUSTRIOUS AND HONOURED SIR,

I have received from you two letters very different in tenor and contents: the first cheerful and entertaining, but the second, of 18 December, bringing the most cruel tidings of the death of our beloved Signor Adamo, which was a bitter blow for me. Indeed, our whole profession should wear deep mourning, for it will not easily bring forth his like again. In my opinion he had not his equal in small figures, in landscapes, and in many another subject. He has died in the prime of his studies, and *adhuc sua messis in herba erat.*[5] Many are the *res numquam vivendae*[6] that could have been expected of him. In short, *ostenderunt terris hunc tantum fata.*[7]

Nothing has ever afflicted me so cruelly as this news, and I shall never be a friend of those who have reduced him to so miserable an

---

[1] Among the gods.   [2] Alive or dead, the rascal shall be flogged.   [3] Even if he joins his begetter in the darkest depths of Erebus.   [4] It is not given to everyone.   [5] His wheat was still in the blade.   [6] Things that are never to be. [7] Fate has only shown him to the world.

end. I pray that God may forgive him the sin of indolence, by whic
he has deprived the world of many beautiful things, brought muc
misery upon himself, and, I believe, driven himself to despair, wherea
he could with his own hands have made his fortune and earned th
respect of all the world.

But enough of these laments. I regret that we have no relics of hir
in these parts and I should be glad if that plate of the Holy Virgin
Flight into Egypt, which you mention, could be acquired by som
compatriot who would bring it to this country. I fear, though, tha
the price of 300 scudi may prove an impediment. Nevertheless, if
cannot readily be sold in Italy, I would advise the widow to send it t
Flanders, where there are many who love the arts. And though
cannot ensure that she will obtain that price, I would gladly help he
to the best of my ability, for the sake of Signor Adamo's cherishe
memory. And now I kiss your hands with all my heart, also on beha
of my brother; he is greatly surprised about the delay of his letter t
Signor Schioppio, who might be reckoned among the antiquities c
Rome, if he were not known for a modern author. I would write als
of Don Alfonso and Martellano, if the matter did not seem out c
harmony with the tragic end of Signor Adamo, which merits a lett
to itself, *a qua exulent risus jocusque*.[1] Again I recommend myself t
your favour and pray Heaven to give you every happiness.

> Your most affectionate servant,
> PIETRO PAUOLO RUBEN

The widow would certainly be well advised to send that picture c
copper (the Flight into Egypt) direct to Antwerp, where there a
very many who are interested in small works. I shall make it m
special concern and shall serve her interests to the best of my abilit
If it should not be sold at once, we shall find some way of sending he
a handsome sum in advance, without prejudice to the sale.

Signor Adamo is Adam Elsheimer, the German painter, whom Ruber
had met in Rome. Jan Faber, Joseph Scaliger, and the vain, unprinciple
Scioppius were amongst Rubens's Roman friends. Faber was a physicia
and had attended the painter in July 1606; in return Rubens had painte
Faber's portrait.

In the first letter to Faber, Rubens tells of the preparations for the we
ding of his brother Philip, who had also been in Rome. Although h
adds 'io non ardirei di mettermi a seguirlo', he was married to Isabel
Brant six months later.

[1] From which laughter and joking be banished.

VIII. MEMORANDUM TO ARCHDUKE ALBERT

Antwerp, 19 March 1614

The Archduke, thanks to his excellent memory, will no doubt remember that two years ago he saw a coloured sketch which I had made in connexion with the triptych for the high altar of Ghent Cathedral, at the instance of the Most Reverend Bishop Maes (may he rest in glory), who had intended the work to be of the utmost magnificence; and it would no doubt have been the greatest and finest ever made in these countries, had not his death intervened. After that, although the Cathedral Chapter had given its full approval, everything remained in abeyance; and I, having been at great pains to make preparations for the whole work, both for the marble decorations and for the picture, received no recompense whatever. I had, indeed, nursed a hope that the present bishop would succeed to this undertaking as he did to the episcopal dignity, but I was sadly mistaken, for he has listened to bad advice and, without once looking at my designs, intends to decorate the altar in a most absurd fashion: there is to be no painting of any kind, but only a statue of St. Bavo in a marble enclosure, with some columns, and behind the altar a receptacle for the Holy Sacrament; but my design, too, allowed for such a repository together with a base above the altar to hold the relics, notwithstanding the painting. The bishop has entered into no agreement yet with the sculptors nor made any provision for the marble; but he has allocated to the project the same sum of money as his predecessor. That so fine an enterprise should be ruined gives me great displeasure, not so much for the sake of my personal interest, which matters little, but because the city will lose such an ornament—unless Your Serene Highness, for the great love he has always shown towards the art of painting and towards me in particular, and in order to enhance the beauty of that cathedral, from the funds of which the cost will be defrayed—unless, I say, Your Highness will think fit to inform the Bishop of Ghent that he has seen my design and found it good and that His Most Reverend Holiness would do well to follow it or at least to examine it before he makes another decision. I should be most obliged to Your Highness if you would support me with such a note to the Bishop of Ghent, assuring him that I have not any profit in view that may accrue to me from the work (indeed, I have at present more commissions for large works than ever before, and some of them I shall bring to Brussels for Your Highness to see, as they are on canvas), but only because I can affirm

upon my conscience as a Christian that this design for Ghent is th
finest thing I have done in all my life. For this reason I am so anxiou
to bring it to completion that this request to Your Highness is per
haps couched in more importunate terms than is proper. I pray ●
God that he may keep you in good health.

> Your Most Serene Highness's most devoted servant,
> PIETRO PAUOLO RUBEN

The Archduke caused a minute to be added in the margin of this lette
'Escrire une lettre au Révérendissime de Gand de la part de Son Altes
qu'il veuille faire venir le tableau d'aultel par ce suppliant peint à
réquisition et par charge de fut Révérendissime évesque Maes, afin de
faire parachever, et le prendre si avant qu'il puisse luy estre désireux ou
son église.' Yet Rubens still did not achieve his purpose. Two successo
of Bishop Maes had different projects which likewise were not carri
out. It was only under Antoine Triest (Bishop of Ghent from 162
that Rubens's painting was put up; it was of course somewhat differe
from his original sketch. See also Note 76 above.

The following letters are concerned with a bargain made by Rube
with Sir Dudley Carleton, English Ambassador at The Hague fro
1616 onwards, who had brought a large collection of sculptures ba
from Venice. Having to travel very frequently, Sir Dudley found I
collection rather cumbersome. Moreover, his taste had changed, as
informed Rubens quite frankly, 'da sculpturi a pittori ma principa
mente al Sig. Rubens'. He had already acquired a 'Wolf Hunt' b
Rubens soon after his arrival in The Hague, for which he had given tl
painter a string of pearls in exchange. When his agent in Antwer
George Gage, called on Rubens and suggested that Sir Dudley's scul
tures should be exchanged for pictures painted by Rubens, the latt
replied as follows.

IX. TO SIR DUDLEY CARLETON

Antwerp, 17 March 16:

To my most excellent and honoured patron, Sir Dudley Carleto
Ambassador of His Most Serene Majesty of Great Britain, in T
Hague.

MOST EXCELLENT SIR,

Having heard from many persons of the rarity of the antiques whi
Your Excellency has collected, I wished to come to see them,
company with your countryman, Mr. George Gage, but owing

...e departure of that gentleman for Spain, and in consequence of ...e pressure of my business, this idea had to be abandoned. Since, ...owever, Your Excellency told Mr. Gage that you were contemplat-...g some exchange with me of those marbles for pictures by my ...and, I, being fond of antiques, would readily be disposed to accept ...y reasonable offer, if Your Excellency is still of the same mind. I ...annot imagine a better method of reaching some agreement than by ...eans of the bearer of this letter, and should Your Excellency be ...illing to show him your collection and to permit him to make an ...ventory, so that he may give me an account of it, I for my part will ...end you a list of those works that I have in my house; or I would ...aint specially such pictures as would be more to Your Excellency's ...aste. In short, we could thus enter upon negotiations which would ...e of advantage to both parties. This gentleman is called Frans ...ieterssen de Grebbel, a native and inhabitant of Haarlem, an honour-...ble and respectable person, in whose honesty we may place the ...reatest confidence. With this I commend myself with all my heart ... Your Excellency's good graces, and pray Heaven to grant you ...appiness and content.

Your Excellency's most humble servant,
PETER PAUL RUBENS

...he Haarlem painter, Frans Pieter de Grebber (not Grebbel), whom ...ubens had probably met on a visit to that town in 1616, enjoyed the ...ainter's full confidence. The message which he brought back to Rubens ...as to the effect that Carleton valued his sculptures at 6,000 florins and ...as prepared to negotiate on this basis.

X. TO SIR DUDLEY CARLETON

Antwerp, 28 April 1618

...o my most excellent and honoured Sir Dudley Carleton, Ambassador ...f His Most Serene Majesty of Great Britain to the Confederate ...tates, in The Hague.

MOST EXCELLENT SIR,

I have learned from my agent that Your Excellency is disposed to ...nake some bargain with me about your antiques; and it has made me ...ope well of this business to see that you are in earnest, having named ...o him the exact price that they cost you: in regard to which, I will ...ely completely on your word as a gentleman. I am also willing to

Q

believe that you purchased them with perfect judgement and pru
dence; although persons of distinction are wont, in buying and selling
to have some disadvantage, because many tend to adjust the price o
the merchandise to the rank of the purchaser, a practice to which I ar
most averse. On the contrary, Your Excellency may be well assure
that I shall assign such prices to my pictures as if I were selling them
for ready money; and in this I entreat you to confide in the word o
an honest man. I have at present in my house a selection from the bes
of my pictures, particularly some which I have retained for my ow
enjoyment; and some that I bought back for a price higher than tha
at which I had sold them to others; but the whole shall be at the dis
posal of Your Excellency, for I like quick bargains, each party givin
and receiving his property at once; and, to speak the truth, I am s
overwhelmed with commissions, both public and private, that fo
some years to come I cannot dispose of myself: nevertheless, if, as
hope, we reach agreement, I will not fail to finish as soon as possibl
all those pictures which are not yet completed, though they ar
named in the list annexed hereto, and those that are finished I woul
send immediately to Your Excellency. In short, if Your Excellenc
will place the same reliance in me that I do in you, the matter i
settled. I am ready to give Your Excellency of the pictures by m
hand, enumerated below, to the value of six thousand florins, at th
price current in ready money, in exchange for all the antiques tha
are in Your Excellency's house, of which I have not yet seen the list
nor do I even know their number; but in everything I trust your word
Those pictures which are finished I will deliver immediately to You
Excellency, and for the others, which remain in my hands to b
finished, I will furnish good security to Your Excellency, and wil
finish them as soon as possible. Meanwhile I submit to whatever You
Excellency may conclude with Mr. Frans Pieterssen, my agent, an
will await your decision, recommending myself in all sincerity to th
good graces of Your Excellency, and with reverence I kiss you
hands.

Your Excellency's most affectionate servant,

PIETRO PAUOLO RUBEN

List of Pictures which are in my house

500 florins. A Prometheus bound on Mount Caucasus, with an eagl
pecking his liver. Original, by my hand, the eagle done by Snyders
6 × 8 f

oo florins. Daniel amidst many lions, which are taken from the life. Original, the whole by my hand. 8 × 12 ft.

oo florins. Leopards, taken from the life, with Satyrs and Nymphs. Original, by my hand, except a most beautiful landscape, done by the hand of a master skilful in that genre. 9 × 11 ft.

oo florins. A Leda, with the Swan and a Cupid. Original by my hand. 7 × 10 ft.

oo florins. Crucifixion, large as life, considered perhaps the best thing I have ever done. 12 × 6 ft.

,200 florins. A Last Judgement, begun by one of my pupils, after one which I did in a much larger size for the Most Serene Prince of Neuburg, who paid me three thousand five hundred florins cash for it; but this, not being finished, would be entirely retouched by my own hand, and by this means will pass as original. 13 × 9 ft.

oo florins. St. Peter taking the tribute money from the fish's mouth, with other fishermen around, taken from the life. Original by my hand. 7 × 8 ft.

oo florins. A Hunt of men on horseback and lions, commenced by one of my pupils, after one that I made for His Serenity of Bavaria, but all retouched by my hand. 8 × 11 ft.

o florins each. The Twelve Apostles, with a Christ, done by my pupils, from originals by my own hand, which the Duke of Lerma has, each having to be retouched by my hand throughout. 4 × 3 ft.

oo florins. A picture of an Achilles clothed as a woman, done by the best of my pupils, and the whole retouched by my hand, a most delightful picture, and full of many beautiful girls. 9 × 10 ft.

oo florins. A St. Sebastian, naked, by my hand. 7 × 4 ft

oo florins. A Susanna, done by one of my pupils, the whole, however, retouched by my hand. 7 × 5 ft

ome of the paintings in this list can be identified: the 'Prometheus' vas later in the museum at Oldenburg, the 'Twelve Apostles' are robably those in the Rospigliosi Collection in Rome, and the 'Achilles' perhaps that in Madrid and the 'St. Sebastian' that in Berlin. But Carleton wanted to accept only pictures by Rubens's own hand, which mounted in the list to a value of only 3,000 florins; for the remaining ,000 florins he wanted Brussels tapestries, which Rubens was to buy for im. But this uggestion was not to the painter's liking.

XI. TO SIR DUDLEY CARLETON

Antwerp, 12 May 16

MOST EXCELLENT SIR,

Your very agreeable letter of the 8th reached me yesterday evenin
I see from it that Your Excellency has in part changed his min
desiring pictures for only half the price of the marbles, and for th
other half tapestries or cash, because without the latter I cannot fir
the former. Your decision seems to be due to the small number of
pictures on my list, Your Excellency having chosen only the original
with which I am perfectly content; yet Your Excellency must n
think that the others are mere copies; they are so well retouched b
my hand that it would be hard to distinguish them from original
notwithstanding which they are assigned a much lower price. But
do not wish to persuade Your Excellency by fine words, for if yo
persisted in your previous intention I could still furnish real origina
up to the total price. But to be quite frank, I imagine that you do no
care to acquire such a quantity of pictures. My reason for preferrin
to give pictures in exchange is clear: for although they do not excee
their just price in my list, they have cost me nothing and you kno
that everyone is more prodigal of the fruits he grows in his garde
than of those he buys in the market. Moreover, I have spent this ye
some thousands of florins on my buildings, and I am unwilling for
caprice to exceed the bounds of good economy. In fact, I am not
prince, but one who *manducat laborem manuum suarum*.[1] By which
mean that, if Your Excellency wishes to have pictures to the fu
amount, be they originals or be they well-retouched copies (which a
well worth their price), I should treat you liberally, and am alwa
willing to refer the price to the arbitration of a competent person. I
however, you are resolved to have some tapestries, I will undertak
to give you tapestries to your satisfaction to the amount of tw
thousand florins, and four thousand florins in pictures: that is, thre
thousand florins for the originals chosen by you, namely, the 'Pre
metheus', the 'Daniel', the 'Leopards', the 'Leda', the 'St. Peter' an
the 'St. Sebastian', and for the remaining thousand florins you ma
choose from the other pictures on my list; or else I pledge myself
give you such originals by my hand for that sum as shall satisfy yo
If you have faith in me, you will take that 'Hunt' on the list, whic
I will make of equal quality to that which Your Excellency alread
has by my hand; the two should then match perfectly together, on

---

[1] Lives upon the labours of his hands.

owing tigers and European huntsmen, the other lions and Moorish
d Turkish cavaliers, a very singular composition. This I would give
: six hundred florins, which leaves four hundred florins, for which
would add the 'Susanna', similarly finished by my hand to your
isfaction, and lastly some other *galanteria* by my hand for the
ndred florins, to make up the four thousand florins. I hope you will
ree to this reasonable arrangement, *consideratis considerandis*,[1] namely,
at I accepted your first offer with frankness and that the present
ange has been made by Your Excellency and not by me. I could
tainly not increase my offer for many reasons. I beg you to inform
e as soon as your decision is taken. Should you be willing to accept
y offer, you may, if you wish, consign the marbles to Mr. Francis
eterssen before your departure for England, and I will do likewise
th those pictures that are ready; the remainder will follow in a few
ys. Regarding the tapestries, I could be of great assistance to your
end the merchant, owing to the great experience I have had of
ussels tapestries, from the many commissions which come to me
om Italy and other countries for such works. Besides I have made
ne perfectly magnificent cartoons at the request of some Genoese
ntlemen; these are now being worked and to say the truth, if one
shes to have exquisite things, they must be made for the purpose.
vill willingly take care that you shall be well served here, though I
fer entirely to your judgement. To conclude, I kiss Your Excel-
cy's hand with all my heart, and *in omnem eventum nostri negotii*,[2] I
ll always be your most devoted servant. Mr. Francesco Pieterssen
s not yet sent me the list of your marbles; and in case we strike
argain, I should also like to have that list of names which, as you
ite, you have found.

PIETRO PAUOLO RUBENS

bens tried to persuade Carleton to accept further pictures to the
ue of 1,000 florins and Carleton agreed to take the 'Susanna' and
e 'Lion Hunt', the latter as pendant to his 'Wolf Hunt'. To make up
1,000 guilders, Rubens was to paint a *galanteria*, which is subse-
ently named as the 'Casting out of Hagar' (later collection of the
ke of Westminster). For the balance of 2,000 florins, Rubens under-
ok to supply tapestries, but being unable to find anything suitable
paid the amount in cash. The next three letters tell of the final
gotiations.

[1] All things considered.   [2] Whatever the outcome of our business.

XII. TO SIR DUDLEY CARLETON

Antwerp, 20 May 16

To the most excellent Sir, my most honoured patron, Sir Dudle
Carleton, Ambassador of His Majesty of Great Britain, in The Hagu

MOST EXCELLENT SIR,

I have this day received news from my friend Pieterssen that Yo
Excellency has finally agreed to my last offer. *Quod utrique nostru
felix faustumque sit.*[1] I have already, during our negotiations, given t
finishing touch to most of the pictures selected by you, and broug
them to such perfection as I am able, so that I trust Your Excellen
will be entirely satisfied with them. The 'Prometheus', the 'Led
the 'Leopards,' the 'St. Sebastian', the 'St. Peter', and the 'Danie
are entirely finished: I am ready to consign them to any person who
you may send to me with the express order to receive them, thoug
they are not yet perfectly dry, but should remain on their stretchi
frames for some days yet, before they can be rolled up witho
danger. On Monday next I shall, with God's help, put hand to t
'Hunt' and the 'Susanna', also to that trifle for the hundred flori
animated more by the desire of honour than by that of profit, kno
ing the importance of preserving the good graces of a person of yo
eminence. Of the tapestries I can say little; I handed the list today
Mr. Lionello, wishing to negotiate with him, but he would not ev
talk to me, as Your Excellency gave him express orders not to con
with anybody. I am only too pleased that it should be so, since it w
save me much trouble, and moreover I am not of an interfering d
position. I also beg Your Excellency to inform me to whom I am
pay the two thousand florins in cash, which I shall not fail to do
sight of your order. I cannot, however, refrain from telling Yo
Excellency that at present there are but few good tapestries in t
workshop at Brussels. That which I consider least bad is a chamb
with the history of Camillus, four braccia and a half in height, eig
pieces, which make a total of 222 braccia, at 10 florins the bracci
A similar tapestry, that is, one depicting the same story, after the sar
cartoons, and of the same quality, made for Mr. Cabbauw, is at T
Hague, where Your Excellency may inspect it and decide accordi
to your judgement. To me, as I have said, it matters nothing; an
shall be well content if Mr. Lionello renders good service to Yo

---

[1] May your decision bring luck and good fortune to both of us.

xcellency, to whose good graces I recommend myself with sin-
city; and with humble reverence I kiss your hands, remaining
ways Your Excellency's most devoted servant.

PIETRO PAUOLO RUBENS

The pictures promised to Your Excellency shall, with God's help,
entirely finished in eight days without fail.

XIII. TO SIR DUDLEY CARLETON

Antwerp, 26 May 1618

OST EXCELLENT SIR,

I have given the exact measurements of all the pictures to that
an of Your Excellency's who came to take them by your order to
ve the frames made, although you had not mentioned this to me in
ur letter. For some time past my brush has not made a single stroke
hich was not in the service of Your Excellency, so that all the
ctures, the 'Hunt', the 'Susanna' and that left to my choice which
oses our account, as well as those of our first agreement, will be
ished by the 28th of this month, according to my promise. I hope
ou will be satisfied with my works, both on account of the variety
the subjects and for the love and desire which urge me to serve
our Excellency with so much zeal. I doubt not in the least that the
Iunt' and the 'Susanna' will appear amongst my originals. The third
painted on wood, about three feet and a half in length by two feet
d a half in height; the subject is altogether original, being neither
cred nor profane, although taken from Holy Writ: namely, Sarah
the act of reproving Hagar, who, pregnant, is leaving the house in
attitude of womanly dignity, with the assistance of the Patriarch
braham. I did not give the measure of this to your man because it
s already a small frame about it; it is done on wood, because small
ings succeed better on it than on canvas; and being so small in size,
will be easy to move. I have engaged, as is my custom, a man very
ilful in his genre, to finish the landscapes, solely to augment the
joyment of Your Excellency. For the rest, I assure you that I have
ot suffered a living soul to put hand to them; for I am anxious not
ly to abide punctiliously by my promise, but also to do more than
ave undertaken, because I wish to live and to die Your Excellency's
ost devoted servant. I cannot, however, state so precisely as I would
ish the exact day when all the pictures will be dry, and to speak the
uth, it appears to me better that they should go away together,

because also the first are newly retouched. If I have the advantage of
bright sunshine and if there is no wind to stir up the dust, which is
injurious to newly painted pictures, they will all be ready for rolling
up after five or six days of fine weather. For myself, I wish I could
consign them immediately, being ready to do everything that is
agreeable to you; but I should be vexed indeed if from too much
freshness they were to suffer damage on the way; this would certainly
cause vexation to Your Excellency, and to me as well. As regards the
tapestries, I can say little, because, to confess the truth, there are at
present no very fine things, and as I wrote, such are rarely to be
found unless they have been wrought on purpose; nevertheless, if the
history of Camillus does not please you, you might like that of Scipio
and Hannibal, of which your agent did not seem to think badly. To
speak frankly, in all these things the choice is arbitrary, their great
excellence not being in dispute; I will send Your Excellency all
measurements of my cartoons of the History of Decius Mus, the
Roman Consul who sacrificed himself for the victory of the Roman
people; but I shall have to write to Brussels to get the exact figures,
having given everything to the master there. Meanwhile, I recommend myself to the good offices of Your Excellency and with humble
affection I kiss your hands.

Your Excellency's most devoted servant,

PIETRO PAUOLO RUBENS

XIV. TO SIR DUDLEY CARLETON

Antwerp, 1 June 161

To my most excellent and honoured Sir Dudley Carleton, Ambassador
of His Majesty of Great Britain in The Hague.

MOST EXCELLENT SIR,

In compliance with Your Excellency's order, I have paid the two
thousand florins to Mr. Lionello; he has given me a receipt in his own
hand, and will report to Your Excellency. I have also delivered the
pictures[1] to Mr. Francis Pieterssen; all in good condition, and packed
with care, and I think Your Excellency will be perfectly satisfied. Mr.
Pieterssen was certainly astonished to see them all, finished *con amore*
and placed neatly in a row. In a word, in exchange for a chamber

[1] (In the margin): The 'Daniel', the 'Leopard', the 'Hunt', the 'St. Peter',
the 'Susanna', the 'St. Sebastian', the 'Prometheus', the 'Leda', 'Sarah and
Hagar'.

furnished with marbles, Your Excellency receives pictures sufficient to adorn an entire palace, quite apart from the tapestries. Touching the measurements, which proved somewhat smaller than you had expected, I did my best, taking the dimensions of the pieces with the measure current in these countries. Let me assure you that this trifling difference does not affect the price, since pictures are valued differently from tapestries; these are purchased by measure, but those for their excellence, subject, and number of figures. Nevertheless, the commission which you gave me is so gratifying and honourable that I consider it a very high favour and shall most willingly send my portrait to Your Excellency, provided you will in turn do me the honour to allow me to have in my house a memorial of your person, as it is only reasonable that I should place a much higher value on you than you on me. I have today received the marbles, but I have not yet been able to see them because Mr. Pieterssen was in such haste to depart. However, I hope they will be equal to my expectations. Mr. Lionello took upon himself the charge of procuring a free passage for your things, having received from me Your Excellency's letter for Brussels many days since. I did not find this a convenient route for my marbles, so that I had these delivered by other means; nevertheless, I remain with infinite obligations towards Your Excellency for all that has been done in my favour, with which I shall make an end, kissing with all my heart Your Excellency's hands, and desiring to be ever

Your most devoted servant,
PIETRO PAUOLO RUBENS

Both parties were satisfied with the bargain and Sir Dudley wrote to a friend: 'I am now saying to my Antiquities *veteres migrate coloni*, having past a contract with Rubens the famous painter of Antwerp for a sute of tapistrie and a certaine number of his pictures, which is a goode bargaine for us both, onely I am blamed by the painters of this country (Holland) who made ydoles of these heads and statuas, but all others commend the change.'

The 'perfectly magnificent cartoons', which had been commissioned from Rubens by Genoese noblemen, were the designs for the 'Decius Mus' cycle, which was woven in Brussels. The cartoons have disappeared; the corresponding paintings, in which Van Dyck also collaborated, are now in the Liechtenstein Gallery in Vienna.

Pieterssen, to whom Rubens refers repeatedly, was his friend Frans Pietersz Grebber, who arranged the transport of the sculptures and paintings. He seems to have been not only a painter, but also an art dealer and commission agent. 'Lionello' was Carleton's agent Lionel Wake, who was then in the southern Netherlands. The 'skilful man' engaged to finish the landscape in the little panel of 'Hagar' was Jan Wildens.

XV. TO PIETER VAN VEEN

Antwerp, 4 January 1619

To Mr. Pieter van Veen, advocate in The Hague.

VERY ILLUSTRIOUS AND HONOURED SIR,

You may think it strange to hear from me after so long a silence. But I assure you I am not one of those who feed on empty compliments and I take it that all men of worth act likewise. So far we have exchanged only greetings sent or returned through friends passing to and fro, but today I am in need of your advice. I would know what steps I must take to obtain a Privilege from the United Provinces authorizing me to publish a number of copper engravings made in my house, in such a way that their imitation in these Provinces is prohibited. Many have advised me to make such an application and, lacking all experience in these matters, I would gladly have your opinion whether you think such a Privilege necessary and whether it is likely to be respected in so free a country. I would also know how to proceed and whether the application would encounter great difficulties. If you grant me the favour of your opinion I am resolved to follow your wise counsel. Finally I kiss your hands with all my heart and pray to God to grant you a very happy New Year.

Your very affectionate servant,
PIETRO PAUOLO RUBENS

XVI. TO PIETER VAN VEEN

Antwerp, 23 January 161

To the honourable, prudent and discreet Mr. Pieter van Veen, advocat in The Hague.

MOST ILLUSTRIOUS SIR,

I am greatly obliged by your courteous offer to assist me in m petition for the privileges. To tell the truth, you risk being taken a your word, for I am one of those who abuse courtesy by accepting a that I am offered. Not all the prints are quite ready, but I think th ne would be saved if negotiations could be begun at once; the bjects could be laid down in writing and I would undertake to bmit, when the time comes, the prints as specified in advance. I all not fail to refund whatever sums you may pay, give, or promise, Secretary Arsens or to others in this matter. The subjects will not use any difficulty; they are in no way political, but straightforward, ithout ambiguity or mystery, as you will see from the list appended ereto.

To be frank, I should like to include some which will not be ready ntil later, to avoid the trouble of new formalities later, and therefore think it expedient to lay down everything in writing without sub- itting copies until the affair is settled—always assuming that this rocedure is practicable, for I do not wish to appear impertinent— nce the subjects are all well known and there cannot be the least ruple concerning them. I will gladly pledge myself to send the pies in good time without fail; in fact, most of them are ready and n be published very soon. I should have preferred an engraver of reater experience in following the prototypes, but I considered it e lesser evil to have them done in my presence by a well-intentioned oung man rather than by any of those great men who work accord- g to their own caprice. I await your reply concerning this at your nvenience. If our aim cannot be reached in this way, we will wait ntil we are ready to do as should be done. In the meantime I recom- end myself to your favour with all my heart and pray that Heaven ay grant you good health and every satisfaction, *publice et privatim*. kiss also with great affection the hands of Signor de Gheyn.

> Your very affectionate servant,
> PIETRO PAUOLO RUBENS

A battle between Greeks and Amazons.
Lot and his family leaving Sodom.
St. Francis receiving the stigmata.
A Nativity of Christ.
A Madonna and Child, with the little St. John and St. Joseph.
A Madonna and Child with St. Joseph returning from Egypt.
Some portraits of men.
An Adoration of the Magi.
A Nativity of Christ.
A Deposition from the Cross.
Elevation of the Cross.

Martyrdom of St. Lawrence.

The Fall of Lucifer.

A Scene from the life of St. Ignatius of Loyola.

Another of Xavier.

A Susanna.

A St. Peter extracting the piece of money from the fish's mouth.

A fable of Leander.

These two letters and Letter XIX below are concerned with the painter's negotiations to secure the copyright of his engravings. The publication of unauthorized copies inflicted not only financial damage upon the head of an engraving workshop (and this was Rubens's status in these negotiations), but did less than justice to the originals, because the master was unable to supervise the reproduction by unknown engravers. The Dutch States-General were not very helpful when Rubens applied for such a privilege; but it must be borne in mind that the two countries were not at peace; a truce, it is true, had been arranged, but strictly speaking, there existed a state of war. An earlier application by Rubens had already been refused in 1614; and therefore he turned now for support to the brother of his teacher, Otto van Veen. Pieter van Veen was a lawyer at the Dutch court and syndicus of the cities of Leyden and The Hague, but in spite of his efforts, Rubens's application was at first refused, and a privilege for seven years was granted only after Sir Dudley Carleton had intervened on the painter's behalf. In the meantime, Rubens had obtained similar protection in France and in the southern Netherlands. The engraver principally employed by Rubens during those years was Lucas Vorsterman, but two years later the two artists fell out (see also p. 9) and some of the subjects mentioned in the letter of 23 January 1619 were either completed later by other engravers (the portraits of men and the 'Elevation of the Cross') or were never engraved ('Hero and Leander').

From the French

XVII. TO WILLIAM TRUMBULL

Antwerp, 26 January 162]

SIR,

The picture that I have painted for my Lord Ambassador Carleton is quite ready and securely packed in a wooden case, in which it can very well be sent to England. I will readily entrust it to the care of Mr. Corham, if he will call or send his porter for it. But as to gainsaying what I have said to our Judges, to wit that the picture is not worth as much, that is not my way of acting. If it had been painted entirely by my own hand, it would indeed be well worth twice a

ich. I have not, however, gone over it lightly, but have touched
d retouched it everywhere. I will conform exactly to all I have said
d although the picture is of that value, the obligation that I am
der to my Lord Ambassador will make me content with whatever
ompense His Excellency may think good and just, without any
nment on my part. I do not know what more to say nor how to
mit myself more entirely to the good pleasure of this gentleman,
om I esteem more than any could believe. The picture by Bassano,
ich I had in exchange, is so spoilt that, such as it is, I will sell it for
een écus to anyone who cares to buy it.

From the French

XVIII. TO WILLIAM TRUMBULL

Antwerp, 13 September 1621

R,

am well content that the picture painted for my Lord Ambassador
rleton be returned to me and that I should paint another hunting
ce less terrible than that of the Lions, making fair abatement, of
urse, for the amount already paid; the new picture to be entirely
my own hand without admixture of the work of others, which I
ll undertake on the word of a gentleman. I regret that there should
ve been any dissatisfaction on the part of Monsieur Carleton, but
would never give me to understand clearly, though I often en-
ated him to do so, whether this picture was to be a complete
ginal or merely one touched by my own hand. I wish for an
portunity to put him again in good humour with me, although it
uld cost me some trouble to oblige him. I am glad that this picture
ll be hung in so eminent a place as the gallery of H.R.H. the
nce of Wales, and I will do all in my power to make it superior
design to that of Holofernes, which I executed in my youth. I have
most finished a large picture entirely by my own hand, and in my
inion one of my best, representing a Hunt of Lions, the figures as
ge as life. It is an order of My Lord Ambassador Digby, to be
esented, I understand, to the Marquis of Hamilton. But as you truly
y, such subjects are more agreeable and have more vehemence in a
ge than in a small picture. I should welcome it if the picture for the
llery of H.R.H. the Prince of Wales were of larger proportions,
cause the size of the picture gives us painters more courage to

represent our ideas with the utmost freedom and semblance
reality, but I am ready under any circumstances to employ mysel
your service, and recommending myself humbly to your favour, c
myself at all times to your notice.

As to His Majesty and H.R.H. the Prince of Wales, I shall alw
be pleased to receive the honour of their commands, and with res
to the Hall in the New Palace, I confess myself to be, by nat
instinct, better fitted to execute works of large size rather than l
curiosities. Each one according to his gifts: my endowments are s
that I have never lacked courage to undertake any design, howe
vast in size or diversified in subject.

Sir, Your very humble servant,
PETER PAUL RUB

Both letters are only copies, perhaps partly shortened, made by Will
Trumbull and sent to Sir Dudley Carleton, whom he assisted with
purchase of paintings; Trumbull was then living in Brussels. His '
leagues' were Tobias Matthew, George Gage and Lionel Wake, v
have been mentioned earlier on. Sir Dudley had once again engage
an exchange of pictures, and had given Rubens a night piece by Bass
in return for a replica of a 'Hunt' which the master had painted for
Duke of Bavaria. This second hunting piece was not intended for Ca
ton's own collection, but for the gallery of the Prince of Wales, l
Charles I. This time neither party was satisfied: Rubens regarded
Bassano as worthless, while Lord Danvers, the Prince of Wales's age
complained in his letters to Carleton that Rubens had supplied a paint
'scarse touched by his own hand'. 'The Prince', he added, 'will
admitt the picture into his galerye.' Rubens agreed to take the pict
back and to supply a better one, of the dimensions and quality of
'Lion Hunt', which he was painting for the Duke of Hamilton. '
'Holofernes', a youthful work in the collection of Charles I,
disappeared and is known only from an engraving by C. Galle. I
interesting that Rubens wished to undertake the decoration of White
Palace; he was given this commission, but not until his visit to Lon
in 1629.

XIX. TO PIETER VAN VEEN

Antwerp, 19 June 1

To the honourable, learned and discreet Mr. Pieter van Veen, P
sionary in The Hague.

ST ILLUSTRIOUS AND HONOURED SIR,

have been prevented from answering before by my travels and
er impediments. From your kind letter of 12 May I can perceive
ch of my prints are not yet in your hands. I regret that they are
ew, because, owing to the derangement of my engraver, I have
le none for some years, but the few that there are I will send you
h pleasure. They are: a 'St. Francis receiving the stigmata', rather
ghly engraved because it was the first attempt; 'the Virgin and
ld returning from Egypt'; a small 'Madonna kissing the Child',
ch seems to me good; a 'Susanna', which I reckon among the best;
rge picture of the 'Fall of Lucifer', which has not come out badly;
'Lot with his wife and daughters leaving Sodom', which was
raved when he first became my assistant. I have also a 'Battle of
Amazons' in six sheets, which requires only a few more days'
k, but I cannot wrest it from the man's hands, though it was paid
three years ago. I should like to send it to you with the others, but
unlikely that I shall be able to do it so soon.

have published also an architectural book on the finest palaces in
ova, about 70 folios including the plans, but do not know whether
will interest you. I should be glad to know how you are minded
ut this and beg you to give orders to some boatman or messenger
know well to collect these things by hand, as it would cost too
ch to send them by courier.

am pleased to hear that you have discovered that secret of drawing
copper upon a white ground which Adam Elsheimer employed—
ess indeed your method is still better. He did as follows: when he
hed to etch on copper by means of acid, he covered the plate with
nd of white paste; when the needle then reached the copper, which
y nature somewhat reddish, it seemed to him as if he were drawing
h red chalk on white paper. I do not remember the ingredients of
paste, though he was good enough to tell me. I understand that
nor Otto Veen, your brother, has published anonymously a little
k on Universal Theory or some such thing. I should much like
ee this and if you would send it to me—as you have no doubt a
y—I shall cherish it and would give you my word as a man of
our that I will keep this favour of yours secret and not speak of it
ny living person. And lastly I kiss your hands with all my heart
pray Heaven to give you every happiness.

                                        Your affectionate servant,
                                        PIETRO PAUOLO RUBENS

This letter, written in Italian as were all Rubens's letters to the cultu
Dutchman, shows how the rupture with Lucas Vorsterman delayed
completion of the engravings. A privilege of the States-General was
effective until a proof had been deposited. The work on architectu
'Palazzi di Genova con le loro piante ed alzati da P. Paolo Rub
delineati', Antwerp 1622. The last paragraph shows once more
master's intimate relationship to Elsheimer, who had even confide
him his secret technique of etching.

The 'certi impedimenti de viaggi' mentioned in the beginning of
letter are an allusion to his visit to Paris in January and February 1
The decoration of the Luxembourg Gallery, which he discussed on
occasion with Maria de' Medici, is the subject of the following
letters.

From the French

XX. TO MONSIEUR DE VALAVEZ

Antwerp, 26 December 1

SIR,

I owe you a reply to two letters, as I received the first too late to
able to answer it by last week's courier, although I was stirred
great haste by your news (coming from the mouth of the Abbé
Saint-Ambroise) that the departure of the King and all the court fr
Paris is to take place in the month of February at the latest, with
being able to discern whether this means the beginning, the mid
or the end of that month. Now I have, by the latest ordinary, recei
a letter from M. de Saint-Ambroise himself, dated 19 December
which he inquires, on behalf of the Queen-Mother, as to the ex
date when I can deliver my works in Paris, without adding anyth
or mentioning the departure of the Court or pressing me in the le
on the contrary, he sends me the measurements of a picture wh
Cardinal Richelieu wishes me to paint for him, and which i
dentally I should have liked to be larger, as I am anxious to pl
such a patron. I have informed M. de Saint-Ambroise that, if
urgency is so great as he gave me to understand through you, I
finish everything, if God gives me life and health, by the end of r
January; but if the matter is not so pressing, it would be better to g
me more time so that the colours can dry at their ease and the pict
can be rolled and packed without danger of damage. Moreover
the roads are in a very bad state, we must allow at least fifteen d
for the coach to take the pictures from Brussels to Paris. Notw
standing this, I engage myself, with the grace of God, to arriv

is with all the pictures by the end of February at the very latest.
should it be necessary for me to be there before, I shall not fail in
duty. I beg him therefore to send me definite instructions as
ckly as possible, so that I shall know what arrangements to make,
I wish on no account to arrive in Paris after the departure of the
urt. I entreat you also to urge M. de Saint-Ambroise to let me
ow with certainty the date fixed for my arrival; and should any
v or different arrangements be made with regard to the King's
arture, I entreat you to inform me at once. Thus you will increase
obligations towards you—if that is still possible. Two days ago
ceived the parcel of books mentioned in your list. The books are
there, but I did not think that they would make such a large packet.
e letters of Cardinal d'Ossat are presented in a better form than I
e seen before, and those of Duplessis-Mornay are also very wel-
ne, for I do not remember having heard them mentioned here,
ugh he is well known and famous for his other works and his
troversy with Du Perron. In return I can give you nothing but my
nks, for I cannot find here anything worthy of your interest or
of your brother. I have not yet consigned to the coachman the
k by Father Scribanius, together with the *Ordonnances des armoi-*
, because I had hoped to find some other work pleasing to you;
I can find nothing except a Latin work published quite recently
M. Chifflet, which seems to me very good, entitled *De sacra
one Vesuntina aut sepultura Christi.*[1] I shall have it tomorrow and
send you all three by the first coach. I have also had a perfect
wing made of the mummy which I have, so that your brother can
y it; but I dare not send it with the books, because it would have
e folded to a very small size. Although it is only a single sheet of
er, I think it will be safer to roll it into one of my pictures; in this
it will also be better protected from damp. But I shall think this
once more, for it is ready and I do not want to keep him in
ense. In the meantime, Monsieur, I beg you to dispose of me
ely and if, by postponing my departure from here, there should
anger that I shall not find you in Paris, I shall not fail to make
e for that reason alone. You will oblige me by advising me in
d time. Recommending myself to your good favour, I assure you
I shall be, Monsieur, as long as I live,

Your very humble servant,
PIETRO PAUOLO RUBENS

On the sacred Winding-sheet at Besançon or the Entombment of Christ'.

This letter and the next give us a vivid picture of the painter's life ar
activities during his work on the Medici cycle. We can see how anxio
he is that everything should be completed in time and to the satisfactic
of his royal patroness. At the same time he is to paint a picture for Ca
dinal Richelieu, a commission he could hardly refuse. Monsieur
Valavez, to whom this letter is addressed, was a brother of the famo
Claude Fabri de Peiresc, a keen antiquarian, with whom Rubens mar
tained a brisk correspondence. On this occasion Rubens sends him t
drawing of a mummy which he owned (see also p. 224). Clau
Maugis, abbot of Saint-Ambroise, was the almoner of Queen Marie
Medici and responsible for the arrangements connected with t
decoration of the Medici Gallery.

From the French

XXI. TO MONSIEUR DE VALAVEZ

Antwerp, 10 January 16

SIR,

I am glad to know that you seem to have received the perpetu
motion in good condition, as the glass tube was not broken. I belie
your brother still has the directions, which I sent him a long time ag
for setting it in motion. But to be sure that nothing is wanting
shall in any case refresh his memory on the first occasion, which
should, indeed, have done already. But I beg you to believe that t
short time remaining to me to finish the paintings for the Quee
Mother in addition to my other work, makes me the busiest and t
most harassed man in the world. I thank you for your minute instru
tions, which are the same as those I received from M. de Sai
Ambroise, namely, that I must be in Paris with all my pictu
on 2, or 3, or, at the latest, on 4 February. Time is so sh
that I shall have to stop painting from today, otherwise the
would be no time for the colours to dry or for the journey fro
Antwerp to Paris. Nevertheless, that will be no great disadvanta
for in any case it would be necessary to retouch the whole work
the spot, I mean in the gallery itself, and whether more or less rema
to be done, it can be done all together; whether I do it at Antwerp
in Paris, is therefore a matter of indifference. Although I believe t
the departure of Madame will be delayed, since there is always so
delay in the affairs of the great, I do not wish to rely upon that,
prefer to be as punctual with my paintings as possible. What wor
me most is that the picture for the Cardinal cannot, in my opinion,

te finished, and if it were, would not be dry enough to bring with
. But though I would fain serve His Lordship, knowing well the
lue of his favour, I do not hold it of much account whether the work
completed at Antwerp or in Paris. In the end he will be, I hope, as
isfied with my diligence as the Queen-Mother and I shall find some
ject to his taste. I am greatly flattered to hear from you that
adame seems to wish to see my pictures before her departure and I
ll be happy to give her this satisfaction. Her husband, the Prince
Wales, is the greatest lover of painting I know among princes. He
s already something by my hand: through the English agent-
ident in Brussels he has so pressed me for my portrait that I could
t refuse it; for though I did not think it fitting to send my own
rtrait to a prince of his eminence, he finally overcame my modesty.
d if the projected alliance had come into being, I should have had to
ke a journey to England; but when that friendship faded away, the
ations between individuals also became cooler, for the fortunes of
great always draw everything else in their train. As for myself,
an assure you that there is no one more dispassionate in public
airs than I, except where my property and my person are con-
ned, by which I mean that—*ceteris paribus*—I look upon the whole
rld as my native country and I believe, too, that I should be wel-
me wherever I went. It is thought here that the Valtellina is lost and
t there is a very good understanding between the King of France
d the Pope. So much for that; but concerning Breda, the Marquis
inola is more and more determined to have the town, which is, I
assure you, so well besieged that no power can save it, unless he
recalled by the express command of his master, to obviate some
back elsewhere (which I do not believe). From the beginning he
never reckoned to take it by assault, but only by blockade. Great
parations are being made for the defence of the Provinces of
tois, Luxembourg, Hainault and Flanders, and God grant that I
y go and return in safety before there is some rupture. I have
thing to add this time except that I kiss your hands very humbly,
ommending myself to your favour with all my heart and assuring
u that I shall remain devoted to you as long as I live.

have consigned to Antoine Soris a little parcel of three books, or
her two, as the *Ordonnances des armoiries* consist only of one folio.
e other two are the *Prince Christiano-Politicus* by Father Scribanius
l *De Linteis Salvatoris* by M. Chifflet. You may be certain that you
l pay a high price for them, for Master Antoine has never charged

less for the carriage than two francs. I leave it to you to deduct
much as you think unreasonable, which is in my opinion more th
half. I am not sending the mummy, which I shall bring with t
pictures.

> Sir, Your very humble servant,
> PIETRO PAUOLO RUBE

XXII. TO PIERRE DUPUY

Antwerp, 15 July 16

MOST ILLUSTRIOUS AND HONOURED SIR,

You have done well to remind me of the inexorability of hum
fate, which does not yield to our desires, but as an agent of t
Supreme Power has no need to justify its actions to us. Its part
absolute dominion over all things, ours is obedience and service;
can do nothing else, it seems to me, than to make that obedience m
sincere and less painful by ready submission. But at this mome
such a course seems to me not easy in practice. You very wis
recommend me to put my faith in Time, which will, I hope, bri
about in me that which should be brought about by reason. But I
not pretend ever to achieve the impassibility of a stoic; nor d
think it wrong that a man should have the human qualities congru
to an object, or that all things of this world are equally insignifica
sed aliqua esse quae potius sint extra vitia quam cum virtutibus,[1] and th
things arouse in our souls a sentiment that is *citra reprehensionem.*[2]

I have, in truth, lost a very good companion, whom one co
love, nay, had to love, with good reason, she having none of
vices common to her sex, and being without morosity and femin
weakness, was all goodness and sincerity, and was loved for th
virtues while she lived, and mourned by all after her death. Such a
seems to me worthy of deep grief. I must, no doubt, hope that
daughter of Time, Oblivion, who cures all sorrows, will grant
relief. But I find it difficult to draw a distinction between the g
for her whom I have lost and the memory of one whom I m
revere and honour so long as I live. I believe that a journey would
the best means of distracting my mind from many things which n
of necessity renew my sorrow, *ut illa sola domo maeret vacua stratis*

[1] But there are some things that belong outside the vices rather than with
virtues.   [2] Beyond reproach.

ctis incubat[1] and the new impressions I should receive abroad would
:upy my imagination and would restrain me from relapsing into
ef. For the rest, it is true *quod mecum peregrinabor et me ipsum circum-
.m;*[2] but believe me, it would be a great comfort to me to see you
l your brother, and to serve you in any way that is to your taste
l in accord with my abilities. Your sympathy and consolation as
r friend, and the correspondence you have promised me while
de Valavez is absent, mean much to me and I shall be your most
mble servant so long as I live.

Your very humble servant,
PIETRO PAUOLO RUBENS

rre Dupuy was a friend of Peiresc and after M. de Valavez, Peiresc's
ther, had given up his residence in Paris in July 1626, he carried on
correspondence with Rubens. He and his brother Jacques had
embled a circle of scholars and writers known as L'Académie or
binet de M. Dupuy. The brothers kept Rubens informed of the news
Paris and he replied regularly every Thursday from Antwerp. The
er of 15 July is one of the first the painter wrote to Dupuy after
king his acquaintance and this fact may explain why he shows a
tain restraint and stoic composure in lamenting his wife's death. It
he more to be regretted that not one of Rubens's family letters has
en preserved.

XXIII. TO PIERRE DUPUY

Antwerp, 29 October 1626

OST ILLUSTRIOUS SIR,

I have read with great attention that poem on the Medici Gallery.
so far as the verses are concerned, it is not for me to judge its quality,
t for some person of that profession. The poet's vein appears to me
pious and fluent and his words and phrases aptly to render his
eaning. If I am not mistaken, the author must be a son or relative
a *maistre de requestes*, named Monsieur Marechot, whom I saw in
ris. I regret only that, while, in general, he has interpreted the
:tures correctly, in some cases he has not perceived their true sense,
for example, the 4th plate, of which he says: *Mariam commendat
cina Rheae*, instead of Florence, *quae tanquam nutrix ulnis excipit*

Like hers, who mourns alone in the empty house and lies down on the
ndoned couch.   [2] That I travel in my own company and am sufficient to
y self.

suam alumnam,[1] which error comes from the fact that the city, bei
depicted with a crown of turrets, resembles a Rhea or a Cybe
Hence that other error, almost the same, at the ninth plate, where
likewise mistakes the city of Lyons, where the marriage was cel
brated, for a Cybele, because it is turreted and has lions by the chario
But to return to the fourth plate, the figures he calls Cupids a
Zephyrs are the Horae of Fortune presiding over the birth of t
Queen, which can be recognized from their butterfly wings and t
fact that they are female. But that young man, who carries the corn
copia filled with sceptres and crowns, is the Queen's good genius, an
above is the ascendant of her horoscope, the Archer. These seem
me more proper and significant. But let this be said only between ou
selves, for our own delectation, and for the rest I am not interested
the least. Nevertheless, it would be possible to find many other thin
which should be noted, but in truth the poem is short, and not ever
thing can be said in a few words, but to say one thing for another do
not make for brevity.

At this moment I receive your very kind letter of the 22nd, t
gether with that of your brother. I rejoice to hear that he has be
restored to health, in which God, I pray, may long preserve him
shall not answer his letter separately, to spare him the trouble
honouring me with a long reply. There is very little news here, exce
that steady progress is being made, in sight of the Dutch camp,
the canal, while the army of Count Henri de Bergues covers t
workmen. That the encounter was not inconsiderable is manife
from the number of prisoners, among them persons of quality, fro
the standards captured, and from the many horses which are no
being sold everywhere, some of the finest having reached Brusse
The version of events published in Holland is completely distort
and Count Henri is said to have been beaten; but such are the tricks
a people's government to keep the populace in good humour. O
court, on the other hand, is, I assure you, very moderate, this bei
due to the Most Serene Infanta and to the prudence of the Marche
Spinola, who abhors such vanities; our commanders take good ca
not to send him false information, for fear lest he know the trut
which would discredit that commander for the future.

Reports from all sources confirm that Tilly and his army ha
advanced to the neighbourhood of Bremen and that he intends
spend the winter laying siege to the city. The Turk has broken wi

[1] Lucina commends Maria to Rhea, who holds her charge in her arms like
nurse.

he Emperor and joined Gabor Bethlen; but letters from Vienna sug-
est that the Hungarians have abandoned Gabor, wishing to remain
eutral and to avoid fighting, which would place him in grave peril;
hat setback, however, has led to the conclusion of some treaty, of
which no details are yet known. This Emperor, who will never arm
imself, must be greatly favoured by Fortune, for in his greatest
alamities, when he seems reduced to desperation, there appears some
eus ex machina who restores him to the top of the wheel. I confess I
ave pronounced him more than once to be a ruined prince, whose
iisplaced zeal would lead him into disaster. But I marvel that the
'urk should choose a moment such as this—when his kingdom is
iternally in so unsettled a condition and the Janissaries are in revolt,
vhen he suffers affront after affront from Persia and is ill served by all
nd obeyed by none—that at such a juncture he should break with
Christendom. That kingdom, it seems to me, is rapidly going to ruin
nd one blow would suffice to bring about its final collapse.

I thank you for the news from France and am glad to hear that the
ecoration of the Queen's palace proceeds apace. The Abbé de
aint-Ambroise must be very busy, for he no longer writes to me,
hough he has occasion to do so. Having naught else to add, I kiss your
ands and those of your brother with all my heart and recommend
iyself to your favour.

Your affectionate servant,
PIETRO PAUOLO RUBENS

ubens's emendations to Morisot's Latin poem in praise of the
Iedici Gallery were embodied in the printed edition of 1628 (*Porticus
Iedicæa*). The letter also shows his interest in the political events of the
'hirty Years' War, and his opinion of the Turks—and of the Dutch.

XXIV. TO NICOLAS CLAUDE FABRI DE PEIRESC

Madrid, 2 December 1628

IOST ILLUSTRIOUS AND HONOURED SIR,

It seems to me that I have not had any news from you for a
10usand years, our correspondence having been interrupted when I
t out for Spain. But the Infanta wished my journey to be so secret
nd immediate that she would not permit me to see any of my friends,
ot even the Spanish Ambassador or the Secretary for Flanders resi-
ent in Paris. Certainly it was hard for me to be compelled to pass

through a city which I love so much, without being able to wait upo
M. Dupuy or M. de Saint-Ambroise and my other friends an
patrons; indeed I can hardly find words to express my vexation an
sorrow. I cannot penetrate the secrets of princes, but it is true that th
King of Spain had ordered me to come post-haste, and the Infant
may well have thought that, on account of the many obligations
have towards the Queen Mother, I might have been delayed for som
days at the French Court.

Here I occupy myself with painting as I do everywhere. I hav
finished the equestrian portrait of His Majesty, to his great pleasur
and satisfaction. This Prince is obviously very fond of painting, and i
my opinion he is gifted with excellent qualities. I already know hir
personally, as my rooms are in the palace and he comes to see me near
ly every day. I have also done, for the Serene Infanta, my mistres
the heads of all the royal family with great fidelity, as they sat to m
at my convenience. The Infanta has given me leave to return by way c
Italy and I therefore hope, if it please God, to take advantage of th
passage of the Queen of Hungary from Barcelona to Genoa, which
expected to take place at the end of next March. It is possible that
can turn aside from the royal route to make a peregrination int
Provence, to enjoy for a few days the much-desired company of m
Signor Peiresc in his own house, which must be a compendium of a
the curiosities in the world. Straying a little from my path, I saw th
siege of La Rochelle, which seemed to me a spectacle worthy of ever
admiration, and I rejoice with you and with all France, nay, with th
whole of Christianity, for the success of that most glorious enterprise
This being all for today, I kiss your hands and those of Signor d
Valavez from the bottom of my heart and beg you to keep me i
your favour.   Your most devoted servant,
                          PIETRO PAUOLO RUBEN

I hope you have now received my portrait, which I consigned t
the brother-in-law of M. Picquery, as you had requested, many day
before my departure from Antwerp. I have met no antiquaries i
this country, nor have I seen any medals or cameos of any sort. Per
haps I have been too busy; therefore I shall inquire with greate
diligence and keep you informed, though I believe this diligence wi
be in vain.

For Peiresc, who lived at Aix-en-Provence, see pp. 222, 238. Ruben
went on a secret mission to the Spanish court to further the peac

gotiations between England and Spain in which he had already taken
active part on the instructions of his patroness, the Infanta Isabella.
t politics did not occupy all his time in Madrid and he soon began
paint. The equestrian portrait of Philip I V was destroyed by fire (copy
Florence, see pp. 138–40); the family portrait has disappeared.
oreover, he took with him from Antwerp eight pictures, which he
d to the King. The portrait of himself, which he consigned to M.
cquery, the husband of Elisabeth Fourment, was not a self-portrait,
t a work by Van Dyck.

On the same day, Rubens wrote a similar letter to Pierre Dupuy (see
Burchard in *Kunstchronik* 54, 1919, 512).

XXV. TO PIERRE DUPUY

London, 8 August 1629

OST ILLUSTRIOUS SIR,

To see so many lands and courts in so short a span of time would
ve been more fitting and useful to me in my youth than it is at my
esent age. Then the body would have had greater vigour to with-
nd the discomforts of travel and the mind could have fitted itself,
the experience, and knowledge of these diverse nations, for greater
ings in the future. But now I am consuming my declining bodily
ength and have no time left to reap the fruits of so many exertions,
i ut, *cum hoc resciero, doctior moriar*.[1] Nevertheless I feel consoled and
warded by the mere enjoyment of the beautiful spectacles I have
n on my peregrinations, amongst them this island, which merits,
my mind, the interest of every gentleman, not only for the amenity
the landscape, the beauty of the nation, and the splendour and
illiance of the material culture, which appears to me extraordinary,
ing that of a wealthy people luxuriating in the deepest peace, but
o for the incredible number of excellent paintings, statues and
cient inscriptions which are to be found at this Court. I will not
ention the Arundel marbles, of which you gave me the first news,
d I confess I have seen nothing in the world so remarkable by reason
their antiquity *quam foedus ictum inter Smyrnenses et Magnesios cum
obus earundem civitatum decretis, et victoriis Publii Citharoedi*.[2] I regret
at Selden, to whom we owe their publication and the commentary,
uld have abandoned the pursuit of learning and *immiscet se turbis*

---

[1] Except that, having seen this, I shall die a wiser man.   [2] Than the alliance
tween the citizens of Smyrna and of Magnesia, with the decrees of both cities
d the victories of Publius Citharoedus.

politicis,[1] which are, in my opinion, so remote from his noble gen
and precise scholarship that he must not blame Fortune if, for popu
contumacy, *regis indignitatis iram provocando*,[2] she has cast him i
prison with other members of Parliament. I have a mind to stay h
for some little time, together with the desire to breathe for a while
air of my own house, which is truly in need of my presence becau
on my return from Spain, I stayed only three or four days in Antwe
I have received here a letter from M. Peiresc, of 2 June, w
complains of this my diversion from my plan of revisiting Italy a
his Provence on my return journey from Spain, which I woul
could do, were it only to enjoy his conversation for a few days. I b
you to forward to him the enclosed letter, the first after a silence
almost a whole year. Thus I conclude and kiss your hands and th
of your brother with all affection, recommending myself to your go
favour from the bottom of my heart.

Your most affectionate servant,
PIETRO PAUOLO RUBE

XXVI. TO NICOLAS CLAUDE FABRI DE PEIRESC

London, 9 August 16

MY MOST HONOURED SIR,

If I were permitted to order my affairs in my own way and *spo
mea componere curas*,[3] I should have been with you before or should
with you at this moment; but some genius, I know not whether go
or evil, has crossed my plans and drawn me along very different pat

It is true that I derive some pleasure from these my peregrinatio
seeing so many diverse lands and *multorum hominum mores et urbe
Certainly in this island I have not found the rudeness which a clim
so remote from the delights of Italy might lead one to expect. N
have I ever seen in one place so many excellent pictures by masters
the first rank as in the collections of the King and of the late Du
of Buckingham. The Earl of Arundel, moreover, has an infinity
Greek and Roman statues, which you will have seen, since they w
published by John Selden, with a very learned commentary worthy
the resourceful and polished genius of this scholar, whose treatise
diis Syris has, as you will have seen, been reprinted *recensitum iter*

---

[1] Has plunged into the turmoil of politics.   [2] Provoking the king's furi
indignation.   [3] To order my sorrows at my own will.   [4] The customs a
cities of many peoples.

auctius.[1] If only he had been content to remain within the limits of the contemplative life! But he has now become implicated in political movements and has been arrested with some others accused of conspiracy against the King and the last Parliament. Then there are here the Cavalier Cotton, a great antiquary and eminent in various fields of learning, and Secretary Boswell, both, no doubt, well known to you and, I expect, your correspondents, as are all men of distinction everywhere. The latter told me a few days ago that he had the supplement of certain lacunae in the *Anecdota* of Procopius, which concern the debaucheries of Theodora and were omitted by Allemannus in his edition, probably out of modesty and pudicity; they have since been found in the Vatican manuscript and transcribed, and he has promised to let me see them. There is little I can tell you about Spain; there is no lack there of learned men but they are devotees *plerumque severioris Minervae, et more theologorum admodum superciliosi*.[2] I have seen the library of San Lorenzo, yet have done no more than see it. But a certain cavalier, Don Francisco Bravo, has come to Flanders, who has caused a great number of manuscripts to be copied; he told me in Madrid that he had discovered over sixty books, hitherto unknown, of the ancient Fathers. I believe he has something *sub praelo in officina Plantiniana*.[3] I have not made the acquaintance of the celebrated philosopher Drebbel, as he lives in the country, at some distance from London; I have met him in the street, though, and exchanged three or four words with him. He is one of those who, as Machiavelli says, appear greater from afar than when they are near, for I am told that he has produced nothing for many years except that optical cannon which, standing upright, enlarges beyond measure the objects placed beneath it, and that perpetual motion in the glass ring which is a mere *bagatelle*. He has also invented some machines and devices for the relief of La Rochelle, but they were a complete failure. However, I will not rely on popular rumour to the prejudice of so illustrious a man, but shall visit him at his house and get to know him, if possible. I do not remember having ever seen a physiognomy so extraordinary as his, *et nescio quod admirandum in homine pannoso elucet neque enim assa lacerna, ut solet in re tenui, deridiculum facit*.[4]

I hope, by the grace of my superiors, to return very soon to my home; I stayed there for four short days on my return from Madrid

---

[1] Revised and enlarged.   [2] Mostly of the stern Minerva and are very haughty is the manner of theologians.   [3] In the press at Plantin's.   [4] Something wonderful shines from the ragged fellow, and not even his thick cloak makes him ridiculous as it would a lesser person.

and my presence is sorely needed after so long an absence. But I have
not lost all hope of keeping my vow to undertake a journey to Italy
Believe me, I long for it more from day to day and I protest that, i
fate denies it me, I shall not die contented. You may rest assured tha
on my way thither and on my return, but more probably on my wa
thither, I shall wait upon you in your blessed Provence and I sha
count this as the greatest happiness of my life.

If I knew that my portrait were still in Antwerp, I would have i
kept there so that I might open the case and see whether it has no
suffered from being kept so long enclosed without air, and whether
the colours, as often happens if they are fresh, have turned yellow, s
that the picture will not be what it was. There is, however, on
remedy, if this happens—to expose the picture several times to th
sun, which will absorb the redundant oil that has caused this change
And if, from time to time, the picture tends to turn brown, it mus
again be exposed to the rays of the sun, which are the only antidot
against that cardiac disease. This is all for today. I kiss your hands wit
great affection and recommend myself most sincerely to your goo
favour and to that of Signor Valavez, being always at your service an
remaining for ever,

Your most humble and affectionate servant,

PIETRO PAUOLO RUBEN

The sudden mission to London was also occasioned by the peac
negotiations between England and Spain, which seemed to drag o
endlessly. At the same time, peace with neighbouring Holland, whic
Rubens desired so keenly, was not even in sight!

John Selden (1584–1654) published a description of the Earl o
Arundel's famous collection of antiques in 1629. Rubens had alread
painted a portrait of this Maecenas with his family in 1620 (Munich
and now he painted another portrait of him (Boston, Isabella Stewar
Gardner Museum). Selden's treatise De diis Syris syntagmata duo wa
reprinted in Holland in 1627. Robert Bruce Cotton (1570–1631) was
well-known bibliophile. Sir William Boswell was at that time secretar
to Lord Carlisle, whom Rubens had met in Spain. Cornelis Drebbe
painter, adventurer and engineer, had invented various strang
machines, for instance a so-called 'perpetual motion', in which Ruber
had been very interested a few years earlier and which he mentior
several times in his letters to Peiresc. Drebbel is also said to have bui
the first submarine. Rubens's references to him are now somewha
ironical, probably with good reason.

XXVII. TO NICOLAS CLAUDE FABRI DE PEIRESC

Antwerp, 18 December 1634

ONOURED AND MOST ILLUSTRIOUS SIR,

Your very welcome letter of the 24th ultimo, which was delivered
me by my brother-in-law, M. Picquery, was such an unexpected
vour that I felt first amazement and incredible joy and then extreme
ipatience to read it, seeing that you continue with even greater
rvour and curiosity than in the past to investigate the mysteries of
oman antiquities. There was no need to excuse your silence, for I
d already imagined that the essential cause was the unwelcome
elter given to certain foreigners who had retired into this country;
d truly, considering the suspicion and malice which poison our
ne, and the high mission I had in this affair, I never thought that
ou could act otherwise. I have for the last three years lived here in
ace and content, having renounced every employment outside my
loved calling. *Experti sumus invicem fortuna et ego*,[1] and indeed I owe
uch to Fortune since I can say without boasting that my missions
d journeys to Spain and England were crowned with great success,
atters of the highest import being brought to a successful conclu-
on, and that I gave complete satisfaction both to those that sent me
d to the other parties.

And that you may know all, to me were later entrusted—and to me
one—the secret negotiations with France concerning the flight of
e Queen-Mother and the Duke of Orleans from the Kingdom of
ance and the asylum granted to them here. I could furnish an
storian with much material and the pure truth concerning those
atters, very different from that which is generally believed. But
hen I found myself in that labyrinth, pestered day and night by
nportunate supplicants, having constantly to attend at Court and to
e away from my own house for the space of nine months, rising
igher and higher in the favour of the Serene Infanta and of the
rincipal ministers of the King, and having given every satisfaction
o the parties abroad, I felt that the time had come for me to constrain
yself to cut the golden knot of ambition in order to recover my
eedom. Such a step has to be taken, in my opinion, while one's star
in the ascendant and not when it is setting, while Fortune smiles and
ot when she has turned her back. Therefore I chose the occasion of a
ecret journey to throw myself at the feet of Her Highness and implore

[1] Fortune and I, we have experience of one another.

her, as sole reward for so many services, to release me from the
duties and allow me to serve her in my own house, to obtain whi
concession from her caused me more difficulty than any other s
has granted me; but in the end she agreed, provided only that I wou
undertake certain negotiations and secret affairs of state, which
could handle without great inconvenience. From that hour onward
have taken no part in the affairs of France and have never repent
taking this decision.

Now I lead, by the grace of God, a quiet life with my wife an
children, as you have heard from M. Picquery, and have no oth
ambition in the world than to live in peace. When I found I was n
yet fitted for a life of celibacy, I resolved to get married again; a
as *primas damus* to continence, *fruimur licita voluptate cum gratiar
actione*,[1] etc. I took a young wife born of honest but humble paren
although all sought to persuade me to marry a lady of the Court. B
I feared *commune illud nobilitatis malum superbiam praesertim in illo sex*
and chose one who would not blush when I took up my brushes. A
to tell you the truth, I was loath to exchange my precious liberty f
the embraces of an old woman. Such is the story of my life since th
suspension of our correspondence. I see that M. Picquery has told yo
of the children of my present marriage. I will add only that m
son Albert is now in Venice and during the whole of this year will
travelling round Italy. On his return he will, God willing, wait up
you, but of this we will speak in due course. Today I am so busy wi
the arrangements for the triumphal entry of the Cardinal-Infante
which will take place at the end of this month—that I have bare
time to live, let alone to write, wherefore I am cheating my art of
few nocturnal hours in order to reply with these inadequate and u
polished lines to your gracious and elegant letter, the Magistrature
this City having charged me with the entire burden of this festival
think that the invention and variety of conceits, the novelty of th
designs and the felicity of their application would not displease yo
It may be that you will see them published one day, adorned with th
fine inscriptions and epigrams of our Signor Gevaerts, who kiss
your hand with sincere affection.

These burdens aforesaid compel me to call a truce, for truly it is n
possible in this conjuncture to fulfil my obligations to you and
answer your questions. I will only say that I still have the antiqu

---

[1] We give the first prize to continence, we may enjoy lawful pleasure, f
which we give thanks. [2] A vice often met with in the nobility, prid
especially in that sex.

on and bowl, which is so light, and the handle so convenient, that
wife used it during her confinements, yet it is neither damaged
corroded. The spoon corresponds exactly to your sketch, but it
not of gold, except for the rivet, which seems to be solid, rather
in gilded. I confess, however, that in my ignorance I mistook that
aich you call the helmet of Mercury for fire, and the purse for an
ple to be thrown into it as an offering. What the round reticulated
ject is meant to be I cannot even guess; some shrewd person here
aintains that it is the shepherd's hoard, the product of the sale of his
ats and hens, and therefore fastened to the top of Mercury's
luceus[1] as a symbol of his trade; he says also that *loculi antiquorum*[2]
re made like reticules, as are certain pouches at the present time,
th tassels on either side to shut them; and from the bulk of the purse
concludes that it is full, etc. The pedestal does not trouble me much,
: it seems of one piece with the turf or mound on which the
epherd is sitting, but it is hard to discern owing to the rough execu-
n. The workmanship of the handle of the bowl is much more
licate, and I therefore deem it to be of a different century. It shows
thing beyond the mask of a Bacchante, a staff with leaves of
yrsus and some fruit, an altar laden with fruit and a pipe, with a
at *quae rodit vitem*;[3] and on either side a scroll which ends in the head
a fish with a long-toothed snout like that of a swordfish or saw-
h. Unless you send me the prints, I can say nothing about the heap
it lies beside the woman, save that I cannot imagine it to be any
id of human body, but rather a sphinx or panther, which seems to
e more likely though by no means certain. The rest of your com-
ands I am compelled to defer until I can deal with them at greater
sure.

I enclose, however, a folio from the Reverend Father Silvestro
Petra Santa's *De symbolis heroicis*, about the mysterious clock (or
ass globe) in a carafe filled with water, of which you will find a
awing and a description. I think you will consider this contrivance
orthy of an Archimedes or Archytas, and will laugh at Drebbel and
s perpetual motion, to which he has never been able to impart a
gular movement. The secret lies in some great sympathy and
agnetic virtue and you must not doubt its efficiency, for I have
oken to ingenious persons who, having seen and operated it with
se, are full of admiration. I have never neglected on my travels to
serve and investigate the antiquities in public or private hands, and

[1] Staff.   [2] The purses of the ancients.   [3] Which nibbles a vine.

to acquire some little curiosity or other; moreover, when I sold son
gems and medals to the Duke of Buckingham, I retained some of tl
rarest and most exquisite, so that I now have a fine and interestir
collection. But of all this I must write with a more tranquil mind.
cannot, however, omit to refresh your memory regarding some ve
singular methods of weighing which I saw in Spain, as I believe I ha
told you already, during my first visit to that Court, thirty years ag
when I met Don Hieronimo de Ayanza, chief assayer of the mines
the West Indies in the King's Council. The first method was deriv
from Aristotle—I found it in his fragment *De subsidentibus aquae*—ar
is very similar to the experiment by which he ascertained the differe:
metals in the crown of Hiero. This Don Hieronimo had a small silv
scale, which appeared to have the proportion and depth of a sectic
of the third part of a perfect globe. On the outside there were mark
an infinite number of circles, each with very tiny numbers, thoug
there seemed hardly enough space between the lines to inscribe thes
He suspended this scale on three or four threads from a mobile ir
beam, in the manner of a balance, so that it could rise and fall, acrc
a second iron bar, which was perpendicular, and in the shape of
half-fork. He then placed upon the scale any weight he pleased ar
let it dip into a basin filled with water, as far as it would go: when l
saw that it would sink no further, he noted the circle which touche
the surface of the water, from which he was able to calculate the exa
weight to an imperceptible difference. His second method of weighir
also seemed to me most ingenious. He had a copper rod erecte
vertically on a plane likewise of copper and levelled horizontally. /
the top of the rod there was a very thin steel needle, so fine that
ended in an indivisible point. He then took a small silver balanc
made with such accuracy that, he assured me, he had worked for ov
six months to adjust it to equal thickness all round; and that is tl
whole secret. The centre of the balance was marked on its conve
base by an indivisible point and when this was placed upon the tip (
the needle, the system rested in equilibrium: but it was so sensitiv
that one tiny particle of human hair placed upon one scale w.
sufficient to set it in motion and to incline it perceptibly to that sid
He had also an infinite number of weights so minute that the smalle
were nearly invisible and the difference in their sizes was too small t
be seen. Each bore a number, and he put them upon one end of tl
balance and the counterpoise on the other; and this, he said, was tl
finest and most exact type of balance in existence. But let it be sai

cerning the antique weights that I do not know whether they ever
ieved such accuracy. And with that I will cease importuning you
depriving myself of what little time I have. I kiss your hands a
lion times with all my heart and remain always

> Your most humble and affectionate servant,
> PIETRO PAULO RUBENS

When I thought to have finished, I recalled to mind that I have an
on pending before the court of the Parliament in Paris against a
ain engraver of German birth who is now a burgher of Paris.
s man has done me great prejudice and damage by copying my
ravings notwithstanding that the privilege granted to me by His
st Christian Majesty was renewed three years ago. My son Albert
sed him to be prosecuted by the *lieutenant civil*, but when judge-
t was given in my favour, the man appealed to the Parliament.
refore I beg you to be good enough to assist me by recommend-
my most just cause to the President or to some of your friends on
Council. You may even be acquainted with the official respon-
e, the Sieur Saulnier, *conseiller en parlement de la seconde chambre des
uestes*. I hope you will do me this favour all the more willingly
e it was through your good offices that I obtained my first
vilege from His Most Christian Majesty. I confess I am very
:nsed and enraged by this affair and your assistance therein would
ige me more than any other favour in matters of greater moment.
: it is urgent, *ne veniat post bellum auxilium*.[1] Forgive me for thus
urbing you etc.

ignor Rockox is alive and well, and kisses your hands with
ere devotion. I still have the drawing and the model of the agate
e you saw (which I bought for two thousand gold scudi), but not
mould. It was, however, no bigger than an ordinary carafe of
newhat thick glass. I remember measuring it and it held exactly
: 'pot', which is the stupid name of this measure in our language.
e jewel itself was sent to the East Indies in a carrack and fell into
hands of the Dutch, *sed periit inter manus rapientium ni fallor*;[2] and
ugh many inquiries were made of the Eastern Company in
isterdam, it has never been heard of again. *Iterum vale*.

much desire to know whether your brother Signor de Valavez
1 good health and beg you to kiss his hands for me and assure him

[1] Lest the assistance arrive after the battle.   [2] But unless I am mistaken, it
shed in the hands of the pirates.

S

that no one remembers better than I his favours and no one is m
eager to serve him.

In addressing your letters to me, it is better to write, instead
'Gentilhomme ordinaire de la maison', 'Secretary to His Cath
Majesty in His Privy Council'. It is not from vanity that I men
this, but to ensure quick and safe delivery of your letters, if they
not pass through the hands of my brother-in-law, M. Picquery.

We have printed this letter in full because it shows Rubens's liv
interest in subjects so different as politics, antiquities, bibliophily, nat
science and art. Peiresc, parliamentary councillor at Aix, was one of
oldest and most intimate friends of the painter. His corresponde
was very extensive and after his death ten thousand letters were fou
In a letter to Dupuy, Rubens says of him: 'Monsieur de Peiresc, in s
of his numerous duties, continues in his zeal for the antiquities, whic
truly astonishing. Indeed, he is as well informed in all the various branc
of knowledge as others are only in their own professions. I can har
understand how one person's mind can do justice to so many differ
occupations.' And this is Peiresc's opinion of the painter in a letter
addressed to Dupuy: 'I have read with singular pleasure the letters fr
Monsieur Rubens, who is born to please and delight in everything
does and says'.

After Marie de' Medici and Gaston d'Orléans had fled to the Net
lands, Peiresc was afraid of incurring suspicion if he continued
correspond with someone as prominent as Rubens. He had theref
entrusted his letter to the painter's brother-in-law, Nicolas Picqu
who had settled in Marseilles as a merchant.

XXVIII. TO NICOLAS CLAUDE FABRI DE PEIRESC

Antwerp, 31 May 1

MY MOST ILLUSTRIOUS AND HONOURED SIR,

You will have already seen from my previous letter that I h
received through Monsieur Le Gris the news of the successful issu
my process in the Parliament, thanks to the favours and good off
of your friends, as I have written at greater length to you with
thanks, though these are far below your deserts, which place
under a perpetual obligation, so long as I have sense and life to hon
and serve you with all my energies. M. Auberey informs me that
opponents will not yield, but have presented a *requeste civile*, wh
has been placed in the hands of Councillor Saunier to look over

ort upon. I do not understand chicanery and am so simple that I
ught that a decree of the Court of Parliament was the final deci-
n of a lawsuit, without appeal or subsequent revision, as the sen-
ces here of the sovereign councils; and I cannot therefore imagine
at can be the object of this *requeste*. I did not fail to send to Mme
nier immediately the impressions of my prints, ordered by M.
Gris on his way through this place. When I inquired from him
at it was necessary to provide for the cost, douceurs, and acknow-
gements due to those who have co-operated in this matter, he
ged me to defer it until his return (excepting only Madame
nier, which he wished should be done at once), because he had the
ount with him and wished to make the distribution with his own
d; in the meanwhile he had left everything in good order so that
hing should be wanting during his absence. He assured me that
Auberey had undertaken to procure everything necessary for the
lement of the whole affair; but he did not tell me that he would
burse any money, whereas I perceive, from the copy of his letter
you, that he has paid 20 *escus quarts* for the fees, of which he makes
mention in his letter to me of 22 May. Now I do not know what
do, whether I should repay only this sum to M. Auberey at once
await the return of M. Le Gris and settle everything together, or
ether I should write to M. Auberey that, as I supposed that he
bursed for the expenses of my suit in the absence of M. Le Gris
at was necessary, I beg him to let me know the amount in order
t I may reimburse him at the first opportunity, and I will do this
edily, adding some trifle as a token of gratitude. As to the query
cerning the triennial interval between the first and last privilege,
rises from the figures of the year marked beneath the smaller
cifixion (1632), which are done with such ambiguity that it can-
be discerned whether the last figure is a 1 or 2; it must, however,
essarily be a 2, though its horns and projections are not sufficiently
icated, for it is known to all the world that in 1631 I was in
gland and this engraving could not have been done in my absence,
t has been retouched, as is always my custom, many times by my
n hand. But since this doubt has not been mooted by our oppo-
ts, there is no need to bring it forward. We shall see what will be
result of this *requeste*.

Ve are in great travail here owing to the passage of the French
y, on its way to assist the Dutch and which, near Marche en
enne, routed Prince Thomas. The action was, however, of greater

import for the disrepute and fright than for the loss, very few havi
been killed; but the greater part of the caissons of the infantry ha
been taken, together with artillery and baggage. This loss is attribut
to the temerity and negligence of the general, who, without spies, a
without being well informed as to the numbers, strength and mov
ments of his adversary, engaged the enemy with so great a d
advantage that he was defeated in less than half an hour. Many sav
themselves in a neighbouring wood or thanks to the roughness of t
terrain. It is certain that the rupture between the two Crowns
come to a head, which gives me great uneasiness, being by nature a
choice a peaceful man and averse to disputes, lawsuits and quarre
whether public or private. Moreover, I do not know whether in ti
of war the privilege of His Majesty will be valid; if not, all c
labours and expenses to obtain the decision in the Parliament, for t
purpose of maintaining it, will have been in vain; and above all, I f
(the States of the United Provinces make me observe their inviolal
privileges in time of open war) that our correspondence will run t
risk of another cessation for some years—not on my part, but beca
you, being a person of eminence and in high office, may not be a
to maintain it without incurring some suspicion. I shall always cc
form, though with infinite displeasure, to whatever may be nec
sary for your tranquillity and security. With this, humbly kissi
your hands from a sincere heart, I remain,

Most illustrious and reverend Sir,
Your most humble and obliged servant.
PETER PAUL RUBE

Another example of the troublesome infringement of the painte
copyright in the engravings and of the onerous negotiations necessa
to protect his privilege. The work of which these unauthorized cop
had been made was the 'Christ on the Cross' ('au coup de poin
engraved by Paulus Pontius.

In the question of the dates Rubens makes two mistakes: the engravi
is dated 1631, and he returned from London in 1630 and married Hélè
Fourment in the following year.

XXIX. TO NICOLAS CLAUDE FABRI DE PEIRESC

Antwerp, 16 March 1e

MOST ILLUSTRIOUS AND HONOURED SIR,
A few days ago I received your most welcome letter of 23 Decemb
already very old, together with the engraving of the anti

ndscape. My reply has been delayed by my absence, for, against my
wishes, I was detained in Brussels by some private business, and not
or the purposes you suppose (I say this in good faith, trusting that
ou will believe me). I admit that at first I was asked to undertake
hat business, but I disliked being given so little scope. There was also
ome dispute concerning my passport, to which was added some
eliberate procrastination—one might almost say tergiversation—on
ay part. Moreover, there was no lack of candidates eager to under-
ke the work, and thus I preserved the leisure of my home, where by
he grace of God I find myself still, very happy, and most ready to
erve you.

As I abhor court life, I have sent my work to England by a third
and. My friends write that it has now been placed in position and
hat His Majesty is entirely satisfied with it. I have not yet received
ay recompense for it, but I should be a novice in the affairs of the
world if that were to surprise me. Long experience has taught me that
rinces are slow where the interests of others are concerned and do
rong more easily than right. Therefore I am not uneasy and do not
uspect any unwillingness to pay me, for my friends at that court
ourish me with hope, assuring me always that the king will use me
a fashion worthy both of his station and of my merit. I know well,
hough, that according to the well-known proverb, he who wants
hould go, he who does not want should send, and therefore I should
o in person if I wish to negotiate well. This I say only that you may
e still more assured of my inclination towards tranquillity of mind
nd my obstinate determination to avoid, so far as it depends upon
e, all perturbation and intrigues. For the same reason I am not
reatly perturbed about my affair in Paris, which has been over-
hadowed by public affairs. M. Le Gris has informed me that my
ivileges remain safe and intact; but as I have not one penny to lose
the whole of France, I fail to see how the King's Attorney has
voured me, as against my adversaries, who had demanded the
onfiscation of the *Planches et images, etc. de Rubens*. M. d'Auberi per-
aps meant *planches des copies condamnées à estre rompues*, or that my
rints in third hands are to be confiscated—a loss which would not
uch me—or that my pictures are to be banned from the Kingdom
France, which again would not disturb me unduly, though such a
ing has never been done in the world.

My lawyers, in fact, could not demand anything except the con-
cation of the costs, which my adversaries owe me by sentence of the

judges; concerning which I cannot understand on what grounds they should be excused from paying costs which they have been condemned to pay; in fact, these by right should go to the royal treasury.

But let us turn from these bagatelles, which do not merit so long and tedious a discourse. The engraving of the antique landscape has given me much pleasure, though it seems to me nothing but a painter's caprice, which does not represent a place *in rerum natura*.[1] Such arches, one upon the other, are found neither in nature nor in art and could hardly subsist in that fashion; those little temples on top of the rock have not the space which such buildings would require, nor is there any path by which priests and worshippers may ascend and descend that round receptacle *non est usus*,[2] since it does not retain the water it receives from above, but discharges them again into the common basin through many very wide outlets, thus losing incomparably more water than it receives. The whole may be called, I should say, a *Nymphaeum*, being like a confluence *multorum fontium undique scaturientium*;[3] the little shrine with three female statues might be dedicated to the nymphs of the place, and those on the summit of the hill to some rustic deities *aut monticolis*.[4] The square building is perchance the tomb of some hero, *nam habet arma suspensa prae foribus*,[5] and has a cippus like a winning-post adorned with foliage and columns with festoons and torches; above the corners *habet calathos*[6] in which to hang fruit and other offerings, *quibus inferias et justa solvebant defunctis et tanquam oblatis fruituris heroibus parentabant*.[7] The goats are sacred to some deity, for they graze without a herdsman, etc. The whole seems to have been painted by a competent hand, but there is too little accuracy in the perspective, for the lines of the buildings do not intersect at a point of equal height on the horizon, or to put it in a nutshell, the entire prospect is wrong. Similar errors can be observed in certain buildings on the backs of medals, particularly in hippodromes given in faulty perspective, though those works are, for the rest, quite good; and some bas-reliefs, even by good masters, have the same defect. Such ignorance, however, is more tolerable in sculpture than in painting, and this suggests that perspective was not as generally known then as it is today, although its principles were laid down very clearly by Euclid and others. And that is all I can tell you on this subject.

[1] In real nature. [2] Is of no use. [3] Of many springs gushing forth from all sides. [4] Or mountain gods. [5] For there are arms hung up at the entrance. [6] It has baskets. [7] Which they offered to their dead as sacrifices and obsequial dues and gave to their heroes to partake of.

I enclose the drawings of the antique helmet, in the same size as the original; also the bas-relief of the Trojan War, which one of my pupils has drawn after the Arundel marble; but as the marble is really antique and the figures have only two feet, the great age has left its marks and but little can now be seen of the perfection of the faces. I hope you have received my views on colours, and as I can think of nothing else this time, I recommend myself to your favour and humbly kissing your hands I remain for ever,

Your most obedient and devoted servant,
PETER PAUL RUBENS

The allusion at the beginning of this letter is to a projected diplomatic mission to Holland. Though there was nothing Rubens desired more than peace with that country, he was not eager to go on this journey, since he had once before, on the occasion of similar negotiations, been treated in a scandalous manner by a jealous professional diplomat at Brussels, the Duc d'Arschot. The pictures dispatched to England were the ceiling paintings on canvas for Whitehall Palace (see p. 120). Rubens was not disappointed in his hope of payment: the £3,000 due to him had been paid in instalments by 1638.

From the Flemish

XXX. TO GEORG GELDORP

SIR,   Antwerp, 25 July 1637

Your agreeable letter, which has now come to hand, has enlightened me at last, for I could not imagine for what purpose an altar-piece would have been wanted in London. I shall need at least a year and a half if I am to work at leisure and to serve your friend willingly. The subject should be chosen according to the dimensions desired, for some subjects are better suited to large dimensions, others to intermediate or small proportions. If I were free to choose a subject from the life of St. Peter, it would be his Crucifixion head downwards, which is very extraordinary and convenient and at the same time very striking. But I leave the choice to those who will bear the cost and will wait until I am informed of the size of the picture.

I have a great affection for the city of Cologne because I was reared here until I was ten years old; and I have long wished to visit it once again after such a long time. But I fear that the perilous times and my own occupations will deprive me of this and other pleasures. And thus

I recommend myself to your good favour from the bottom of m<
heart and remain for ever,

Sir,

Your affectionate servant,

PIETRO PAUOLO RUBEN<

Georg Geldorp, an artist from Cologne, who had settled in Londor
commissioned an altar-piece for the church of St. Peter in Cologne o
behalf of the well-known banker Eberhard Jabach. See also Lette<
XXXII.

XXXI. TO JOSSE SUSTERMANS

Antwerp, 12 March 163<

I hope that you have received my answer to your letter of 10 Fet
ruary, in which I acknowledged receipt of the Tragedy and du<
thanked you for this favour.

Now I must tell you that Signor Schutter came to my house toda<
and paid me 142 florins and 14 'pracq', to complete the payment <
that picture which I made to your order, and I gave Signor Schutt<
my receipt. To be able to speak of it with certainty, I made enquiri<
of Signor Annoni, who tells me that three weeks ago he dispatche<
the case containing your picture to Lille, whence it will proceed <
Italy. Please God that you may receive it soon and in good conditio<
and this I hope will be so, for since the capture of Hanau and th
defeat of the Duke of Weimar the roads of Germany will be clear <
all impediments. Concerning the subject of the picture, this is pe<
fectly clear, and since I gave you some idea of it before, your pen<
trating eye will soon discern the rest, better perhaps than with an
description of mine. Nevertheless, since you so command me, I w<
explain it in a few words. The principal figure is Mars, who, leavin<
open the temple of Janus (which it was a Roman custom to kee
closed in time of peace), advances with his shield and his bloodstaine
sword, threatening the nations with great devastation and payin<
little heed to Venus his lady, who strives with caresses and embrac<
to restrain him, she being accompanied by her Amors and Cupid
On the other side, Mars is drawn on by the Fury Alecto, holding
torch in her hand. Nearby are monsters, representing Pestilence an<
Famine, the inseparable companions of war. On the ground lies
woman with a broken lute, signifying Harmony, which is incom
patible with the discord of war; there is also a mother with her bab<
in her arms, denoting that fecundity, generation and charity a<

versed by war, which corrupts and destroys all things. In addition,
re is an architect, lying with his instruments in his hand, to show
at that which is built for the commodity and ornament of a city, is
d in ruins and overthrown by the violence of arms. I believe, if I
member aright, that you will also find on the ground, beneath the
et of Mars, a book and some drawings on paper, to show that he
mples on literature and other arts. There is also, I believe, a bundle
arrows, with the cord which bound them together undone, they,
nen bound together, being the emblem of Concord, and I also
inted, lying beside them, the caduceus and the olive, the symbol of
ace. That lugubrious matron, clad in black and with her veil torn,
spoiled of her jewels and every other ornament, is unhappy
urope, afflicted for so many years by rapine, outrage and misery,
hich, as they are so harmful to all, need not be specified. Her attri-
te is that globe, supported by a *putto* or genius, and surmounted
a cross, which denotes the Christian orb. This is all that I can tell
u, and it appears to me too much, since with your own sagacity
u will have easily penetrated the meaning. Having nothing further
ith which to entertain or weary you, I recommend myself with all
y heart to your good graces and remain for ever.

S. I fear that, remaining rolled and packed for so long, the colours
this newly done painting may suffer a little, and, in particular, that
e flesh-tints and white lead may turn rather yellow. But you, being
great a man in our profession, will easily remedy this by exposing
to the sun at intervals. If need be, you have my permission to set
ur hand to it, retouching it wherever it may be needful, as the
sult of accident or of my carelessness.

stus Sustermans, born at Antwerp, was court painter to Duke
osimo II of Florence, and the famous painting (see also p. 113 above)
as probably intended from the first for the Duke, Sustermans acting
erely as intermediary. Rubens's description of the picture shows his
traordinary optical memory. Another instance of the vividness of his
collection is the rendering of the Escurial landscape, see Letter
xxvi below.

From the Flemish

XXXII. TO GEORG GELDORP

Antwerp, 2 April 1638

R,
Having heard through M. van Lemmens that you would fain know
hat progress I have made on the painting for your friend in Cologne,

which I began on your instructions, I will not fail to inform you th
it is well advanced and that I hope it will be one of the best pictu
I have ever made. You may tell your friend so quite frankly; bu
must add that I do not like being pressed and would ask you to
me work at my discretion and convenience so that I can take pleas
in completing it. For although I am overburdened with other wor
this subject interests me more than any other I have in hand. I ha
not written to your friend in Cologne, because I have not made
acquaintance and think that it is better done through you. Thu
recommend myself cordially to your favour and remain for ever, S

Your affectionate servant,
PIETRO PAUOLO RUBE

See Letter xxx above. The picture in question is the 'Crucifixi
of St. Peter', which Rubens had undertaken a year before. It was still
his studio when he died, and was not set up in the Cologne church un
1642.

From the Flemish

XXXIII. TO LUCAS FAID'HERBE

Steen, 17 August 16

To Mr. Lucas Faid'herbe, in the house of Mr. Peter Paul Rubens
Antwerp, express, express, express.

MY DEAR AND BELOVED FRIEND LUCAS,

I hope that this letter will find you still at Antwerp, for I ne
badly a panel on which there are three heads in life-size, painted
my own hand: one of a furious soldier wearing a black bonnet, t
others of a man crying and one laughing. I should be very glad if y
would send this panel to me at once; or if you are coming here, plea
bring it with you. You should cover it with one or two inferi
panels to protect it in order that it cannot be seen on the journey.
seems strange to us that we have heard nothing of the bottles of wi
from Ay; of the wine which we brought with us, not a drop is le
And so my best wishes for your health and for Caroline and Suzann
and I am, with all my heart,

Your devoted friend,
PIETRO PAUOLO RUBE

P.S. Make sure before you leave that everything is safely locked a
that no originals, whether pictures or sketches, remain in the stud

mind William the gardener that he is to send us the Rosalie pears
en they are ripe, also figs in their season, or some other delicacy
m the garden.

cas Faid'herbe, an Antwerp sculptor, had been Rubens's pupil and,
this letter shows, enjoyed his special confidence. While Rubens
s staying in the country, Faid'herbe was in charge of the large town
.ise and was responsible for the workshop and the apprentices.

From the French

XXXIV. TO SIR BALTHASAR GERBIER

R,   Antwerp, 15 March 1640

It is true that M. Norgate, when he visited me, paid much attention
the picture of St. Lawrence in Escurial, without showing much
erest for anything else. I saw no need at the time to open his eyes
cause I did not wish to cross him; but now that I am forced to
real the truth, in order not to deceive His Majesty of Great Britain,
dmit that the said picture is not by my hand, but by a very me-
)cre painter of this city, called Verhulst, who painted it after a
awing I had made on the spot. It is in no way worthy of appearing
.ong the marvels of the royal cabinet. His Majesty may at all times
pose of everything that is mine as well as of myself, his very
mble servant. I entreat you to keep me in his favour, and in yours
), and to honour me with your commands whenever occasion offers.

Sir,

Your very humble servant,

PIETRO PAUOLO RUBENS

is view of the Escurial is discussed on p. 150 above. See also
tter XXXVI. Balthasar Gerbier, court painter and political agent of
ng Charles I. was an old friend of Rubens and had acted together
th him in political matters.

From the French

XXXV. TO FRANÇOIS DUQUESNOY

Antwerp, 17 April 1640

annot express to you my obligation for the models you have sent
, as also for the plaster casts of the two admirable children from the

tomb of M. van den (Huffel), in the Chiesa dell'Anima. Nor ca
find words to praise them as they deserve. It is not art, it is natu
herself who has formed them, and the marble seems softened to fles
The praises bestowed on the statue of St. Andrew just unveiled ha
come to my ears and I, together with our whole nation, share yo
joy in your fame. If I were not detained by my age, and by the gc
which cripples me, I would instantly depart, and go to admire, wi
my own eyes, the perfection of this fine work. But since I cannot ha
that satisfaction, I hope, at least, that I shall see you among us, a
that our beloved Flanders will one day be resplendent with yo
illustrious works. Please Heaven that this may happen before dea
which will soon close my eyes for ever, deprives me of the sight
the marvels executed by your hand, which I kiss from the bottom
my heart, praying that God may give you long life and happiness.

Your very affectionate and very obliged servant,

PIETRO PAUÓLO RUBE

François Duquesnoy, a well-known Flemish sculptor, who had liv
in Italy since 1618, executed works for several Roman churches.

From the French

XXXVI. TO SIR BALTHASAR GERBIER

SIR, Antwerp, April 16

Here is the picture of St. Lawrence in Escurial, finished accordi
to the capacity of the Master, but under my direction. Please God t
extravagance of the subject may give some recreation to His Majes
The mountain, which is called Sierra de S. Juan in Malagon, is ve
high and steep, and very difficult to ascend and descend, so that t
clouds were far beneath us, the sky above remaining quite clear a
serene. There is, at the summit, a great wooden cross, which may
easily discerned from Madrid, and nearby a little church dedicated
St. John, which could not be represented in the picture, since it w
behind our backs; a hermit lives there who is here seen with his mu
I need scarcely say that below is the superb building St. Lawrence
Escurial, with the village and its avenues of trees, with the Frisne
and its two ponds, and the road towards Madrid, which appe
above, near the horizon. The mountain covered with clouds is cal
Sierra Tocada, because it has almost always a kind of veil round

ummit. There is a tower and a house on one side, but I do not
remember their names particularly, though I know the king went
there at times when hunting. The mountain quite to the left is La
sierra y puerto de butrago. Which is all I can say on this subject.

Remaining ever, Sir,
Your very humble servant,
PETER PAUL RUBENS

forgot to say that, at the summit, we met with plenty of *forse inayson*,[1] as is represented in the picture.

From the Flemish

XXXVII. TO LUCAS FAID'HERBE

SIR,   Antwerp, 9 May 1640

I rejoice to hear that on May Day you planted the maypole in your
beloved's garden, and hope it may flourish and bring forth fruit in
time. I and my wife, and my two sons, wish you and your beloved
with all our hearts great happiness and perfect, lasting contentedness
in your new station. There is no need for haste concerning the ivory
child, for you now have children of greater importance in hand; but
your visit will always be welcome. My wife will, I believe, shortly
pass through Malines on her way to Steen, and so she will have the
pleasure of wishing you happiness by word of mouth. In the meantime, give my hearty greetings to your father-in-law and mother-in-
law, who will, I hope, rejoice more every day in this union and in
your person. I wish the same to your father and to your mother, who
must be laughing in her sleeve, because your journey to Italy has been
abandoned and instead of losing her dear son she has won a new
daughter, who will soon, with God's help, make her a grandmother.
And so I remain ever with all my heart, etc.

The last letter of Rubens that has come down to us (in a copy only).
This jocular and affectionate tone would certainly be found more often
in his correspondence if, instead of the letters dealing with political,
scientific and business matters, those to Isabella Brant, to Hélène
Fourment and to his children had been preserved.

---

[1] Gerbier has added—He means deare which is called venson when putt in
a crust.

PLATES

I. THE APOSTLE SIMON
1603. Madrid, Prado

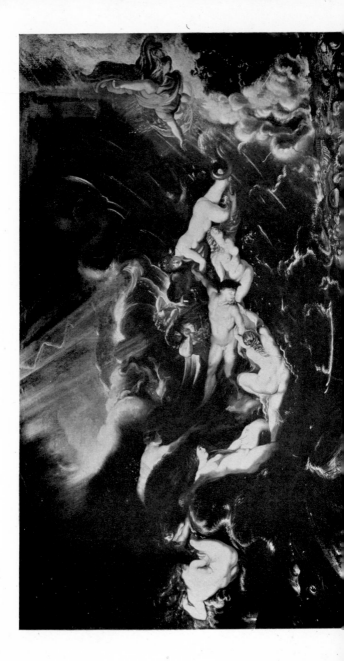

3. THE TRANSFIGURATION. 1605. Nancy, Museum

4. THE TRINITY
1605. Mantua, Academy

5. THE GONZAGA FAMILY ADORING THE TRINITY
1605. Mantua, Academy

6. THE CIRCUMCISION
1606–7. (Modello for the altar-piece in Sant' Ambrogio, Genoa.)
Vienna, Academy

7. THE DUKE OF LERMA
1603. Madrid, Conde Valdelagrana

8. MARCHESA BRIGIDA SPINOLA DORIA
About 1606. Duveen Bros. Inc., New York

9. ARCHDUKE ALBERT
About 1609. Vienna, Kunsthistorisches Museum

IO. INFANTA ISABELLA
About 1609. Vienna, Kunsthistorisches Museum

II. THE ANNUNCIATION
About 1609. Vienna, Kunsthistorisches Museum

12. 'DISPUTA'
1609–10. Antwerp, St. Paul

14. Detail of Plate 13

15. THE RAISING OF THE CROSS
1610–11. Antwerp, Cathedral

16–17. INNER WINGS OF 'THE RAISING OF THE CROSS'
1610–11. Antwerp, Cathedral

18. THE DESCENT FROM THE CROSS
1611–14. Antwerp, Cathedral

19–20. INNER WINGS OF 'THE DESCENT FROM THE CROSS'
1611–14. Antwerp, Cathedral

21. THE FOUR PHILOSOPHERS
About 1611–12. Florence, Galleria Pitti

22. MICHIEL OPHOVIUS
About 1618. The Hague, Mauritshuis

23. THE DRUNKEN HERCULES
About 1612. Dresden, Gemäldegalerie

24. THE CROWNING OF THE HERO
About 1612. Munich, Alte Pinakothek

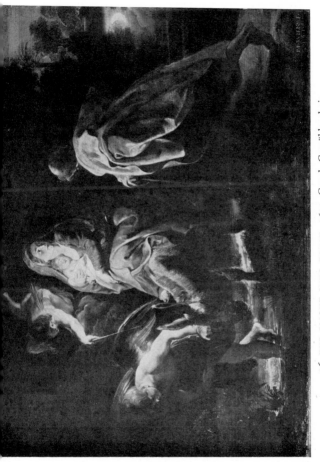

26. THE FLIGHT INTO EGYPT. 1614. Cassel, Gemäldegalerie

27. VENUS AND ADONIS
About 1610. Düsseldorf, Gemäldegalerie

28. MAGDALEN AND MARTHA
1612–15. Vienna, Kunsthistorisches Museum

29. THE STIGMATIZATION OF ST. FRANCIS
1614–15. Cologne, Wallraf-Richartz Museum

30. THE ASSUMPTION OF THE VIRGIN
ut 1616. (From the altar of the Church of the Carmelites.) Brussels, Museum

31. THE LARGE LAST JUDGEMENT
About 1616. Munich, Alte Pinakothek

32. Detail of Plate 31

34. LION HUNT. About 1617. Munich, Alte Pinakothek

36. THE BATTLE OF THE AMAZONS. About 1618. Munich, Alte Pinakothek

37. DECIUS MUS OFFERING HIMSELF UP, 1617. Vienna, Liechtenstein Gallery

38. THE DEATH OF DECIUS MUS IN BATTLE. 1617. Vienna, Liechtenstein Gallery

39. THE RAPE OF THE DAUGHTERS OF LEUCIPPUS
About 1619. Munich, Alte Pinakothek

40. ROMULUS AND REMUS
About 1618. Rome, Galleria Capitolina

42. THE MIRACULOUS DRAUGHT OF FISHES. 1618–19. Malines, Notre Dame

43. Detail of Plate 42

44. CHRIST WITH THE FOUR GREAT PENITENTS
About 1620. Munich, Alte Pinakothek

45. ST. AMBROSIUS AND THE EMPEROR THEODOSIUS
About 1619. Vienna, Kunsthistorisches Museum

46. THE MIRACLE OF ST. IGNATIUS LOYOLA
1619. (From the altar of the Jesuit Church, Antwerp.)
Vienna, Kunsthistorisches Museum

47. THE MIRACLE OF ST. FRANCIS XAVIER
1619. (Sketch for the altar of the Jesuit Church at Antwerp.)
Vienna, Kunsthistorisches Museum

48. THE LAST COMMUNION OF ST. FRANCIS OF ASSISI
1619. (From the altar of the Church of Recollects.) Antwerp, Museum

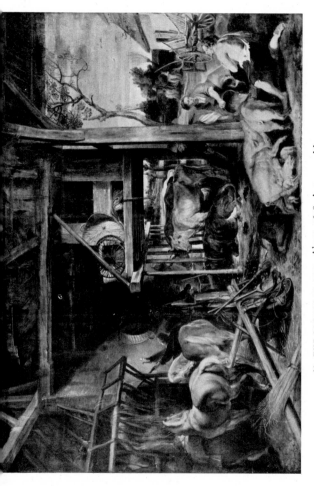

50. THE PRODIGAL SON. About 1618. Antwerp, Museum

52. THE HEAD OF CYRUS BROUGHT TO QUEEN TOMYRIS. About 1620. Boston, Museum of Fine Arts

53. Detail of Plate 52

54. 'LE COUP DE LANCE'
620. (From the altar of the Church of the Recollects.) Antwerp, Museum

55. THE DEATH OF SAINT LUCIA
1620. (Sketch for the ceiling panel of the Jesuit Church at Antwerp.)
Quimper, Musée des Beaux-Arts

56. ST. BARBARA FLEEING
1620. (Sketch for the ceiling panel of the Jesuit Church at Antwerp.)
Dulwich College

57. THE RAISING OF THE CROSS

620. (Sketch for the ceiling of the Jesuit Church at Antwerp.) Paris, Louvre

58. THOMAS HOWARD, EARL OF ARUNDEL, AND HIS WIFE, ALATHEA TALB
1620. Munich, Alte Pinakothek

59. 'LE CHAPEAU DE PAILLE'
About 1620. London, National Gallery

61. THE CORONATION OF THE QUEEN

About 1622. (Second sketch for the cycle 'History of Marie de' Medici'.) Munich, Alte Pinakothek

63. HENRY IV RECEIVING THE PORTRAIT OF

62. THE EDUCATION OF THE PRINCESS

64. THE WEDDING OF THE PRINCESS

65. RECEPTION OF THE NEWLY MARRIED QUEEN AT
THE HARBOUR OF MARSEILLES

About 1622. (Sketches for the cycle 'History of Marie de' Medici'.) Munich, Alte Pinakothek

66 THE COMING OF AGE OF LUDWIG XII

67 THE QUEEN TAKEN PRISONER

68. THE FLEMISH KERMESSE. About 1622. Paris, Louvre

69. THE FALL OF THE ANGELS: 'THE SMALL LAST JUDGEMENT'
About 1620. Munich, Alte Pinakothek

70. THE ADORATION OF THE MAGI

624. (From the high altar of St. Michael's Church.) Antwerp, Museum

71. LANDSCAPE WITH THE SHIPWRECK OF AENEAS. 1628–30. Berlin, Kaiser-Friedrich Museum

72. LANDSCAPE WITH PHILEMON AND BAUCIS. About 1625. Vienna, Kunsthistorisches Museum

74. THE TRIUMPH OF THE SACRAMENT OVER HERESY
1625–8. (Design for the wall-tapestry of the Clarisses Convent at Madrid.) Madrid, Prado

75. THE BETROTHAL OF ST. CATHERINE
1627–8. Antwerp, St. Augustine

76. HENRY IV AND MARIE DE' MEDICI
1628–31. (Sketch for the cycle 'History of Henry IV'.)
London, Wallace Collection

77. THE CAPTURE OF PARIS BY HENRY IV

1628–31. (Sketch for the cycle 'History of Henry IV'.) Berlin, Kaiser-Friedrich Museum

78. ENTRY OF HENRY IV INTO PARIS

1628–31. (Sketch for the cycle 'History of Henry IV'.) London, Wallace Collection

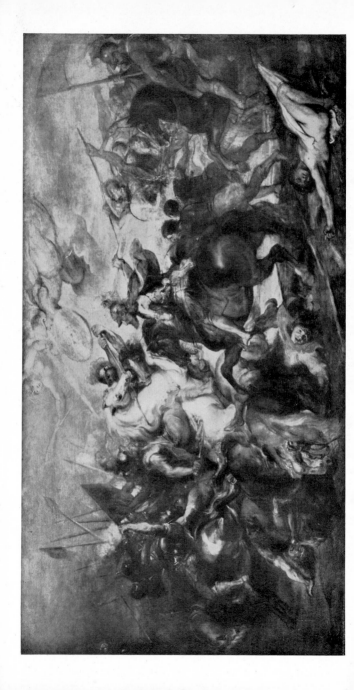

80. WAR AND PEACE. 1629–30. London, National Gallery

81. SACRIFICE TO VENUS
About 1628. Stockholm, National Museum

82. HÉLÈNE FOURMENT IN HER WEDDING DRESS
1630–1. Munich, Alte Pinakothek

83. LANDSCAPE WITH ULYSSES AND NAUSICAA. 1630-5. Florence Galleria Pitti

84. RUBENS WITH HIS SECOND WIFE IN THE GARDEN. About 1631. Munich, Alte Pinakothek

85. Detail of Plate 84

86. SUSANNA FOURMENT
About 1631. London, National Gallery (Gulbenkian Loan)

87. CHIRON EDUCATING ACHILLES
About 1630–2. Rotterdam, Boymans Museum

88. THETIS BATHING ACHILLES IN THE STYX
About 1630–2. Rotterdam, Boymans Museum

89. ACHILLES WITH THE DAUGHTERS OF LYCOMEDES
1630–2. Rotterdam, Boymans Museum

90. WISDOM EXPELLING WAR AND DISCORD FROM THE THRONE OF JAMES I
About 1632. (Sketch for the ceiling fresco in Whitehall Palace.) Vienna, Academy

91. ENGLAND AND SCOTLAND CROWNING CHARLES I
About 1632. (Sketch for the ceiling fresco in Whitehall Palace.)
Vierhouten, Coll. D. G. van Beuningen

92. CALVARY
About 1634. (From the altar of the Abbey of Afflighem.) Brussels, Museum

93. THE ILDEFONSO ALTAR-PIECE (CENTRE-PANEL)
1630–2. (From the altar of S. Jacques-sur-Coudenberg, Brussels.)
Vienna, Kunsthistorisches Museum

94–5. ARCHDUKE ALBERT WITH ST. ALBRECHT · INFANTA ISABELLA
WITH ST. ELIZABETH: INNER WINGS OF THE ILDEFONSO ALTAR-PIECE

96. THE HOLY FAMILY UNDER THE APPLE TREE
1630–2. (Outer wings of the Ildefonso Altar-piece.)
Vienna, Kunsthistorisches Museum

97. TRIUMPHAL COACH

38. (Design for the Triumphal Car made for the 'Pompa Introitus Ferdinandi'.)
Antwerp, Museum

99. THE GARDEN OF LOVE. 1632–4. Madrid, Prado

101. THE RAPE OF THE SABINE WOMEN. About 1635. London, National Gallery

386. THE MIRACLES OF THE INNOCENTS, after. Munich, Alte Pinakothek

103. THE JUDGEMENT OF PARIS. About 1635-7. London, National Gallery

104. THE MARTYRDOM OF ST. LIEVIN
About 1635. (From the high altar of the Jesuit Church at Ghent.) Brussels, Muse

105. MADONNA AND SAINTS
1636–40. Antwerp, S. Jacques

107. LANDSCAPE WITH CASTLE STEEN. About 1635–7. London, National Gallery

108. TOURNEY AT THE CASTLE. 1635–40. Paris, Louvre

109. LANDSCAPE WITH BIRDCATCHER. 1635–40. Paris, Louvre

III. THE OUTBREAK OF WAR. 1637–8. Florence, Galleria Pitti

113. MERCURY AND ARGUS. About 1636–8. (Belonging to the decoration of the Torre de la Parada.) Madrid, Prado

114. THE FALL OF THE TITANS

About 1636. (Sketch for a painting in the Torre de la Parada.) Brussels, Museum

115. THE RAPE OF HIPPODAMEIA

About 1636. (Sketch for a painting in the Torre de la Parada.) Brussels, Museum

116. NEREID AND TRITON
About 1636. (Sketch for a painting in the Torre de la Parada.)
Rotterdam, Boymans Museum

117. PASTORAL SCENE
About 1638. Munich, Alte Pinakothek

118. ST. CECILIA PLAYING THE ORGAN
1638–40. Berlin, Kaiser-Friedrich Museum

119. THE THREE GRACES
1638–40. Madrid, Prado

120. SELF-PORTRAIT. 1623–4. Windsor Castle
Reproduced by gracious permission of His Majesty The King

INDEXES AND
BIBLIOGRAPHICAL NOTE

INDEX OF COLLECTIONS

INDEX OF RUBENS'S WORKS

BIBLIOGRAPHICAL NOTE

ORIGINAL EDITIONS:

First edition: Jacob Burckhardt, *Erinnerungen aus Rubens*, Basle, 1898. Second edition 1898.

MODERN EDITIONS:

Jacob Burckhardt, *Gesamtausgabe*, vol. 13, 1934, pp. 367 ff. (With an introduction by H. Wölfflin.)

Jacob Burckhardt, *Erinnerungen aus Rubens*, Leipzig, 1928. (With forty-four illustrations, postscript and notes by H. Kauffmann.)

Jacob Burckhardt, *Rubens*. Grosse illustrierte Phaidon-Ausgabe, Vienna, 1938. (With 400 illustrations and notes by L. Goldscheider.)

LITERATURE:

Wilhelm Waetzoldt, *Deutsche Kunsthistoriker*, vol. 2, pp. 172 ff., Leipzig, 1924.

Carl Neumann, *Jacob Burckhardt*, Munich, 1927.

Heinrich Wölfflin, *Jacob Burckhardt*, in *Gedanken zur Kunstgeschichte*, 2nd ed., 1941.

O. Bock von Wülfingen, *Rubens in der deutschen Kunstbetrachtung*, Berlin, 1947. (With a chapter on Burckhardt.)

DATE DUE

APR 2 7 2009	